"*Guts and Grace* is a brave, bold invitation into a new paradigm for women's leadership—one that values wholeness, the wisdom of the body, deep listening, reflection, and authentic action. Each chapter contains simple, yet powerful, daily practices designed to deepen the important work of connecting with our innermost truth."

Eileen Fisher, founder and co-CEO of EILEEN FISHER, Inc.

"Throughout human history, leadership has largely been a male and masculine energy-dominated undertaking. This has led to considerable progress, but at a staggering and unnecessary cost in human suffering. Today we need more feminine energy in leadership to balance masculine energy and restore it to its healthy rather than toxic version. LeeAnn Mallorie has written a compelling, highly readable, practical, and authoritative book that will help women lead from a place of authenticity and deep connection to self. Refreshing in its approach and compelling in its inner logic, *Guts and Grace* is destined to occupy a place of significance in the pantheon of leadership books."

Raj Sisodia, cofounder of Conscious Capitalism Inc., and coauthor of *Shakti Leadership: Embracing Feminine and Masculine Power in Business* and *The Healing Organization*

"*Guts and Grace* is a robust guide to leading and living more effectively. In it, LeeAnn Mallorie offers a call to arms that shows women can serve others and care for themselves in parallel—a foundation of fully conscious leadership. This book is filled with novel ideas and practices that will energize you and the people you lead!"

Tom Rath, author of *StrengthsFinder 2.0* and *Are You Fully Charged?*

"The time has come to rebalance the masculine and feminine in business. While many books on women's leadership tell us what we need to do to change the tide, *Guts and Grace* finally offers simple, practical, and compelling answers to the question, "How?" This is a book that speaks deeply to where women are now as we emerge and take our rightful role in business and in all of life. Buy this book. Read this book. Step out and lead!"

Lynne Twist, founder of the Pachamama Alliance and author of *The Soul of Money*

"LeeAnn's work hits at the heart of one of the essential conundrums of being a Purpose-driven woman—*how do I give everything I've got when I've got nothing left to give*. Filled with practical tools and practices for nourishing the body, mind, and spirit, *Guts and Grace* will give you everything you need to navigate life and leadership beautifully, whole-heartedly, and sustainably. This book is a MUST for any leader who aspires to attend to the needs of the world and the needs of their own soul at the same time."

Haley Rushing, cofounder of and chief purposologist at The Purpose Institute

"*Guts and Grace* is for women leaders who aren't just about winning the rat race but determined to change the game. LeeAnn Mallorie offers a roadmap to authentic, innovative, purpose-driven leadership that will help organizations become great places to work for all."

Michael C. Bush, CEO of Great Place to Work

"LeeAnn Mallorie has a pulse on the deepest challenges facing women leaders and incredible insight on how we can overcome those challenges to become our best selves in all areas of our life. If read and practiced, this book can kick-start a journey of personal transformation that will have positive effects for the reader and all they touch. If 'the future is female,' this is the manual we all need."

Zahra Kassam, founder and CEO of Monti Kids, Inc.

"The journey of leadership isn't just about getting things done—it's about how you treat yourself and everyone else in the process. In *Guts and Grace*, LeeAnn Mallorie lays out how to be a successful leader with raw power and drive as well as genuine self-acceptance and resilience. For you, your team, and everyone you impact."

Sheryl O'Laughlin, former CEO of REBBL and Clif Bar & Company,
cofounder of Plum Organics

"Hell yes! It's time to make way for more feminine leadership! For too long, we've let the era of competitiveness overwhelm our instincts for compassion and empathy at work. I'm so thrilled to witness this paradigm shift in leadership. *Guts and Grace* is the modern woman's guide for how to bring your whole self to your work. An absolute must-read!"

Jennifer Graham, cofounder and CEO of Civic Dinners

"In a sea of voices proclaiming the importance of vulnerability, whole-heartedness, and authentic self-expression at work, *Guts and Grace* offers a concrete roadmap to help us get there. LeeAnn Mallorie gets inside the head of women at all levels of leadership, addressing both why it's tough and why it matters. If you are a woman who wants to make a bigger impact and still feel like yourself, I highly recommend this book!"

Meg Wheeler, founder and CEO of One for Women

"*Guts and Grace* is stupendous. It's full of the kind of truth and wisdom that I wish I'd known sooner, as I navigated increasing responsibilities in my own leadership journey. Today I run a global fellowship for women leaders, and so much of what we teach is covered within the pages of this powerful book. As a tribute to an inspiring mother and role model, this beautiful book truly warmed my heart!"

Julie Castro Abrams, founder of How Women Lead

"*Guts and Grace* is a book for all women (and men!) who want to step into their world in way that reflects their true essence. It is especially relevant for anyone who wants to lead—a company, a team, a foundation, a movement—in an authentic, honest, and empowering way. For too long it's been a survival of the fittest to get to the top. LeeAnn Mallorie offers an alternative that releases the need to strive at all costs. She demonstrates the innate strength, power, and grace within all of us for a new way forward in leadership and in life."

Jodie Priess, founder and CEO of Inspiring a Difference

"*Guts and Grace* is a remarkable achievement. LeeAnn Mallorie combines the latest work from the science of psychology with snapshots from her coaching clients and her own personal experience to provide a comprehensive roadmap to healthier, more empowered, and more fulfilling leadership. *Guts and Grace* targets women, but most of the men I know would benefit enormously from this book."

Barry Schwartz, UC Berkeley Haas School of Business, author of
The Paradox of Choice, *Practical Wisdom*, and *Why We Work*

"Today, many of us are so consumed by a culture of doing that we rarely have downtime to sit and reflect. This constant cycle even plagues us in our sleep. And the moment you open your eyes in the morning, the cycle begins again. *Guts and Grace* gives you a reason to slow down and engage in an introspective journey that can transform your life for the better. Walking down the pathway LeeAnn has created provides many thoughtful exercises, heartfelt stories, and inspiring ways to come home into your body. There is something here for anyone wanting to expand, grow, and lead in a deeper, more fulfilling way."

Leisa Peterson, author of *The Mindful Millionaire* and founder of WealthClinic

"*Guts and Grace* is a wake-up call for women leaders. It is an important reference book to help women realign their values and energy—and it provides embodiment exercises that can empower and fuel their leadership. The author hits home with the message that for many of us, this journey begins with accepting and loving ourselves. Changing the narrative for all conscious female leaders starts with each of us examining our personal stories and practices so that we can make a bigger impact together."

Laura Hall, partner at WHYZ Partners

"In *Guts and Grace*, LeeAnn Mallorie expertly lays out many of the leadership myths so many women succumb to from the start of their career. The advice contained within *Guts and Grace* beautifully reveals these social and corporate behaviors and importantly how to overcome them with kindness to yourself and others. Treat yourself to not only reading *Guts and Grace* but to practicing the techniques Mallorie recommends. You will find inner peace in conjunction with the wisdom you have to offer at work and in life."

Elizabeth Baron, vice president of Immersive Solutions at Silverdraft, LLC

"At a time when humanity calls upon women to be the agents of change, LeeAnn encourages this generation of feminine leaders to unlearn the current paradigm that has drained them of their inner power, and to operate from the one place that nourishes rather than diminishes the woman of service—her wisdom from within. *Guts and Grace* is a practical manifesto for women leaders who understand that true leadership must be both sustainable and conscious, and that their full service in the world can ONLY be achieved when they establishes the permissions and habits to nourish themselves FIRST."

David Bayer, CEO of David Bayer Industries, author of *Mind Hack*, and creator of The Powerful Living Experience

Guts & GRACE

LEEANN MALLORIE

Guts & GRACE

A WOMAN'S GUIDE TO **FULL-BODIED LEADERSHIP**

How to Lead Consciously,
Dissolve Glass Ceilings,
and Dismantle the Patriarchy Within

Conscious Capitalism Press
www.consciouscapitalism.org/press

Round Table Companies
Packaging, production, and distribution services
www.roundtablecompanies.com

Executive Editing	*Agata Antonow*
Cover Design	*Christy Bui*
Interior Design	*Sunny DiMartino*
Proofreading	*Adam Lawrence*
	Carly Cohen

Printed in the United States of America

First Edition: January 2020
10 9 8 7 6 5 4 3 2 1

Library of Congress Cataloging-in-Publication Data
Guts and Grace: a woman's guide to full-bodied leadership
/ LeeAnn Mallorie.—1st ed. p. cm.
ISBN Hardcover: 978-1-950466-09-2
ISBN Paperback: 978-1-950466-08-5
ISBN Digital: 978-1-950466-10-8
Library of Congress Control Number: 2019916955

For Karen Mallorie-Gerber,
Sylvia Seybert, Della Traister,
and all of our mothers,
who are doing the best they can.

THE FOUR KEYS TO FULLY EMBODIED LEADERSHIP

Embody

Embodiment is about wholeness—reclaiming any parts of yourself that you left behind in order to succeed earlier in your career. An effective, embodied leader knows how to bring all of herself to work, in a way that adds, rather than detracts from her professional impact.

Empower

Empowerment is about taking effective action, especially when the going gets tough. Rather than just looking okay on the surface, an empowered leader takes responsibility for her triggers, emotions, and thoughts, and uses them in a truly productive way.

Activate

Activation is about honesty of purpose—knowing what matters most to you, both in your personal life and at work, and taking aligned action. An activated leader takes the risk to honor her inner longing, rather than selling herself short and playing small.

Inspire

Inspiration is the moment where you take what's inside and share it with others. It's about being generous with what you think, feel, see, and know. An inspired leader dares to speak up in a way that invites others to stand beside her. In so doing, she becomes the catalysts—and the embodiment—of the change she wants to see in the world.

CONTENTS

PREFACE

I wrote this book in honor of my mother, because her story is where my story starts. Despite the fact that I intend this book to be a compelling volume on new-paradigm leadership, I know in my heart that every woman who is leading today got her chops from somewhere. And I've seen how that same "somewhere" plays a role—be it small or large—in the way we approach our work by default. Our early stories make us who we are. And whether we love them or hate them, we must *consider them* if we are to become fully conscious leaders of change.

From the time I was a young girl, I looked up to my mother for her spirit, passion, and miraculous ability to do everything that needed to be done in twenty-four hours and never get tired. At least that's what I saw at the time. At seven or ten years old, I was privy only to the grace with which she carried herself as she managed my sister and I, along with her business, our household logistics, family relations, and even the monthly budget. She was the executive director of our vibrant working-class household, the dotted-line supervisor of my father's marginally profitable division, and the CEO of a local business that taught discipline and rigor to school-aged community members under the guise of the arts.

She was my first baby-boomer superhero. For her, no task seemed too hard. Not only was she my protector, confidant, and mentor, but she played that role for several hundred other young women in our town who were served by her work. She was a brave, bold, and audacious woman who was willing to stand up for what mattered to her most. And she was an inspiration.

There was just one thing I remember questioning at the time . . . she didn't seem to eat. I remember thinking that after such a long day of hard work serving the world, I would have been hungry. And I was. Ravenous. I was a small child with an incredible appetite—both for food, and for new experiences. As I grew older, my search for the deeper truths in life took me first across the country, then around the world. I studied human psychology with the rigor of a top-notch academic, taught ESL in China with a grand plan about how uniting the East and the West could save the world, and eventually moved to the San Francisco Bay Area to pursue my small-town pipe dream: to change the culture of large organizations for the better.

On my journey, I began to see that while the lessons I had learned from my mother's determined and dogged lifestyle got me ahead in my career, they nonetheless left me feeling empty inside. As the unexplainable magic of my childhood ideals began to wear off, and the realities of womanhood set in, I found myself wilting. And grasping. Sometimes suffocating. And often longing. What I was longing for, I wasn't entirely sure. But despite how hard I tried to fill myself up with food, sex, love, or a higher paying job, the hole in me still remained.

I also began to see that I was not the only woman left starving by the lifestyle that I had ultimately created for myself. After co-facilitating ten years of deep-dive personal development workshops, delivering hundreds of business coaching sessions that secretly focused on the "human" side of our work dysfunctions, and putting myself through thousands of hours of training in mindset, somatics, energy healing, personal mastery, positive psychology, and transformational leadership, I was finally able to see clearly what my childhood intuition had already foreshadowed: *we must take the time to know and to nourish ourselves, if we are to live our lives—and lead others—sustainably.* This lesson became the foundation of my work.

The women I've supported over the past fifteen years have shared with me story after story of their breakdowns. And even my own mother, I began to notice, was feeling weighed down by the difficult things in life. Today, the cracks around the edges of who I—who *we*—were supposed to be as women are now starting to show. It isn't personal. It isn't about you, or them, and nobody is to blame. It's an epidemic. The physical, mental, and emotional wreckage that piles up when we put others first far too often, and stop listening to the admonitions of our own tender bodies, is striking. When the voice inside of us is tired of begging for our attention, it stops asking and starts demanding an audience. And there are costs. We get sick. We make a dramatic and costly mistake at work. Our husbands look elsewhere for love, or come to us with an unexpected request for divorce. Like a broken record, these stories seem to run, over and over, through our modern lives, and, when left unchecked, they become the legacies we pass on to the next generation.

Between hearing my early clients' stories and reflecting on my own story, I could not help but wonder: was all of this the inevitable fate of a woman in leadership? And if not, what was I doing that fed the re-creation of those patterns in my own life? At twenty-seven years old, I decided to become my own research project—a living, breathing exploration of conscious leadership, courageous embodiment, real authenticity, and radical self-care. I would do my part to stop the legacy that so many of us carry. I would tackle the various ways that our out-of-balance, performance-driven lives are killing us—starting with me first. I made the choice not because I'm a righteous person. But because, truly, *where else could I possibly start?* "We must be the change we wish to see in the world" isn't Gandhi's clever invitation. It's his experience-driven declaration of a universal truth.

Guts and Grace is your personal invitation to do your own version of the same experiment I've been doing for over a decade: to practice greater consciousness, get real with your vulnerabilities, get back in your body, and right the balance inside of yourself. And, in so doing, to help rewrite the paradigm of women's leadership, for good.

WHY THIS? WHY NOW?

Though I began my personal research project around 2007, I didn't opt to publish this book right away. I wanted to be 100 percent clear that there would be a viable audience when I finally released it into the world. Now, after the tidal wave of women choosing to *Lean In*, and on the heels of the #MeToo movement, I believe the time is finally right.

Today, it has become abundantly clear that a change in the way we do business, politics, policy—and therefore leadership—is needed. Our way of working has enabled societies to amass an incredible stockpile of wealth, in the form of financial gains, a rapid increase in knowledge, and unprecedented technological breakthroughs. At first glance, we appear to have become powerful beyond measure. Yet this progress has come at a cost to diverse peoples and to the planet. I believe it is time to fully empower new-paradigm leaders—especially women—who hear the call to lead in more conscious and sustainable ways. I believe it is time for these emerging voices to guide us in making some radically different moves.

The idea of women leading change isn't new. A growing body of evidence shows that many companies with women at the helm are now outperforming their counterparts in the global market,[1] and investors who have chosen to back start-ups headed by women are often seeing greater, and more reliable, returns on their investment. These statistics have taken both the internet, and the stages of women's empowerment conferences across the globe, by storm.

Yet, far too many of the go-to books on women's leadership for our generation are still teaching skills that harken to, and frankly ballast, the old paradigm of business. Rather than teach us how to authentically, painstakingly, and courageously rewrite the rules, these books teach us how to amass power, wealth, and success inside of the structures that currently exist. This isn't a bad thing. Sometimes women need to "play the game" for a while in order to earn the right to change it. But if we follow *only* these guidelines, we end up literally working against ourselves in the long run. While *inside* we may be receiving the impulse to take actions that would change business for the better, we are simultaneously juggling myriad messages about "the right way to get there" that are born of (and are perpetuated by) an outdated approach. This leads to confusion. Resentment. Exhaustion. Burnout. Faltering confidence. Wasted energy and wasted time. In other words, real progress just takes longer.

When we try to re-create hopeful statistics by teaching women to beat their male peers at the old game, we basically miss the larger opportunity. It's women who are doing it *their way*—paragons like Eileen Fisher, Mandy Cabot, Beth Comstock, and Elizabeth Barron—who have been going against the grain for *years*, whose innovative moves are truly changing the face of business today. This book is about backing *us*—the next generation of female leaders—to become *more like ourselves* and therefore do business in new ways we have yet to imagine. The first step is to *unlearn* the past.

Having served now for over a decade as an executive coach for conscious, forward-thinking business leaders (often the rebellious types who see a better future and are ready to take a stand for it), I've witnessed the same unconscious, self-sabotaging patterns play out again and again among my female clients. These patterns, which stem from chasing the old paradigm of leadership, prevent the very women who could be building our future from trusting their guts and taking the risks to make it happen.

In my work today, I help these women bring their whole selves forward—including their visions for organizational change—by breaking these unconscious habits for good. My clients are rethinking the evaluation of education programs in inner cities, stewarding sustainability efforts at Fortune 500 companies, rebuilding new-hire training and development programs for the Department of Defense, and challenging the financial industry to think differently about the social and environmental impact of their investment dollars. Through literally hundreds of hours of intimate, sometimes heart-wrenching, vulnerable and passionate conversations with these women, I have come know the territory well.

This experience, paired with my own personal and professional experimentation, led me to develop the leadership curriculum contained in this book. I am thrilled to share the insights—and surprisingly simple, life-hacking solutions—we have uncovered with you. Many of the lessons it contains were initially written while I lived in the UK from 2008 through 2010. It was a time of great change in my life. I had moved abroad to spend time with a new lover, having recently ended an eight-year relationship that was both deeply fulfilling and deeply toxic at the same time. In that relationship I came to see how I'd lost a huge part of myself in the wake of striving to be perfect for everyone else. I knew that something had to change, and, though I wasn't sure *how* to do it, I knew that I couldn't wait any longer.

I could sense that the change would begin to unravel a family legacy of women diminishing themselves through the supposed gift of service—both to their families and to their careers. And since service was deeply important to me, I wasn't willing to throw the baby out with the bathwater. Rather, I was committed to uncovering and re-righting the ways in which my own shadow and egoic needs perverted the potentially nourishing process of giving, turning it into a life-sapping endeavor. I was (and still am) unwilling to accept "either–or" in this case. Thus, the "*and*"—of *Guts and Grace*—was born. I believe that as women, we *can* have it all. We can serve others and care for ourselves at the same time. I believe this is a critical *foundation* of fully conscious leadership, and I am taking a stand that we do so.

At that time, however, I wasn't entirely sure where to start. I was still coaching executives for a San Francisco–based training firm, while living abroad. Working remotely gave me the flexibility of schedule I'd been missing in years prior. I knew my body was longing to be nourished, so I started to dance more. I both attended and taught classes several days a week. Feeding my own longing for a deep personal reconnection, while serving my clients who were hungry for the same, I began to write a weekly blog called *Living in Motion*. The blog offered my readers a single "somatic focus," or body-based mindfulness practice, to try each week. Those who also attended local classes would share about their experiences as part of each week's lesson.

Slowly, a synergy began to form. The topics that created the most profound changes in me also resonated deeply with my female students *and* the female leaders I was coaching. And vice versa—challenges that came up in our coaching sessions would find their way into the blog, and would influence my personal practice the following week. Thus, the blog became a tool for integration, helping me make sense of my own journey toward wholeness, developing new tools for my clients, and inviting everyone else to come along for the ride. The chapters in *Guts and Grace* are inspired by this body-based exploration.

BUT WHAT DOES THE BODY HAVE TO DO WITH LEADERSHIP?

As you make your way through this book, you will be reintroduced to the power and wisdom of your own body, using technologies like mindfulness, somatics, and positive psychology. While it may sound counterintuitive, I have observed that increasing our *embodiment* is one of the fastest and most direct routes to ignite new-paradigm leadership. Here's why: *it rehabilitates our innate capacity to find our own way.*

What I've found is that most people—especially women—unconsciously begin to ignore their bodies, and disconnect from their intuition, in order to get ahead in today's business context. And I'm not just talking about failing to exercise or meditate. We learn at an early age to favor rational thought, facts, and data over what we deeply feel. We learn to trust "the experts" over our inner knowing. We learn that we can overperform, running ourselves into exhaustion, in order to win the next contract. And at the same time, we learn that "driving" uninterrupted toward ever-increasing linear growth is not only possible, but desirable—and that any urge to the contrary can and should be overridden, for the sake of the bottom line.

I strongly believe that these collective tendencies (which have become synonymous with corporate culture) are at the root of what leads businesses to neglect certain stakeholders, build cultures that deplete rather than engage, exercise command-and-control leadership, and chase dividends over a higher purpose. The thirteen practices I teach in this book are designed to directly counter those tendencies and help you develop new, more conscious, integrated, and *sustainable* leadership habits, without making the old models wrong. They are designed to support your growth as a leader in both obvious and unexpected ways. Using your own embodied presence as a doorway, they will help you recover native superpowers you left behind earlier in your career and exponentially increase your capacity to lead.

Given these declarations, it's important for me to restate explicitly that every practice in this book was initially sourced *from the inside out*. Slowly.

Through deep listening. Through shared practice, through personal observation, and through client experimentation. While many of the practices contained in the following pages are now backed by cutting-edge research in neuroscience and positive psychology, no doctor or scientist had the first say in the birth of this work. I did have some help from my mentors in the expanding field of somatics, who taught me how to listen to my own body well. But after that, *the practice itself* became my teacher. In other words, the curriculum contained in this book was born from the practice of painstakingly conscious, full-bodied, new-paradigm leadership.

As you make your way through the book, you too will learn how to listen to your own intuition and trust the wisdom of your own body as an ever-present, universally available, original source of information from which innovative ideas and authentic approaches can be birthed. The wisdom of the body is accessible across lines of class, race, and religion. It is 100 percent open source. If you live in a human body, you're in. There is no application process. There are no fancy degrees required. All you need is an ounce of trust, the patience to listen, and the willingness to surrender your mind in service of your deeper longings. We all have this. It's in-built, and it's our birthright. This book is intended to be equal parts permission slip and user's manual, if you are ready to learn how to listen.

And, in case you are a woman who has some trepidation about going "off the grid" so to speak, I will *also* provide all the science you need to feel comfortable that the wisdom of your body does jive with what's "good, right, and true" from a modern scientific perspective. For your reassurance, I recently returned to academia in order to earn my masters of positive psychology (MAPP) degree at the University of Pennsylvania. I wanted to know if my own inner research matched the recommendations of this burgeoning new field that is turning the self-help and academic psychology worlds upside down. Long story short—it did.

In the pages of this book you will therefore also find references to some exciting new research that backs what our bodies have been whispering to us for decades. For example, science now demonstrates that money doesn't necessarily lead to happiness, that the body does inform the mind, that you're more likely to stick with your daily workout if you enjoy it, and that feeling good is actually good for you. Just remember that good science is designed to reveal and articulate the experience of the masses. It is only useful to you when the deeper wisdom of your own body-listening agrees. When there's a gap, I encourage you to listen *inside* first (i.e., trust your gut) and follow the thread you find there with rigor. It's through such audacious behavior that surprising new scientific discoveries—like the field positive psychology itself—are born.

In addition to science, this book has also been directly and indirectly influenced by ancient wisdom; spiritual guides; authors like Julia Cameron, Brené Brown, and Oriah Mountain Dreamer; embodied teachers like Richard Strozzi-Heckler, Debbie and Carlos Rosas, Samantha Sweetwater, Anna Halprin, and Claire Nuer; poets like Rainer Maria Rilke, Hafiz, Mary Oliver, and David Whyte; and many others. I have done my best to reference them, weaving their influence with my own stories and body wisdom.

I have also built in opportunities for you to develop *your own* reflections on the questions this book ignites, so that you can add *your own* wisdom to the living lineage of which you are now a part. This book isn't the first twelve-step program for personal transformation, nor will it be the last. But I do believe it is a powerful invitation—written for *these* times—when our relationship with self-care is still broken, and the costs of unconscious business are higher than ever before, for both people and the planet.

A ROADMAP FOR YOUR JOURNEY

Guts and Grace is organized in four sections: Embody, Empower, Activate, and Inspire. These are the pillars of conscious, full-bodied women's leadership. They also mirror the trajectory of my own personal and professional transformation. As I often say to my clients, I have been (and will be!) on this journey with you every step of the way.

In the first half of the book, you will learn how to enhance your resilience and emotional intelligence by consciously reconnecting with your own natural, body-driven impulses and learning from their wisdom. Together we will tackle six common leadership myths and their *uncommon* antidotes. We will also identify and deconstruct the core self-sabotage mechanism that makes up your own personal *internal glass ceiling* in order to help you reach your professional next level.

In the second half of the book, you will learn how to trust your gut and enhance your intuition in the context of your leadership. From this place of deeper listening, you will tackle questions of purpose, explore your untapped strengths and leadership "superpowers," and use embodied practices to manifest original leadership initiatives. Together we will focus on stoking your visionary flame, while at the same time building confidence, self-trust, and a comfortable relationship with both ambiguity and raw power, in order to bring those big visions to life.

The chapters of *Guts and Grace* build upon one another, taking you through a self-guided process of evolution. Each chapter includes vivid examples of common challenges facing women leaders, delivered via personal stories, client results, and scientific data. Each chapter also includes practical tools that address each challenge directly. By starting with resilience and emotional intelligence, and by weaving grounded, embodied practice through your entire journey, you will literally turn the rules of leadership upside down. My goal is to create a "permission factor" that will help you start taking yourself—and your instincts—seriously again. By frontloading with the stuff that's most missing in traditional leadership models (e.g., Joy), we will build your confidence to challenge the status quo on issues that matter down the road.

As you dive into the pages that follow, please promise me *one thing*. *Please don't just think about it!* Please, please do the practices. This wisdom came from the human body. It was born of a consciousness greater than thought. If there's one thing I know for sure, it's that *thinking more about it* is not going to get you (or us!) to the next level. This book is designed to be digested fully through embodied practice—and practice alone will lead to the results you desire. I urge you to give yourself that delicious and most precious gift.

INTRODUCTION
LEADING WITH GUTS . . . AND GRACE

I choose to risk my significance,
to live so that which came to me as seed
goes to the next as blossom,
and that which came to me as blossom,
goes on as fruit.

—DAWNA MARKOVA

WELCOME TO THE JOURNEY

Greetings brave, bold, and powerful woman.

I think I know why you're here. You are passionate, and you are stretched. Maybe you are even a bit overwhelmed, though you might not want to admit it. You know how to run fast . . . and you know what it feels like to run out of steam. You care about people, and you serve something bigger than yourself. You are committed to changing the tide in your organization, your community, or your industry. You do it well. And sometimes, it leaves you exhausted.

You got word about a book whose author suggests that it *might* be possible to have it all—to break through what's left of your glass ceiling . . . without burning out. And despite the little nagging voice in the back of your head that whispers, "No way, can't be; **there's a tradeoff between success and well-being—between drive and self-love—and that's not gonna change**," some part of you still wants to believe in miracles. That same part of you is longing for something beyond "Leaning In." Something different than "climbing the ladder." Something as empowering as "#MeToo"—but with clearly defined next steps. Something real, sustainable, and right for these unique and challenging times.

If I am right, you are anxious to take hold of your life and learn what it *really* means to thrive as a woman in leadership. Or maybe you've got a big vision that you want to take to the next level—to really *be the change* you wish to see in the world around you. But you're not quite sure how to walk that path in a way that both nourishes you and best serves others *at the same time*. What's more, you are probably riding on years of proof that all of this is *hard* to do. It might feel damn near impossible. And perhaps, if you're anything like me, a recent (or not-so-recent event) has shown up in your life that feels like a wake-up call. Does that even make sense? Do people get called to wake up? Who knows? But if it *is* a wake-up call, you don't want to miss your opportunity to answer.

This may seem like a strange proposal . . . but let's start here: think back to last time you hit a wall. A personal crash and burn moment. A phone call. An illness. A breakup. A lost client. An expensive business mistake. Can you remember a moment like that in your life? Were you taken by surprise? Did you feel upset, afraid, frustrated? Excited? Anxious? Without calling on any particular set of religious beliefs, I invite you to imagine that this moment was, in fact, a purposeful *adjustment*. In other words, just for a moment, try entertaining the thought that the event was neither good nor bad. Rather, it was simply a stimulus that required your response. And that "your response" may have been a needed course-correction on the path of your life. Let's call it a change in your trajectory; an opportunity to dance with the circumstance. Dare I say . . . a chance to become *even more fully* yourself?

If you're already feeling annoyed or anxious about what I'm suggesting, we might be on the right track. I don't take these kinds of situations lightly, make no mistake. But I am about to offer you a tool that begins where frustration ends . . . and helps you start listening to the wisdom of your body to get more of the results you want day to day. Take note of your feelings, take a deep breath, and keep on reading.

About ten years ago, at an early peak in my professional career, my doctor discovered a lump in my breast. I remember feeling as though time had slowed down. Something was different now, and my life was never going to be the same. Like the jerk of a knee when tapped by a hammer, I felt an instant shift in my physical body. Anger welled up inside me, and also fear. What am I going to do? The pain! The fear! The inconvenience! The money! How could this happen to me? Me, the unsuspecting victim. ALL those voices in my head were singing their angry songs. It wasn't my fault—and I didn't want to deal with it. And then . . . something surprising happened. In the back of my mind just a few seconds later, I got curious and I got a lot more present. In that moment, one question came to mind that summed it all up: *So now what?*

Now, what is needed in this moment? My mind stilled and cleared. My anxiety settled. Suddenly, the diagnosis became a piece of information like any other fact, and my own capacity to take action became the opportunity for a useful (or not-so-useful) response. I thought, *What is the very next step I need to take?*

The matter-of-factness of it caught me off guard. The truth is, I had been a self-declared drama queen for most of my life. My best friend even "majored in drama"—literally and figuratively—and we would often boast about it jokingly when things came to a head in our lives. What's more (though I hate to admit it), I'd been very comfortable playing the part of the righteous victim. Ah, yes. "Just let me just tell you how unfair the world is!"

But at that moment, something started to change. It was as though, on some level, the fear was so BIG that I had no other choice but to get present with the realness of the situation, and ask myself, "Okay, so now what?" Stimulus. Response. Information. Choice. Like a compass, I found that I could listen to the signals from my body to adjust course in the moment. I'll tell you now, from the vantage point of over ten years of deliberate practice: this choice is *always* available. It's actually how our bodies and intuition begin to teach us—*if* we are willing to listen.

The shift I made in that moment has become the foundation of my own healing and my professional trajectory as a leader. I will come back to this story again in chapter 6. The practices it inspired is are a fundamental part of the learning we'll be doing together as you make your way through the pages of this book. So. Now. What?

Even if you haven't faced any big life challenges lately, I will teach you how to harness challenging day-to-day events and use them to grow into the very best version of your self—in life, work, and leadership. Whether we're talking about reacting to a *major wake-up call*, or making a proactive choice to step in the direction of something deep that is *calling you forward* in a bigger way, that same act of pausing, slowing down, and tapping in can bring you to a new level of clarity. It can also have a massive impact on what you do next. (And how you do it.)

In my story, "so now what?" lead me to relax into a challenging and inconvenient situation . . . and take lots of deep breaths. Rather than spend energy on resistance, I rallied my energy to be present for my life, and the path became clear. Over a string of meaningful weeks, months, and years, I got to course-correct from a lifelong habit of righteous independence toward a series of vulnerable conversations, lots of asking for help, receiving care and support. I learned how to be more present with clients, family, and friends. And, by listening to the messages from my own body, I got clearer and clearer about the *one thing* I absolutely needed to change in order to fully heal . . . but more on this later.

In *your* story, "so now what?" might go something like this: So you started thinking about what it would be like to take action on behalf of your deepest longings, despite your already full and busy life . . . and in the process, you started reading a provocative book called *Guts and Grace*, because you are a woman who wants to have it all. You want thrive, body, mind, and spirit. You are committed to living in full alignment with your purpose every day. You want to shift from dancing with overwhelm toward cultivating a state of joyful, radical well-being, that allows you to sustain the energy and passion it takes to lead positive change—without burning out. And you want to be the kind of woman who models that for the world. You are choosing to dive in.

On that note, I want to say two things: Congratulations. And welcome to the journey.

Congratulations, because by deciding to pick up this book, you have already taken an important step toward activating your next level of potential. You invested your some of your precious dollars and committed to spend some of your precious time on yourself. I don't take that lightly. If you're anything like me, making time for yourself could be a big leap—perhaps not something you're used to doing every day. (Though THAT, my dear, is going to change . . . but don't worry, you'll be ready for it when it does!) The point is, you have already proven that you know something about how to take care of yourself, and you are willing to take a stand for what you need. If this book was about going to battle . . . well, then half of the battle would already be won.

But it isn't. Which leads me to the second thing: *Welcome to the journey.* One of the most important and fundamental principles of this book is that conscious leadership is a *path*, not a destination. That's why I use phrases like "sustainable leadership lifestyle" and "cultivating your *self* as a leader." While I've described this book as a twelve-week (or twelve-month) self-study program, I've got to be honest at the start: you're not going to bust every internal glass ceiling, achieve every dream, and thwart every bad habit you have in just twelve weeks. Some of the tools may take years to fully embody—it's a journey, and you can come back to these teachings again and again as you evolve.

That being said, you *can* experience massive breakthroughs in your leadership from the beginning to the end of reading this book. If you use the tools, you will likely experience a better relationship with your body, an increase in confidence, self-trust, and empowerment, and a lot more JOY. But I can't promise to give those things to you. Nor *could* I give them, even if I promised. As the old adage goes, this book isn't about me *giving you a fish* . . . it's about *you learning how to fish*. This type of gift can span the journey of lifetime. My promise is to be your compassionate and fierce tour guide along the way.

By the way, this is a gift that I didn't fully receive from my own family, while growing up. They couldn't teach me because they didn't know how. Back then, there were bills to pay, kids to feed, and wolves at the door. This kind of thriving was the last thing on my parents' mind most of the time. Maybe your family has a similar story? If so, this book is also about breaking the *legacy* of overworked, depleted, underactivated, and frustrated women in each of our lives. My commitment is that the journey we take together will help you become the woman you were truly born to be.

STEPPING IN: A MINDFULNESS PRACTICE

And so we begin. As we do, I invite you to *Step In*.

"*Step In*?" you may be thinking. "What does that mean?" If it sounds like a martial arts move, it is. At the beginning of any self-cultivation practice, it's helpful to set your focus and begin with a sense of purpose. In doing so, you lay the foundation for the richest possible experience to unfold. Have you ever spent an hour doing a task, only to find afterward that you didn't remember a thing? Your mind was on something else like work, the laundry, or whether there was enough dog food left in the bag to last till your next shopping trip . . . and the joyous feeling of being present got missed. *Stepping In* is a metaphor for any meaningful ritual that helps you initiate something consciously.

Here's an example. At the start of a Nia Technique class (one of my favorite forms of movement medicine), we *Step In*. Literally, we take a few steps forward while clearing our minds of the distractions from the day. This practice comes from the martial arts. Imagine a robed sensei and her students bowing slowly before setting foot on the practice mat. They do it together, and they do it with purpose. The goal is to become as fully present as possible. Though it may seem quite simple, it's incredible the difference this intentional entrance can create.

One of my clients, Krystina, recently shared that of the many practices I teach, this one made the biggest difference in her life. A badass millennial woman who had no problem tackling huge challenges in pursuit of a sense of accomplishment (when we met, she was readying to climb Mt. Kilimanjaro), she nonetheless felt deep down that she wasn't getting the traction she desired in her career. Krystina had a habit of rushing through the "small stuff" at work. After several months of self-observation, she realized she did this as a way of unconsciously avoiding full responsibility for successful outcomes, out of fear. Through our work together, she learned that a conscious beginning has the power to curb self-sabotage and set the tone for her full engagement in the long run. She started creating her own *Stepping In* rituals at work—and what a difference it made!

Perhaps you can relate? As we begin our journey together, you can use *Stepping In* as a way to set the tone for your experience—both here at the start of the book and at each new milestone along the way. Like a ceremony, or rite of passage, this ritual marks a new beginning. That was then . . . and this is now. I am ready.

Here's how to do it. Design a simple, physical ritual that helps you take a momentary pause with a purpose (e.g., a deeper breath, a bow, walking more slowly, feeling your back against the chair). Imagine it represents pressing a reset button that clears your mind and readies your spirit. You may also choose to answer these few questions in your mind. They will add clarity to your intention: Why are you doing this? What do you want to create in your life? How do you intend this very next action to serve you? Then, see yourself letting go of the past . . . set your intention . . . and *Step In*.

There really is no way to do it wrong. Just be sure to do it.

As you make your way through this book, I will regularly invite you to pause and take a few notes for yourself—starting now. The goal of this invitation is to help you make the learning your own. It's so easy to read this type of book like a tourist: "that's interesting . . . I'll take a picture and come back again later." But the magic of personal and professional growth *only* happens when you start bringing *yourself* to the table (i.e., taking action).

To support this process, I've included potent, relevant questions at the end of each segment for you to consider on the spot. You can also come back to them when you get to the end of the chapter, in addition or instead. I suggest brainstorming a few notes now, then setting aside some time mid-week for a deeper-dive journaling session.

As I suggest to my clients: "Don't think about it too hard; just let your hand write. First thought, best thought."

Stepping In: Reflection Questions

- Why are you reading this book? And why now?
- What changes do you want to create in your life, work, or leadership starting ASAP?
- What are you letting go of in order to be fully present with yourself right now?

SURRENDER AND ALLOWING WHAT IS—OR *GRACE*

Well done. Let's move on to the next step.

In order for you to get the most out of reading this book, there are a few other suggestions I'd like to make at the start. These are both tools and mindsets that have helped me along the way in my own journey. And here's the punchline: I don't expect you to "get" them right off the bat. In fact, most people don't. Rather, I'm telling you about them up front so that they can start sinking in. These tools *may* actually be the most difficult ones in the book. (Let me repeat that: These tools *may* actually be the most difficult ones in the book). Yet over time, they will become a part of your conscious leadership lifestyle—natural and embodied tools that you can access whenever you need them.

The first one is the tool of *surrender*—or *grace*. I also like to affectionately call this tool *allowing what is*. While it may sound cliché, I have found that the art of surrender is actually a practice. It's a very real and ancient kind of medicine, and it begins with your physical body sensations.

Think back again to the last time you hit a wall. At that moment, did you resist? Struggle? Push back? Or by chance, did you allow yourself to be carried through with grace? I hold no judgment either way (and neither should you!) But it is interesting to notice your automatic reaction to life's curve balls, large and small. I encourage you to take note. What's your go-to habit in these moments?

A few years ago, I was working with a client named Nora for whom *surrender* was the final frontier. Nora was a tough, no-nonsense East Coast woman who was good at getting things done. Yet, she'd hit a plateau in her career. Nora grew up in a man's world, having spent her entire career in the banking industry. She was often the only woman in the room, and she'd worked hard to prove her worth. In Nora's office, qualities like strength and control were held in high regard. But she didn't stop in the boardroom. Nora had started to bring these qualities home as well. She was the boss with her husband and kids, as she was back at work. As her duties and responsibilities increased, she was beginning to buckle under the strain of everything she was single-handedly holding up.

So that we could better understand the importance of qualities like strength and control in her life, Nora and I did some research into her past. We explored her growing-up years and found that her tendency to take responsibility for other people had started at a very young age. Stories from her childhood reflected her steadfastness and unwavering competence. For Nora, *surrender* meant giving up. It meant letting things fall apart and, in so doing, letting down the people she loved.

In one coaching session, things came to a head. Nora was scheduled to deliver some critical work on the same day her teenage daughter needed support with an important school project. We tried on *surrender* as a possible antidote to her stuck and frustrated feelings—feelings that had left her temporarily paralyzed. Nora envisioned a single-legged stool that represented her holding up the heavy world alone. She envisioned the stool growing two more legs while the weight above stayed the same. Nora's job was to welcome the support of the other two legs, while simultaneously trusting that the perceived burden of the weight above could be handled with help from others. Shortly after our session, a family friend whom the daughter loved offered to help out by attending the school function.

By surrendering to the support of others, Nora was able to hold a lot more, with less effort. And thank goodness she did. In the months that followed, her daughter faced several health challenges, her husband's job changed, her son entered the military, and she was offered a larger position at work. The practice of surrender became a new starting point. Like a trusted friend, it helped her expand her capacity and face these trials with grace.

You may or may not agree with the approach that Nora took in story above. Nonetheless, I invite you to take a moment and consider your own relationship with *surrender*—or *allowing what is.* When unexpected challenges come your way, do you tend to resist them? If so, where in your body do you feel the tension? In what ways does your approach seem to work? How does it serve you? And how, if at all, does it get in your way?

For example, in my own body, resistance feels like a rigidness that creeps into my muscles and joints. It shows up when I think I know best. Or when I think I am supposed to know best. The feeling starts in my shoulders. It's subtle at first, like a hardening, as though the soft flesh draped over my neck and back are turning slowly into cement. It creeps down to my chest and lungs, and my breathing shallows, even stops. My limbs pull inward. My voice becomes constricted, higher pitched. I speak faster. The space through which my vital energies flow becomes narrower, and, as a result, I also think more shallowly.

When I'm planning or acting from that mode, I am looking for solutions and certainties. I am stuck on the same old ideas that play like a broken record from my past. I am out of touch with possibility, with creativity. I worry about getting it right. I fear the worst-case scenario. I feel an overwhelming urge to construct a plan B and C and D . . . just in case. This mode feels safe. "I'm going to *make sure* things turn out well."

The problem is, it doesn't actually work—at least not in the long run (though frequently not in the short run either, if you count the ancillary costs). On top of that, it's frantic and exhausting. As my old friend and fellow life coach Charlene Wilson reminded me once, "The Universe wants to love you. It's just that you keep getting in the way." When I struggle to stay "in charge" and resist *allowing what is*, I keep myself one extra layer away from receiving the gift of my apparent misfortune and moving through it.

Now please don't get me wrong, I'm not talking about "giving in" to something bad happening, or "giving up" on your determination to get through it. I just mean that it's simply not necessary to work so hard against it. As in Nora's story, giving in and surrendering are actually quite different approaches. When you relax, breathe, soften, and *surrender*, it's amazing what can unfold. And what you can learn.

This practice can be applied to all types of challenges, from trials at work to difficult relationships to breakdowns in personal health. One of the biggest reasons it's difficult to change our physical bodies is that we spend very little time in genuine relationship with them. The same goes for our bad habits and counterproductive behaviors. *Allowing what is* doesn't mean ceasing to care about them. It doesn't mean ignoring a change that needs to take place. Rather, *allowing what is* is actually the first step we rarely let ourselves take.

As you read each of the chapters in this book, I encourage you to work with the embodied practice of *surrender* as an integral part of your journey—the *grace* in *Guts and Grace*. Give yourself this uncommon gift. As a starting point, you might try the following exercise: make the commitment for the next seven days to absolutely surrender to the person, place, and thing you are experiencing in any given moment. Instead of pushing against, look for ways to soften and go *through*. If you try it, take note of what unfolds.

By the way, since I first started teaching these tools in 2008, mindfulness and meditation practices have become much more popular in mainstream culture. This tool, of course, has deep roots in such traditions. Nonetheless, I'm continually surprised at how challenging this tool can be *in practice* for even the most experienced meditator. *Whether you're brand-new to the idea of surrender, or have been grappling with it for years, I challenge you to let yourself be a beginner here.*

Surrender: Reflection Questions

- What would it mean to "allow what is" in your life right now?
- What will be easy or difficult about that for you? How do you resist the sensation of surrender *in your body*?
- In what ways or domains, if any, are you already practiced at this tool? In what domains do you most resist it?

YOUR PACE AND NATURAL TIME

The second introductory tool I'd like to offer is something teachers in the Nia Technique community affectionately call "*natural time*." This tool is about trusting your personal rhythm and pace. In short: I encourage you to listen to your own body for cues about the pace with which you move through this book, and through your own life, starting now.

As Henry David Thoreau wrote: "If a man does not keep pace with his companions, perhaps it is because he hears a different drummer. Let him step to the music which he hears, however measured or far away."[2] While this quote is often used to reference the habits of eccentric people and community outliers, I believe Thoreau was onto something that's important for *everyone*. The truth is, we *all* have our own natural sense of pace, though many of us have forgotten how to listen. In a busy workplace, it's easy to absorb messages about how quickly you should be moving. Yet those messages may not jive with what's actually most effective for you. While social pressure has many of us look outside of ourselves for validation, our own bodies are often the best judges of *what we need*—and *when* we need it.

As a leadership coach, I have learned that many of my clients have a slightly different internal time clock than I do. The book is designed to

THE SCIENCE: RE-GOALING

Chris Feudtner, MD, is a doctor in the Department of Pediatrics at the Children's Hospital of Philadelphia, specializing in pediatric palliative care. He is also one of the world's leading experts on *hope*. For Feudtner, hope is not an idealistic state of Pollyannaish optimism. Rather, it is a reflection of the type of goals we choose. This reframe allows him to help families find hope in the most dire situations: the end of a child's life. Dr. Feudtner's engages with the strong emotions of frustrated parents, who feel "stuck" when all efforts to improve the child's health have failed. Effectively, there is very little that can be done. Nonetheless, the parents' mindset can make a huge difference for both the family and the child.

In these moments, Feudtner employs a process that he calls "re-goaling." He asks the parents, "Given the bad news, what are you hoping for now?" His question affirms the gravity of the situation and acknowledges that it needs to be reckoned with as is. Yet it also offers a possible way forward, in which the parents can choose to *engage with the inevitable* in a way that feels empowering. Often, they shift from a *quantity of life* goal (let's ensure she lives as many more days as possible, no matter what the cost) to a *quality of life* goal (let's do what it takes to ensure that her last days are as comfortable and happy as possible). This practice opens up possibilities for emotional healing and deeper connection. It also impacts the decisions they make in the following days, often leading to more positive outcomes than imagined, given the circumstance.

While Feudtner's research focuses on end-of-life care, it also can be applied outside the hospital walls, in our daily lives. When an outcome you were attached to suddenly becomes unavailable, you might find yourself wishing it weren't so. Re-goaling is a practical way to accept what is, while also maintaining an authentic feeling of empowerment. It can also help you identify the next best step to take, in the face of a surprising or challenging situation.

C. Feudtner, "Hope and the Prospects of Healing at the End of Life," *The Journal of Alternative and Complimentary Medicine* 11, no. 1 (2005): S-23–S-30.

be a twelve-week practice guide. But if you find yourself struggling to move from one chapter to the next in a single week (or month!), feel free to go at your own pace. For some women, twelve weeks may feel too long. For those who like to go deeper, or spend more time engaging with each practice, the right timing may be significantly longer. Remember, this book is about you *learning how to fish*—not about me giving you a fish. You can always come back to any of the lessons later or take longer to do them than I propose.

That's the book—but what about everything else? You can apply the *natural time* practice to your health, your work schedule, or any other domain in your life. If you are committed to learning how to thrive—to break through your glass ceiling *without* burning out—I encourage you to take every opportunity available to listen to your body. Ask it: What do I need right now? Do I need to speed up? Slow down? How might I need to tweak, adjust, or adapt the timing to best suit me?

When I was first introduced to *natural time*, it felt like a personal revelation. The truth about MY body-mind system is that it moves a lot more slowly than most people in some ways . . . and a lot more quickly in other ways. I was the last kid in my primary school gymnastics class to finally master the back walkover. But I often knew the answers to difficult test questions before the teacher had finished asking. This left me scrambling at times, bored at others, and typically feeling like there was something wrong with me . . . or everyone else.

When I finally took seriously the possibility that this timing problem was true for *most everyone* (especially women!), it freed me up to be less judgmental, more compassionate toward others, more creative, and ultimately more patient with myself. It also led me to confidently take actions that might at first seem countercultural for the sake of designing a life that enhances—rather than chips away at—my natural capacity to achieve.

For the skeptics: I do get that there are real external constraints we need to meet. The IRS isn't interested in your natural time on April 15. I understand you have bills to pay, kids to feed, and wolves at the door. Those external stressors may not change their demands . . . and surely aren't going away any time soon. The goal is to practice *listening to your body* in spite of that . . . and when you hear that your body's needs are in conflict with those stressors, try looking for *new ways to negotiate*. The first step is to STOP using "there's nothing I can do about it . . ." as an excuse to turn a deaf ear toward your own needs, and to start really listening. This practice is about learning to trust your body. Doing so takes practice and a clear intention.

There is also one small caveat I want to share. As you work with this tool, you may want to periodically check your own *honesty* about your timing and pace. While honoring your natural time can dramatically increase your effectiveness when done well, there can sometimes be a fine line between *natural time* and *habitual resistance*. For example, you might find yourself resisting diving into an activity, while telling yourself, "It's just my pace, I need to slow down." Over time, it is possible to get good at making the distinction between avoiding something because it's scary or difficult . . . versus honoring your own natural pacing.

There's a *lot* of juice in this distinction. It's part of the foundation of *Guts and Grace*, and many of the tools in the book will help you to make it. Learning the difference can restore lost power and reenergize your daily life—but it might take some practice. Trust that life will challenge you on this. Don't hesitate to challenge it back.

Your Pace and Natural Time: Reflection Questions

- How do you know when you're ignoring your natural time and pace? What signs does your body give you?
- What would it mean to honor your natural time as you move through this book?
- What do you suspect will be easy or difficult about that for you?
- Have you ever used your "pace" as an excuse to avoid something you needed to face? If so, how?

GOING THROUGH THE WALL—OR *GUTS*

Now brace yourself, because I'm about to add something that might sound contradictory. It's related to the caveat above. And I promise, it isn't *actually* contradictory. Your mission is to live with the tension, and, whatever you do, don't foreclose on a belief that one of these tools is truer, more valid, or more important. The truth depends on a mix of your personality, typical habits, and the characteristics of the situation in any given moment. Set a goal to find the place of "both–and" between everything I just introduced a moment ago and this one last critical piece of our introductory work together. I call this last practice: *going through the wall*, when resistance is high. This is the *guts* in *Guts and Grace*.

Can you remember the last time you reached a threshold where your mind rebelled? "Enough! I'm not cut out for this!" Or "Enough! I can go no farther." Or perhaps it sounded more like "Enough. I really don't like doing . . ." or ". . . just isn't for me." Or even "Enough. I'll never be able to . . . I quit."

I suspect that you are a strong woman who *gets things done*, so I've focused many of the early lessons on self-compassion and self-care. As the chapters unfold, I will be inviting you to listen deeply to the voice of your body and to trust the messages it has to offer. I will encourage you to make adjustments. To be more kind to yourself. To set boundaries around your time and energy, and to make choices from the wisdom of your body's deeper needs for the sake of your physical, mental, and emotional health. It's part of the overarching mission of this book—and it's a topic I am incredibly passionate about.

But sometimes—and this is a mission-critical distinction—*we let ourselves off the hook, when in fact, we shouldn't*. Sometimes . . . *enough* is NOT enough. What? When? Why? It's in the moments where our *resistance is high*, because we are about to break through something and really grow. Here's the punchline: To become a conscious leader, and to truly thrive, you will need to recognize those moments, and then muster your courage to *go through the wall*.

In my own practice I've come to realize, without contradicting myself or my strong stand for self-care, that I also am committed to "sticking with it." This practice builds character and strength. In summary, here's what it looks like: I regularly exercise a healthy degree of skepticism when it comes to activities that irritate, annoy, stretch, or scare me. This practice, though not easy, has helped me through difficult situations and enabled me to surpass myself time and time again.

As I sit here today revising this chapter—written originally more than ten years ago—I am surrounded by empty space. My new office is void of furniture, save one small chair and end table. The walls and the hardwood floors are bare but for a few white dog hairs. The air is thick with the haze of late summer California fires, and dark spots of mold peak out from the baseboard on the floor to my right. Currently, I await the forensic specialist who will test the mold and unveil the next steps in an already lengthy process of settling in.

This wasn't my plan. I was supposed to move into a clean, spacious, and freshly painted apartment and quickly get down to work. I was supposed to receive my furniture a few days later, host a housewarming party to reconnect with local friends, and finish revisions by mid-September. But the moving truck never arrived. After four weeks of sleeping on an air mattress *waiting* for the right moment to begin writing again, I realized this moment was simply another opportunity to hold myself deeply accountable to my own desires. Rather than let myself off the hook—which isn't hard when your friends think "it's crazy" that things haven't got better yet—I decided that under these frustrating and uncomfortable circumstances, *writing anyhow* would be the quickest way to truly get free. I decided that my desire to share this message with you was *more important* to me than the discomfort. I decided to *go through the wall.*

Here's how the tool works. Whether it be in learning a new fitness routine with music that I don't immediately love, or *repeating* a confronting conversation with a colleague *because* we didn't quite get on the same page the first time, I frequently put myself in non-dangerous but challenging situations that invite me to grow. Emphasis on "non-dangerous." In my experience, I have found there is something magical about the tension between "taking care of myself by bowing out" and "staying in so that I can stretch myself." Detecting the incredibly subtle but important difference requires a degree of intuition and the willingness to be 100 percent honest with yourself.

In writing this chapter, I asked myself, "*How do you know* which is which?" The truthful answer is sometimes I don't. But chances are, if I really feel positive (or feel a sense of nervous excitement) about an activity before I begin, and suddenly I change my mind in the middle because something catches me off guard, then it might be a good time to engage this practice. In this case, it's likely that I am on the right track and a lot could be gained by going through the discomfort.

Amanda is a friend and former client for whom the practice of *going through the wall* made a huge difference. A visual artist by trade, she had dedicated her life to fully honoring her inner compass. She was good at listening to her body and taking its cues about her own personal emotions, needs, and creative impulses. She trusted those impulses and took action accordingly. Interestingly enough, her body always seemed to have something to say.

When Amanda and I met, she was going through a period of drought in her business and suffering from a mild depression. Her mood swings affected her eating, leading her to consume more sugar and wheat than her system would tolerate. This led to sleepy, unproductive mornings that were often followed by afternoons of beating herself up. Despite the genuine sensitivity of her emotional state at the time, I knew that for Amanda, adding a measure of fierceness to both her work and self-care regimen would make a difference. In our coaching sessions, we explored the ways in which she typically "let herself off the hook" when she wasn't feeling well.

We discovered that depression, and her health reactions stemming from poor food choices, had become a self-fulfilling loop that unconsciously helped her avoid taking the next step in her business.

Amanda chose to put in place a few practices that would help her *go through the wall* and take the hard steps she needed to take in order to get traction. Slowly, as her work started to pick up as a result of these steps, her health and mood also began to improve. With practice, she came to recognize the difference between the moments when she really did need to stay in bed an extra hour to take care of herself, and the moments when her ego was using that desire as a strategy to prevent her from breaking through.

Amanda's example offers some real food for thought when it comes to the relationship between our work and our physical or mental health. Let's take a look at the key characteristics of her *going through the wall* scenario:

1. It was related to something she cared about a great deal.
2. It was uncomfortable to stick with it.
3. She assessed that seeing the work through, though challenging, would not actually be dangerous to her health.
4. There was a lot to be gained by going through the discomfort.

For many of us, the most important actions on our path to thriving, and living a life of purpose, involve these very same characteristics. Think about your own life for a moment. Can you remember an important time when you were challenged, stuck with it, and broke through? In this situation, *enough* wasn't enough.

Of course, there will also be times when you genuinely discover midstream that you made a poor choice that your body, mind, or spirit can't handle. In that case, it's okay to admit you were wrong (e.g., I thought I could handle this . . . but in fact it's just not a healthy situation for me . . .) and renegotiate. Emphasis on *renegotiate* (versus quit)—especially if it *is* something you care about a great deal. This is the "both-and" of *Guts and Grace*. Listen. Pace yourself. *And* know when to *go through the wall*.

Many of the women I support actually avoid diving into their life purpose all together because of the tension between these distinctions. They are *afraid* that if they commit to listening to their intuition, they will *lose* the "getting things done" superpower that helped them advance in their early careers. They fear that if they start taking better care of themselves, they will also start to fail when it really matters. They are afraid of becoming sloppy, giving in, and being "too soft." Mastering these distinctions is the solution. Using both, in the right moments at the right times, will help you cultivate a leadership style that is hallmarked by guts AND grace, in just the right measure. (That's what I call a sustainable, full-bodied leadership lifestyle. And THAT, by the way, is what I believe it means to TRULY lead like a woman.)

THE SCIENCE: GRIT

In the field of positive psychology, the practice of *going through the wall* is backed by research on a character trait known as *grit*. This construct has rapidly gained popularity among executive coaches and thought leaders in organizational leadership. Grit researcher Angela Duckworth defines grit as "perseverance and passion for long term goals." Having *grit* entails putting forth continued effort in the face of challenges, over the long haul, despite apparent failure, adversity, and inevitable plateaus in progress.

The payoffs of grit can be high. Individuals high in grit finish what they begin because they are determined to do so. They set their sights on what they want and go after it with vigor. Rather than changing their minds when the going gets tough, they are willing to stick with it and go through the fire until they reach the other side. In Duckworth's research, grit has been shown to predict the attainment of higher educational degrees. Grit also predicts higher GPA in students, above and beyond their natural intelligence. Gritty children work longer and harder than their peers. In so doing, they are more likely to accomplish their goals.

While there are upsides and downsides to the dogged pursuit of a goal, there is no doubt that exercising some grit in the face of what's *most* important to you can have a positive impact. It has been said that in order to achieve mastery in any discipline, ten thousand hours of practice are required. This applies to your life purpose as well as your thriving. If you are a person for whom grit is a growth edge, consider the ways in which adding *grit* to your toolbox could help you on your journey. On the flip side, if you are a person for whom grit is your typical MO, take some time to take stock of where and when your gritty nature is helpful . . . and where it may be a liability.

A. L. Duckworth, C. Peterson, M. D. Matthews, and D. R. Kelly, "Grit: Perseverance and Passion for Long Term Goals," *Journal of Personality and Social Psychology* 92, no 6 (2007): 1087–1101.

As we embark on this journey together, I encourage you to start developing your intuition for when "enough isn't enough," and to commit to going through your resistance. At the same time, I encourage you to listen for the true and deeper needs of your own body when it comes to your *natural time*. Confusing as it may be *in writing*, I assure you that in the dojo[3] of your own life, the distinction will become clear with practice. It may be the case that you're already better at one of these skills than the other. If so, choose the one that's harder and focus on that for a few weeks. Building a healthy relationship with *both* skills and learning which to choose in order to get the results you really want is what Aristotle called *phronesis*, or *practical wisdom*—the elusive golden mean.

Going through the Wall: Reflection Questions

- Why is breaking through your own glass ceiling and truly thriving so important to you right now?
- What do you want to learn so badly that even if you are afraid, you will stick with it?
- What have you been avoiding that you *know* would be really good for you?
- What are some fears (or judgments) you may need go to through in order to get what you want?

SUMMARY

It's time to begin. Because you picked up this book, I know that becoming a conscious leader—breaking through your own glass ceiling while thriving both at home and at work—is genuinely important to you. My promise to you is that these tools will help you develop a stronger intuition about the most effective way forward. Toss them in your pack, and let's start walking.

When you engage with *guts*—going through the initial "enough" to discover what lies on the other side of your wall—so much growth is possible. When you engage with *grace*, trusting your own body, and learning to dance with the curve balls that come your way, you will have access to a greater sense of flow. In balance, these tools will become the through line for our journey together. You are a powerful woman with an incredible capacity to impact the world. And I can't *wait* to see what unfolds.

In the next two sections, I offer a few additional pointers before you dive into chapter 1. They will help adopt the right mindset so that you can get the best possible return on your investment of time and energy throughout the learning process. They also include information on the materials you will need to gather before you begin, and a few key actions that will help set the gears of positive change in motion.

Good luck, have fun, and whatever happens next . . . enjoy the journey!

FINAL THOUGHTS: HOW TO USE THIS BOOK

Guts and Grace is designed to serve as a roadmap that guides you through the maze of your own feminine psyche and increases the impact of your leadership. Feel free to make your way through the chapters slowly. When you start from the beginning, reading one chapter at a time and implementing the practices contained therein, you will begin to re-access your natural, embodied wisdom. This process can happen quickly for some. For others, it can take a few weeks to get into the groove. It all depends on your starting point. Counterintuitively, if you self-assess that you're starting from a pretty unhealthy place (whatever that means to you), you may begin to see results *more* quickly. In other words, any small change can make a big difference when you're pretty far off the rails. Have at it!

In contrast, if you already have a lot of positive lifestyle practices in place, you may find that some chapters simply support you to anchor and deepen what you've already been doing. In your case, the larger, more feelable impact will come in one of two situations: 1) when you "bump into" a chapter that holds the key to a single, critical shift that you've been missing; or 2) when you uncover a small but critical nuance in a section that you previously thought you'd already mastered. Be sure to pay special attention in those situations. Challenge yourself to go deeper. When it comes to personal and professional transformation, taking a beginner's mind approach can mean the difference between glossing over a vein of gold and finally breaking through.

In either case, I generally recommend *working with the book from start to finish*. The chapters are designed to build upon one another, helping you to *see* and *feel* way that each ingredient supports you to construct a more solid foundation. The ingredients in each chapter interact with one another to form a positive synergy, similar to a chemical reaction, that can lead to upward spirals in all domains. To my delight, when I started running women's courses using the *Guts and Grace* process, one of the overwhelming pieces of feedback I received from clients was, "I can't believe it! When I looked at this week's lesson, I realized I had already

THE SCIENCE: PRACTICAL WISDOM

As far back as Aristotle, a paradox has existed in relation to our human virtues and skills. Even when a personal characteristic is highly *practiced* and *adored*, simply using it all the time isn't a good thing. Aristotle pointed out that the over- or underuse of a virtue—or the use of that virtue in a moment when something else entirely was needed—would ultimately lead to ineffectiveness. To address this issue, Aristotle coined the term *phronesis*, which loosely translates to *practical wisdom*. From Aristotle's perspective, *phronesis* was indeed the master of all other virtues. Without it, one could be rich in many other character strengths while moving through the world in ways that were unproductive or, worse, brought great harm to others.

Positive psychology and business scholar Barry Schwartz writes about this master virtue in his book *Practical Wisdom: The Right Way to Do the Right Thing*. According to Schwartz, practical wisdom requires 1) having cultivated the *skill* that is being called for the moment and 2) having the *will* to exercise that skill when it is needed. Neither one is enough on its own—and both steps pose an opportunity for possible failure when it comes to doing the right thing, in the right way, at the right time. If I don't have the skill, I am unable to execute the most relevant action. If I don't have the will, I may default to something easier or more within the range of my general comfort zone.

Schwartz references the behavior of expert firefighters as an example of practical wisdom in action. Rather than relying on a cookie-cutter set of rules (which would be hard to do, since the exact nature of every fire is a bit different), or always using one signature approach (which could be fatal, if that approach was not the right one for the situation), these firefighters would hold a general set of guidelines in mind, bring along their entire bag of tools and skills, and read the situation quickly to decide exactly which approach to take. Take a moment to consider your greatest strength. Have you ever applied it in the wrong moment and gotten hideous results? *Practical wisdom* is about just that. It is more than balance . . . it is elegance in motion. As you move through the book, this tool can be helpful when dealing with inevitable paradoxes between the tools you will learn along the way.

Barry Schwartz and K. E. Sharpe, *Practical Wisdom: The Right Way to Do the Right Thing* (New York, NY: Riverhead Books, 2010).

naturally started thinking about (or doing) *exactly that*, based on what I learned last week!" The same thing may happen to you. If so, having this kind of *visceral* experience of synergy will help you remember weeks, months, and even years later why it's important to *keep* those practices in your life, even when the going gets tough.

All of that said, there is one potential caveat. You may have picked up this book with a very *specific challenge* in mind (e.g., I'm totally burned out, I'm desperate to understand my purpose, etc.). If that's the case, you can choose to start at the beginning of the *section* (Embody, Empower, Activate, and Inspire) that seems most related to your challenge. Begin with the *first* chapter in that section—even if you're not sure why it matters—then progress through the sections that follow in a circular fashion (10, 11, 12, 1, 2, 3 . . .), ending with the chapter just before the chapter with which you began. By following the order in this way, you will still receive the benefit of the alchemy between the chapters mentioned above.

TAKING ACTION: YOUR FIRST "HOMEWORK" ASSIGNMENTS

Now that we've got through some of the introductory course philosophy, and logistics, it's time to move into action. Each chapter of this book ends with a section called "The Practice," which provides detailed instructions for several embodied practices and new actions that will activate your learning. (You can also find a library of practice downloads, organized by chapter, at www.gutsandgrace.com/book-resources/). The foundation of this book—and the program it teaches—is based on taking concrete steps. Doing. Moving your desires, dreams, and needs out of idea form and bringing them to life. While that may sound obvious, you might be surprised at your own resistance when you're actually about to begin.

So, before you dive into the next chapter, there are a few small but powerful things I'd like you to do first. My clients and I lovingly call these types of assignments "homework," purposefully taking back a negative word from their younger years. We use it to refer to the positive life-giving practices, actions, and rituals that they elect in order to make a change for the better. The goal of these actions is to start building the foundations of your conscious, full-bodied leadership lifestyle and to support your ultimate thriving. The truth is your life will only change when you choose to begin. You know this already, of course, but it can be so tempting to read a book cover to cover before even considering taking a single step. It's our habit. And it's our comfort zone.

I will never forget the day a client told me she wasn't going to start exercising yet *because she wasn't fit enough*. This kind of thinking keeps us stuck! Creating a new lifestyle isn't about getting it right or even being ready. It's about taking those vulnerable first steps while practicing self-acceptance, self-love, and self-forgiveness . . . learning to be your own personal accountability buddy.

In other words, just do it. I promise, you will be glad you did!

The Practice

Ready to get started? I challenge you to start *today* and take at least one action on this list. If you resist . . . that's part of the learning process. These first actions may seem deceptively simple—even juvenile. Remember, the learning is in the *doing* itself. Whether you're a new manager or the CEO of a Fortune 500 company, you can trust that each one has been hand-selected to catalyze a particular aspect of your personal and professional growth immediately. Some of these actions may be totally new to you, while some may be things you have already done before. Some may be easy for you, and some may be hard. If it's all new (or all difficult), don't worry. It doesn't matter. Pick one. Start with what inspires you. Or . . . start with what scares you! Why not?

ACTION 1: ADJUST YOUR PACE

You made a big investment in yourself just by picking up this book. In order to get the most out of your experience, I challenge you *slow down* and make some space in your life to use it well. Take a look at your calendar and carve out a bit of time (one to two hours a week) for reading a chapter, journaling, and engaging in activities that support your learning. I know that you are a busy woman. I *know* that might sound like a lot—especially if you've got too much on your plate or you feel burned out. It may sound cliché, but this is *exactly* the time when you need it most. This book is designed to make sure that you put in enough positive, proactive time to counterbalance the things that are currently draining you. I promise there will be no "busy work"—every minute you invest in the activities will serve to generate more energy and directly impact your mood *and* effectiveness each week.

ACTION 2: GET A REALLY GREAT JOURNAL

Treat yourself. Go to your favorite bookstore or art shop and by yourself a brand-new journal. Designate it specifically for this course. Choose the one that makes your eyes sparkle when you look at the cover. If you have a creative streak, you may want to choose the kind with some lined pages and some blank pages. It will be your companion for the journey.

Starting immediately, write a page or so on whatever comes to mind. Try doing this every day for a week. You can do this in the morning or evening . . . or any time you feel as though you really need it. You can write hopes and wishes and inspirations. You can also dump your fears, worries, musings, etc. You can jot down stuff you're learning or questions that you have. It's okay to draw or doodle, too! There is no way to do it wrong. This practice builds self-awareness, which will be critical for your progress over the next few months.

ACTION 3: GATHER YOUR *GUTS AND GRACE* PLAYLIST

Music speaks to the body and soul. Wherever you gather music, start an empty playlist. Call it "G&G Music." Add one or two songs that have been calling to you lately. Over time, your assignment is to create a collection of songs that either reflect your current mood or reflect how you'd like to feel. They don't have to all be happy! Feel free to include songs that feel positive *and* negative. Happy, uplifting, sad, angry, fearful . . . don't leave any emotions behind if you feel called to include them. Any time you hear a new song that seems to fit, you can add it to your playlist. I will also include a few of my favorites that resonate with the lessons for each chapter. You may love or hate mine, of course. Music is very personal! If you'd like to explore the relationship between mood and playlist more in more detail, check out the book: *Your Playlist Can Change Your Life.*[4]

ACTION 4: DIET AND THIRTY-DAY CHALLENGE

I've never been a fan of extreme diets. Rather, I advocate that women really listen to their bodies and make tiny, authentic changes that align with how they most want to feel on a daily basis. If you've already made a dietary change recently as part of your intention to become a more conscious leader, you're done! Just do what you've already committed to. If not, I invite you to set one simple, doable nutritional goal today. Research shows that kicking off a lifestyle overhaul with *one simple and doable commitment* helps build momentum and leads to greater success.

Choose a goal you know you can reach and stick with it for the next thirty days. Choose by trusting your intuition and being honest with yourself. What would make a difference for you? For example: no alcohol, only drink water, eat green veggies, cut sugar, cut carbs, less coffee, stop smoking. Start immediately. Then, over the next four weeks, pay careful attention to how your body feels, having made this change. Notice how it changes over time. Take note of anything you observe in your journal several times per week.

PS. Don't pick something you "should do" that would make you miserable. Pick something you want to do. The goal of is *not* to leave you feeling deprived. The goal is to give yourself a small, meaningful win. Start TODAY!

BONUS: TAKE YOURSELF ON A ME-DATE

This action may be the juiciest. As a fun bonus, *I invite you to take yourself on a ME-DATE to celebrate the big step you just took by choosing to invest in yourself.* Here are the rules: The date must be two hours minimum. It can include eating your favorite food or doing anything else you LOVE. You must do this totally alone. It's about enjoying the time with yourself. I'm not kidding. And I dare you to do it before you read the next chapter.

Of course, none of the actions proposed in this segment—including the date—is a deal-breaker. They are all for you, to support you on your path. You are still allowed to read the next chapter, even if you don't do them. But if you find yourself resisting, it's not a bad idea to ask yourself "why?" What's so bad, so tough, or so inconvenient about doing these few things for you this week?

Most importantly . . . whatever you do . . . don't beat yourself up. Do them when it feels right—or like a special treat, when you need a break from the hustle and bustle of your daily grind. Have fun and enjoy the ride!

Guts and Grace Playlist Suggestions

"Footsteps in the Stars" – Deya Dova

"Hello" – Antigone Rising

"Hello Bonjour" – Michael Franti

"Lost and Found" – The Polish Ambassador

"Grace Fully" – Wildlight

"Send Me on My Way" – Rusted Root

Embody

"Every experience I've had in my life is a resource in my body."

—ANNA HALPRIN[5]

Embodiment is the pursuit of wholeness—body, mind, and spirit. It's about reclaiming and integrating parts of yourself that you may have left behind in order to succeed earlier in your career. Ultimately, a compelling and effective leader knows how to bring all of herself to work in a way that adds, rather than detracts from, her professional impact. In this section, I introduce practices that help you refuel your energy tank and make space for your whole self.

LEADERSHIP MYTH

When you're striving hard to make an impact,
and you're already exhausted . . .
your body—and your joy—must come last.

LEADERSHIP TRUTH

Powerful and compelling leadership starts
with a full tank of positive energy. So the first
order of business is to get back in your body
and prioritize feeling good.

Chapter 1

THE JOY WORKOUTS

O keep squeezing drops of the Sun
From your prayers and work and music
And from your companions' beautiful laughter
And from the most insignificant movements
Of your own holy body.
Now, sweet one, be wise.
Cast all your votes for Dancing!

—HAFIZ

ANABOLIC PRACTICES FOR THE BODY, MIND, AND SPIRIT

They say that a journey of a thousand miles begins with a single step. While we tend to take that expression as a beautiful metaphor, I've also found it useful to take it literally. In this first official chapter of *Guts and Grace*, we will start our journey together by moving forward—in the flesh. In this chapter, you will lay the basic foundation for conscious, sustainable, and thriving feminine leadership by designing your first Joy Workout. Through this practice, you will evolve your relationship with *movement* itself.

Wherever you are *now* is the perfect place to start. This practice is appropriate for women of every fitness level. Whether you have an existing exercise routine, or whether the idea of moving regularly reminds you of how tired you already are, this chapter is designed to help you build energy. Over the last decade of coaching, I have seen time and time again that the first major energy leak in most women's lives is their failure to "get moving" often enough. This may sound counterintuitive. We need energy in order to move, right? So . . . isn't movement itself an energy leak? This line of thinking leads to the following leadership myth: ***When you're striving hard to make an impact, and you're already exhausted . . . your body—and your joy—must come last.***

But the science tells a very different tale. In fact, movement itself not only increases energy and boosts your mood, but it has been found to improve your cognitive function as well. Clinical trials show that regular exercise is more effective at reducing fatigue than prescription drugs. And that's *good news*! Compared to drugs, exercise is better for your body, easier to access, and costs a lot less. The truth is: ***Powerful and compelling leadership starts with a full tank of positive energy. So the first order of business is to get back in your body and prioritize feeling good.***

You may have already heard these striking statistics. They may or may not have inspired you to get moving. You may be thinking, "Yeah, I know I should . . . but I still don't." Or you do, but you still feel drained. It's all good. Again, wherever you are now is the perfect place to start. In this chapter I will add fuel to the fire of your curiosity by suggesting that not only *what* you do but also *how* you do it make a big difference. In the spirit of playful exploration, we will use movement as a metaphor for life . . . and as a way to hold yourself accountable to what you deeply want. But first, I'm curious . . .

Have you ever had a morning when it was tough to get out of bed?

When you're stretched, it's easy to feel heavy or sluggish in the morning. Or, in contrast, you might find yourself on overdrive—hyped up on natural adrenaline and determined to get everything done from the moment your head leaves the pillow. Unfortunately, both states create a negative internal landscape, in which your stress is more likely to thrive than you are! What you need is a real antidote—something that helps create a positive internal landscape and genuinely builds up energy instead of further depleting it. That antidote is Joy. And your body holds the key.

In his book *Flourish: A Visionary New Understanding of Happiness and Well-Being*,[6] positive psychology founder Martin Seligman shares cutting-edge research that challenges our current approach to the treatment of depression and other mood disorders. He puts forth a five-pronged approach to human flourishing that includes cultivating positive emotions. It's not enough, he argues, to simply reduce negative emotions. Why? Because as human beings, we don't just want to *not* feel *bad*. We want to feel *good*. What's more, positive emotional states broaden our perspective on life and build resources that can be drawn upon in times of stress. In his book, Dr. Seligman describes a variety of simple activities that people can use to *increase* their experience of positive emotion. But how does that apply to the physical body?

Making a similar case in a different domain, alternative cancer treatment specialist and Mederi Center founder Donald Yance argues that "anabolic" treatments that *rebuild* the body's immune system are both hugely missing in standard cancer treatment programs . . . and also critical to the success and survival rate of high-risk cancer patients. Yance advocates for supplementing standard medical treatment plans with immune-rebuilding activities that affect the physical body, emotions, mind, and spirit. As a jazz musician, he particularly likes treatments that include music.

These experts' research findings give us good reason to consider how we spend our time. Think for a moment about the activities that put you in a good mood, promote your physical wellness, raise your spirits, or otherwise bring a sense of Joy and well-being to your life. I'm curious . . . what is your favorite "Joy" practice? This may be an activity you do often or one you've all but left behind. If nothing comes to mind, think all the way back to your childhood. Even if you're not doing it now, was there something you once loved to do that made you really happy? When you have an answer (even if you're not sure it's the best answer), take a few notes about it in your journal.

Anabolic Practices: Reflection Questions

- What is your favorite "Joy" practice, and what do you love about it?
- How often do you do it right now? How come?

BORN TO DANCE

If the idea of practicing Joy is already rocking your world, then hold onto your seat—I'm about to propose an answer to the question, "How do I do that?" which may sound surprising at first. While it is by no means the *only* viable option, I've seen *so many* evolving female leaders have great success with this practice that I couldn't dare deny you the chance to try it out for yourself.

It's also the one I love best. Having tried everything from downhill skiing to long distance cycling to improvisational singing to retail therapy (yes! that's a technical term), I nevertheless keep coming back to this practice. My favorite Joy practice—what I call my personal movement medicine, and the one we will use as a tool in this chapter—is dance. Why? *Because I believe that human beings were born to dance.*

Wait, don't stop reading! Even if you're skeptical, or have never danced a step in your life, stay with me for a just a few more pages and hear me out. Whatever reaction that last sentence evoked—be it "yay!" or "holy crap!"—take note. If you want to make a change, getting out of your comfort zone is bound to be a part of the process. Many of us have connotations that make it tough to entertain the thought of dancing—especially in public! But dancing is a fantastic metaphor for a way of life that's more conscious, honest, and engaged than the rote, half-checked-out ways we move through life when we're in default mode.

If you watch a great dancer, you can see unequivocally that there is a clear emotional connection in the execution of each move, and also a sense of transcendence—of tapping into something larger. *Feeling* is present, both emotion and physical sensation. The music serves as the undercurrent of *flow* that carries the dancer through each intentionally executed step.

THE SCIENCE: FLOURISHING

What *are* the ingredients for a happy life? When positive psychology founder Martin Seligman moved away from his research on learned helplessness and started studying the good things in life, he observed that most of mainstream psychology was focused on *dis*-ease. The number of recognizable, diagnosable mental disorders listed in the DSM (*Diagnostic and Statistical Manual of Mental Disorders*) was increasing at a rapid rate. Yet little was known about the positive aspects of the human condition like hope, meaning, relationships, flow, spirituality, happiness, which make life worth living. While traditional psychology aims to bring people who are suffering back to baseline (*I am okay*), positive psychology aims to leave its beneficiaries with a positive net gain (*I am better than I was before*).

With his colleague Chris Peterson, Seligman set out to create a classification of personal virtues and strengths that would become the positive equivalent of the DSM in the twenty-first century. These character strengths can now be measured using a simple self-report measure called the VIA (Values in Action) strengths assessment.

Seligman also put forward a model called PERMA-V that summarizes his research on the key ingredients of a flourishing life. The acronym stands for: positive emotions, engagement, relationships, meaning, achievement, and vitality. If you are feeling low, this model can help you assess what areas of your life may be the cause. It also indicates what kind of "positive medicine" (e.g., increasing your sense of meaning), if taken in the right dose, would help to rebuild your system and refuel your life. Many of the lessons you will find in *Guts and Grace* fall into one or more of the PERMA-V categories.

The dancer is a channel for the universal *life force*, or *God*, through which miracles appear to easily unfold. This type of dance can reflect the *human spirit* in action.

What's more, when practiced in a healthy and self-honoring way, dance can leave your body feeling great! Physically, dance warms up the muscles and loosens the joints. Energetically, dance begins to move stuck energy around the body, allowing you to feel lighter and freer. Dance, like other movement, also releases endorphins, which elevate your mood, and other chemicals that trigger the body's natural healing systems. And if you get moving vigorously enough, you can counteract the buildup of stress hormones that have accumulated in your body throughout the day.

Lastly . . . have you ever met a joyful toddler who didn't know how to dance? It's a built-in part of our human operating system. For all of these reasons, I invite you to try the idea (and the practice) on. Ask yourself this question, "How could it serve me to remember how to dance?" and see what comes to the surface. Below are a few more reflection questions to get you started.

Born to Dance: Reflection Questions

- In general, how do you feel about dance?
- What, if anything, do you *love* about dance? What do you *hate* about it?
- What is your historical relationship with dance? In other words, what was it like for you when you danced in the past?
- What's your hunch about how it might it serve you to dance (in body or in spirit) at this time in your life?

MOVING IS HEALING

Of course, there are many different kinds of dance. For our journey together, I suggest exploring a genre called "conscious dance." Frankly, though, any dance will do, if you approach it with the right attitude. I love the conscious dance movement because it *isn't* about getting the steps right, being perfect, or aspiring to stardom on stage. Instead, this genre encourages an attitude that supports healing and personal growth. Some forms of conscious dance are designed to provide a great workout. Others release everyday stress and negative emotions. Some teach skills for deeper intimacy. Still others focus on healing childhood trauma. For me, the expression *conscious dance* loosely translates as "dance that's about loving how it *feels* to be in your body rather than looking perfect or getting it right."

Some forms of conscious dance have steps, and some simply ask you to move in a way that feels good to you with no particular guidelines or rules. My own weekly practice includes a fusion fitness form called the Nia Technique[7] and a guided freeform movement practice called Dancing Freedom, which works with the five elements (earth, water, fire, air, and ether). These two practices have provided a foundation for the embodiment practices discussed in the rest of this chapter.

Let me tell you why I chose them. First, these two dance forms both offer a direct pathway to Freedom and Joy (in fact, the Joy of Movement is literally the first principle all Nia Technique instructors learn to teach). Here, I don't necessarily mean the emotion of Joy. Rather, I'm referring to the pleasurable *physical* sensation that happens when we free our mind from fears, worries, criticisms, and distractions and just enjoy moving our bodies in a way that feels good.

When practicing Nia—or any form of dance—you can practice *choosing Joy* (a powerful skill that can also transfer into the rest of your life!). That means, in each moment, you shift your attention away from any distracting thoughts and bring it back to the sensations in your body. You ask yourself how it feels—does it feel good? Pleasurable? Painful? Uncomfortable? Tense? Relaxed? First, you notice what is, without judgment (sound familiar?). Then you remember that you have a choice.

Choice is a critical ingredient in cultivating Joy—both on and off the dance floor. If you're not feeling good, you can always choose to tweak something about the way you're moving in that moment. This creates more room for the physical sensation Nia Technique instructors call "the Joy of Movement." So, rather than focusing on getting it right, doing it perfectly, or looking like the instructor . . . you learn to move in such a way that it maximizes the pleasurable physical sensations of movement in your body. (Remember . . . you are learning to fish.) If this sounds like fun, I encourage you to try it! Dancing this way allows you to be the starting point of what *you* want to feel. And by the way, it can be a blast.

The second reason I endorse these forms of conscious dance is that both encourage the dancer to access the full *range* of what's possible for them—physically, mentally, emotionally, and spiritually. Based on our unique past experiences (even traumatic ones), many of us have shut down certain thoughts, emotions, or areas in our bodies. Check in with yourself for a moment: are there parts of you that you typically keep under wraps? Practicing dance is a great, nonintrusive way to start unlocking and unthawing yourself without a lot of heady dialogue . . . and to enjoy yourself while doing it.

When I first met Sabina, she had recently ended a difficult intimate relationship and was struggling to stand her ground in the face of a negative and critical boss. While I experienced her as a deep and fiery woman, she seemed to shrink in the face of these challenges in a way that surprised me. In addition to coaching, Sabina decided to attend some of my local movement classes as part of her personal journey. In one particularly rich class, we'd been doing a series of martial arts punches and kicks. Sabina approached me after class, with her eyes wide in wonder.

"You'll never believe what popped into my head while dancing!" she exclaimed. As you can imagine, I was curious. She went on. "I heard a voice—my own voice, I think. It said, 'Who taught you that you are so weak? Actually, you are *strong*!'" Through movement that evoked her fierceness, she was able to reclaim a part of herself that had been hiding in the shadows for many years. It happened without effort—by accident, in fact. Upon later reflection, she realized that she had heard those messages many times, growing up as a woman in her strongly masculine household. Through the physical practice of conscious movement, Sabina was able to reclaim her power. By bringing the essence of that breakthrough into her life at large, she was also able to take charge in new ways back at work.

Having heard Sabina's story, you may wonder, *What if my body isn't made to do THAT?* Perhaps powerful tae kwon do punches just aren't your thing. Or perhaps your hips don't have the mobility of a seasoned salsa dancer. It's okay! At the risk of sounding like a broken record, wherever you are is the perfect place to start. You can choose a conscious movement practice that works *with* the design of the body rather than against it. These practices will help you learn to listen to your body for guidance. Every BODY moves differently. And every BODY can find a safe, pleasurable way to move.

In their book *Nia Technique*,[8] Debbie and Carlos Rosas reveal how the structure and design of the body let us know that human beings were built to move in many more ways that we typically do. The body's design says that our muscles were built to extend and contract but also to spiral. Our bones were built to serve as the frame—a coat-hanger-like structure upon which the rest of our body rests. Even more importantly, the body's design calls for our life-force energy to be in constant motion. The body itself loves energetic contrasts: fast and slow, strong and soft, agile, flexible, start and stop . . . even the emotional expression of a variety of moods (happy, sad, angry, excited, afraid) can contribute a great deal to the physical health of the body.

For these reasons, our modern-day sedentary lifestyle takes a massive toll on our physical, mental, and emotional well-being. Listening keenly to the design of our bodies is a powerful way to enhance our physical, mental, and emotional sustainability—and feel good while doing it! But this practice isn't just for couch potatoes. It's for any woman who sometimes asks her body to do things it's not built to do (e.g., sit still for long hours, uninterrupted). It's about listening *to* your body for the antidote and slowly expanding your physical and emotional range—so that you can access the right energy, in the right moment, when you need it. Whether you're an experienced athlete or just getting started, I'm willing to bet there are some benefits you will get from deeper listening, an orientation toward Joy, and the call to "dance" that you just may not find anywhere else.

Dr. Tasha is a high-performance athlete and exercise physiologist, who was running an in-home physical therapy program that served local corporations when we first met. When she joined my women's program, she was struggling with burnout, despite her healthy eating habits and solid exercise regimen. She told me she was looking for tips on stress reduction and better time management. Even though she already saw herself as an expert in the domain of movement, she decided to try this practice on . . . and, boy, was she glad she did!

After a few weeks of radio silence, she showed up to one of our group coaching sessions and told us the practice had changed her life. When we asked what happened, she exclaimed, "Joy! I've been working out every day, but I never pay much attention to how I actually feel. I tried the dance a few times, and that was fun. But mostly I just brought a totally different mindset to the exercise I was already doing. I listened to my body and made changes so that it actually felt good." For Tasha, it was a revelation. She was able to take her breakthrough off the track and into the office as well. By observing her tendency to drive hard while exercising, she realized she took a similar approach to running her business. Tasha started placing more focus on Joy and paying greater attention to how her body felt day to day. She was soon able to delegate with less effort and finally make space in her life for an unexpected and very pleasant surprise—a new baby girl, who turned life upside down in the best of ways a few months later.

Dr. Tasha's breakthrough was a turning point for me as well. She was already a serious athlete . . . but this practice still made a difference. Her revelation helped me to better articulate how the simple invitation to dance can instigate diverse approaches to self-healing—and diverse benefits—for leaders of all kinds.

So that you don't get hung up on whether or not you're *actually* going to dance this week, I'd like to propose this metaphor: let's say *dancing* is about first saying "yes" to the challenge, then letting go of the outcome and relaxing into the mystery that unfolds. It's about riding the wave, trusting your competence, and really *feeling* your body as you execute the steps you previously would have feared were impossible. Human beings have a natural capacity to thrive. *Daring to dance*—both in metaphor and in actual practice—is one way to get there.

Moving Is Healing: Reflection Questions

- If you take dance as a metaphor, how could it represent the way you want to live your life or run your business?
- What parts of you that have been hidden for a while might get uncovered if you started dancing more (in body or in spirit)?
- Having digested the ideas in this chapter so far, what excites you about the idea dancing?
- What, if anything, still scares you?

I DON'T FEEL LIKE DANCING

At this point, you may or may not be sold on the relevancy of dance to your evolving leadership. If you're easygoing enough (or you already love to dance!), you might just take my word for it and try it out. Or you might need to choose a goal related to confidence, resilience, or another leadership skill you already desire to make the effort feel worth your while. Regardless, I want to posit that taking on a practice that challenges your comfort zone is itself a powerful leadership move. Full stop.

Brené Brown, world-renowned TED speaker and researcher on vulnerability and shame, addresses this point in relation to corporate innovation. In her book *Daring Greatly*,[9] she recounts an interaction with Kevin Surace, *Inc.* magazine's 2009 CEO of the year. In it, she asks him what he sees as the greatest barrier to innovation inside of organizations. His answer comes back loud and clear: the fear of introducing an idea, and being ridiculed, laughed at, and belittled. In other words, when we are *afraid* to step out of our comfort zones, a whole host of other leadership moves—including creativity and innovation—are also not possible. The cost? The big ideas you are daring only to dream may never get birthed into reality.

That's why taking the risk to teach your body-mind system something different or new can have massive ripple effects over time. Courageously diving into a new physical practice will boost your capacity to make new moves in other domains, from the boardroom all the way to the bedroom. That said, I want to return to the myth we busted at the start of this chapter: *When you're striving to make an impact, your body—and your Joy—comes last.* If you're like most women, your non-urgent self-care practice is one of the first things to go when your plate fills up with urgent, important work that needs your attention now. This is *especially* true if it *also* challenges your comfort zone. While the benefits are great, this can be the toughest kind of practice to show up for when you're tired, frustrated, or just plain feeling like crap.

So then . . . what is the relationship between dancing, exhaustion, and overwhelm? And what happens on those inevitable days when you just don't feel like getting up and moving? In my experience, these are the VERY days we need to dance the most! But don't take my word for it . . . think about your own experience for a moment.

Have you ever had a day like this:

I'm feeling down, my emotions are low, I'm bordering on the verge of exhaustion. In that moment, when I receive an invitation to move, my response is, ". . . I just don't feel like dancing." Or running, or swimming, or riding my horse. It literally sounds like the LAST thing I want to do. Yet, I remember that in the past, I'd often feel better after a few minutes of riding than I did before getting on the horse . . .

Can you relate to these feelings? Physical movement tends to create an emotional shift in the body. This has been true in my own personal practice, and it's also backed by a ton of science. In his book *Are You Fully Charged,*[10] *New York Times* bestselling author Tom Rath describes three areas of a fully charged life: energy, meaning, and relationships. Rath, a cancer survivor and former researcher on Gallup's large data polls, argues that physical movement is a critical, energy-generating strategy that should not be ignored. He notes that exercise can lead to boosts in mood that can last up to twelve hours after we work out.

Metaphorically—and energetically—your Joy Workout practice is about propelling something that was stuck into motion. The fact is, it's

THE SCIENCE: BUILT TO MOVE

Despite the advances in technology and medicine over the past few decades, both physical and mental disease are on the rise. On the surface, it doesn't make sense. Shouldn't humanity be doing *better* than it was before? What is root cause of all of this disease and disorder? John Ratey, a clinical associate professor at Harvard Medical School, is interested in exactly these questions. Ratey's work explores the relationship between human beings' evolutionary biology and our current predominantly sedentary lifestyle. In his research, he looks at some of the world's leading causes of death (heart disease, obesity, depression, and cancer) and notes that they did not exist at the same frequency in our recent historical past. In his book *Go Wild*, Ratey argues that many of these "diseases of civilization" are the result of lifestyle choices that violate the conditions of our original biological design.

In laymen's terms, much of Ratey's work can be summed up in a single phrase: *human beings were built to move*. By design, our bodies will be at their optimal level of functioning when we engage with our world in ways that are similar to our biological predecessors. Daily walking and running were an integral part of life for our ancestors. Without this daily dose of physical stimulation, our biological systems are running at a sub-optimal state the majority of the time.

As a case in point, he cites the highly successful residential autism treatment program at the Center for Discovery in upstate New York. The remarkable progress their clients make is attributable in large part to their exercise regimen, which includes regular running, jumping, and dancing, as well as rhythm and music. In his research, Ratey also looks at our patterns of nutrition and our lack of connection with the outdoors from the same evolutionary perspective. According to Ratey, finding ways to return to our wilder, more original nature is exactly the medicine we modern-day human beings most need.

John Ratey and R. Manning, *Go Wild: Free Your Body and Mind from the Afflictions of Civilization* (New York: Little, Brown & Company, 2014).

impossible to move and stay stuck at the same time. If you want to make progress . . . start moving forward. Yes, it's obvious. And yes, many of us still don't do it often or regularly enough. It doesn't entirely matter how you choose to move. Just move.

For example, I happen to be one of those lucky people who owns a dog. I don't have a garden or yard attached to my apartment. For me that means that for the past twelve years, be it rain or shine, I would go walking outside at least twice a day. Even on the days when I wake up feeling irritated, resentful, or rushed, I usually walk the dog back in our front door thirty minutes later with a greater lightness in my step. Without her insistent demands, it would be all too easy for me to resist getting into motion on the tougher days. But my commitment to her care is able to override my resistance. It helps me take the first few steps. On those days, I literally walk my way back to higher emotional ground.

One of the gifts in this little story is the power of commitment. If you want to use movement to shift your emotions, ask yourself, "What do I care about *more* than my inertia, resistance, self-consciousness, depression, overwhelm, or fear of getting moving?" Or, if you like to exercise but find you're just *too busy*, ask yourself, "What do I care about MORE than my tactical to-do list? Health? Well-being? Peak performance? Furthering the company mission? Or my personal mission? Being able to show up for my children in five, ten, twenty years?"

If you haven't already done it, TODAY I challenge you to make an inescapable commitment to move *no matter what*. Although I suggest dancing, I actually don't mind what kind of movement you choose, as long as your choice 1) connects you with your body and 2) brings you a sense of Joy. Clearly declare that you are doing it in service of a greater cause. Let others know. Give them permission to remind you how much it matters, in moments when you forget. Then move! Take the first few steps and let your momentum do the rest. On this rare occasion, I can *promise* that you *will* feel the effects very soon.

I Don't Feel Like Dancing: Reflection Questions

- What big leadership goal or personal dream would warrant you daring to get out of your comfort zone?
- What do you care about *more* than any inertia, resistance, self-consciousness, depression, overwhelm, or fear you may feel about getting moving?
- What do you care about *more* than items on your tactical to-do list that tend to fill up your day?

The Practice

The somatic (a.k.a. embodied) practice for chapter 1 lays a critical foundation for our work together. I encourage you to dive in and get started right away. In getting yourself moving, you will build momentum that will serve as fuel for the next steps you want to take. In brief summary, your practice for chapter 1 is to commit to a regular weekly Joy Workout. In order to establish a new and nourishing routine, I invite you to "try on" a few different kinds of dancing to see what medicine or magic they may contain for you. I also invite you to revisit your own loves by reengaging with *old favorite activities* that get you out of the daily grind and bring your soul to life.

Below are a couple of the core practices I recommend. In order to design the perfect Joy Workout practice for you, feel free to get creative. You can find more ideas, along with downloadable guided video and audio practices, at www.gutsandgrace.com/book-resources/.

PRACTICE 1: COMMIT TO A JOY WORKOUT CLASS

Attend ONE *weekly class on any physical activity that brings you Joy.* It's okay to try a few different classes as you begin your chapter 1 exploration. But do choose one *new* or *revived* Joy Workout practice you're committed to doing once per week for the next four weeks. Choose something that excites you—bonus points if it's a type of *dance.* Your practice could be an activity you've always wanted to try but never "had the time for." Or something you enjoyed in your younger years but have let go as an adult.

For example, my clients have chosen activities like pottery, poetry, cooking, Zumba, painting, singing, martial arts, ballroom dance, distance cycling, rock climbing, calligraphy, Spanish, piano . . . the possibilities are endless. The number one most important factor in your choice is that it MUST be something that brings you Joy. Period. Do not choose something that is a "should," that feels heavy, or feels like terrible, hard work. Do not choose something that will make you miserable trying to do it perfectly. It must be something that is not directly related to your work (yes . . . this is about play!). It must be something that you would love to do, just for the sake of doing it.

ACTIVE INGREDIENTS	conscious physical movement, emotional engagement, joyful upliftment
WHY IT WORKS	This practice builds resilience and refills your inner energy reserves by bringing your body into an optional physical and emotional state, at least once a week.

A Few More Suggestions

- Remember, this practice is *not* simply about "working out." If you get a workout in the process, bravo! But the practice is *really* about giving your body–mind–spirit system a weekly boost of positive energy. Choose something that leaves you feeling more alive . . . makes you believe you are worth it . . . and gives you permission to finally have it.
- Your Joy Workout doesn't have to involve rigorous physical movement. However, it MUST be something that is physically, emotionally, or spiritually engaging for you. Better yet, it can be all three!
- If you already attend a weekly class that you *love* and that you think it fits the bill, great! Commit to going consistently over the next four weeks. Pay close attention to what benefits it adds to your week. Let it really count.
- Or feel free to choose a different kind of class for your Joy Workout. As long as the addition of a second class doesn't leave you feeling overwhelmed, there are no rules about getting "too much" of a good thing here.
- Lastly, if you already attend a regular class, but you're not feeling the Joy, you can choose to focus on *increasing your experience of physical and emotional Joy* while doing your practice. Track the positive sensations in your body. Tweak, shift, or adjust your movement to invite more of what feels good.
- And if you want a taste of what it's like to dance with *me*, you can download guided mini Joy Workouts on the *Guts and Grace* website.

PRACTICE 2: DAILY HAPPY DANCE

Take a ten-minute "daily dance break" every day for thirty days. Stanford Design School professor B. J. Fogg called dance the new wave that will soon take the world by storm. Fogg, an expert in behavior change, studies ingrained behavior. His research shows how "tiny habits" can add up to big change in the long run. Fogg predicts that people will soon dance daily, for the sake of pleasure, health, healing, connection, and to expand their creativity. I happen to agree. My own personal dance-related Joy Workout involves rolling out of bed and onto "the dance floor" (a small, open carpeted area in my office) at the start of my day. When I began this practice a decade ago, I literally chose just *one short song* and danced in any way I felt like dancing, from the beginning to the end. You could also set a timer for five or ten minutes and hit shuffle on your *Guts and Grace* playlist. If you're feeling good when the timer ends, you can always choose to continue.

ACTIVE INGREDIENTS	joy, active energy, your inner child, creativity, play
WHY IT WORKS	It only takes a few minutes to change your mood. This practice interrupts negative low-energy trends and powerfully resets the mind and body.

A Few More Suggestions

- If your schedule allows, pick a consistent time and stick with it as often as possible.
- Start by using the same one or two songs every day. Choose music you find uplifting and don't mind hearing regularly.
- If you you're not sure *what* to do, start with a few basic steps from a former dance or aerobics class—or just imagine you're at your favorite club, and rock out.

REFLECTIONS ON THE JOY WORKOUTS PRACTICES

After the first or second week, use the questions below to reflect on your practice:

- What are you learning from engaging with the Joy Workouts practices this week?
- What Joy Workout did you chose, and why? What do you LOVE about it?
- What are you noticing about the benefits you get from your practice?
- If you haven't done *any* of these practices, or seem to be avoiding them . . . why? What's still in the way of you diving in?

Guts and Grace Playlist Recommendations

"Let the Rhythm Just" – The Polish Ambassador

"Feel Good" – Lira

"The Motown Song" – Rod Stewart

"Bone Dance" – Deya Dova

"Everybody Ona Move" – Michael Franti

"I Hope You Dance" – Lee Ann Womack

LEADERSHIP MYTH

There is not enough time, because my time is not my own. I'm at the mercy of other people and deadlines.

LEADERSHIP TRUTH

Your time is more malleable than you think. When you exercise healthy disbelief and challenge your constraints, you can create space and bend time.

Chapter 2

TIME FOR ME

In that first hardly noticed moment in which you wake,
coming back to this life from the other
more secret, moveable and frighteningly honest world
where everything began,
there is a small opening into the new day
which closes the moment you begin your plans.

—DAVID WHYTE

TAKING BACK THE REINS

In order to develop a truly impactful, conscious, and sustainable leadership style, it is essential that you create space to rest and rejuice. What's more, it's *also* essential that you make time for creating thinking, strategic priorities and unstructured activities that support real innovation. You probably already know this. But knowing doesn't necessarily equal successful implementation. In fact, while time management is not too tough for most people to understand, it is one of the *toughest* challenges for most of my clients to actually break through. If you are still feeling burned out, or simply have less energy than you'd like to admit, then there is undoubtedly some work for us to do in this domain.

Once again, we'll turn to the body for guidance. What is the real problem here? And how can we fix it? Research on high-performance athletics shows that both our physical muscles and our minds function best when they are stretched to capacity, then given downtime to rebuild. Literally everything in nature is built to expand . . . and then contract. In other words, the contraction is part of the cycle of life. Without it, we're only living into *half* of our natural potential. Whether we notice it or not, we are significantly less effective when we are running forward to infinity on a half-empty tank than when we are fully resourced. Sacrificing things that matter in order to "get more done" prevents us from ever completely filling our tanks. Likewise, barreling forward in business on last year's strategy without pausing to take stock of shifting market trends, employee morale, and client needs is your one-way ticket to chaotic, reactive recovery—or even irrelevance—in the long run.

Unfortunately, cultural norms don't help us out much here. As a society we're used to feeling busy, being busy, and talking about being busy. Not only is busy an acceptable state of being, it's often worn like a badge of honor. "Let me tell you about the week I had last week!" This leads to another leadership myth: ***There is not enough time, because my time is not my own. I'm at the mercy of other people and deadlines.*** Unconsciously, we use this myth as a way to connect with others. And others expect it from us. Unconsciously, it's seen as par for the course at work.

It makes sense. In the past hundred years, our cultural norms shifted to meet the demands of our rapidly industrializing societies. Now, we are racing to keep up. During this time, human beings have undergone a transition of mindset—from allowing growth via the natural cycle of expansion and contraction (intense motion followed by an equally rejuvenating pause) to expecting growth in a straight line, continually increasing on both the x and y axis, into infinity.

The thing is, our bodies simply weren't built to function this way. When we perform nonstop, our delicate machine parts begin to wear out. And, as one of my mentors says, in the end, the body always wins. The good news is, we still have choice—and choice is power. Here's the truth: ***Your time is more malleable than you think. When you exercise healthy disbelief and challenge your constraints, you can create space and bend time.*** In this chapter, you will learn how to restore balance in your body and in your calendar.

So what *would* an ideal day, week, or month look like if you operated on "the body's time"? It would include *both* periods of exertion and periods of rest, in right proportion. You would feel awake and alert (rather than overwhelmed and exhausted) the vast majority of the time. And you would be directing the right amount of attention to the concerns that matter most. Sound like a fantasy? It's not. Most Olympic athletes actually design their lives this way. And you *know* they get some amazing stuff done. Yet many of us derail our daydreams about how our ideal schedule would look and feel, with even stronger beliefs about why it's just not possible. Or why we don't deserve it. We also practice unconscious habits that can keep us on the hamster wheel without us even noticing. Through our own self-fulfilling actions, we prove our beliefs "right" on a daily basis. This chapter is about getting real. It's about loving yourself, challenging your beliefs, and taking a new stand immediately.

Take a deep breath and get ready to dive in. Just like Rome wasn't built in a day, you may not have an ideal calendar in place by the end of this week (or ever!). Nonetheless, I promise that if you take the following practices seriously, things *will* get better. This simple but not easy lesson is about finding creative ways to build the kind of relationship with time that you've been craving . . . step-by-step.

EMPTY

Have you ever noticed that even when you have the best of intentions, your day can get away from you even before it begins?

Often, we think of a new day as a metaphorical "blank slate." Yet it's rare that we actually live that way. If we did, it might actually be scary as hell! Think about it: a blank slate. That means *empty*. A sense of nothingness. Like a bottomless pit. Full ambiguity. Not knowing the answers yet. In this place, we could easily get lost. Or worse . . . In this place, we might have to face the deeper fears and whispers that creep in when the busyness of the daily grind falls away.

Last year I moved across the country from Boston, Massachusetts, to Oakland, California. I had just received the acceptance of this book proposal, and I couldn't wait to land in my new home and get down to writing. Using the tools I'm about to share, I cleared space in my calendar and was ready to go. There was just one problem . . . the moving truck hadn't arrived. Sitting alone in a completely empty two-bedroom apartment with no plans, no housemates, no research materials, and no furniture, I found myself in a waiting game with literally nothing to do but write.

On the one hand, it should have been the ideal scenario. No distractions . . . just a big goal and a ton of time to achieve it. Instead, it turned out to be one of the most anxiety-ridden weeks of my year. While I knew I *could* and *should* get a lot done, it was far more difficult to make use of the empty space than I had imagined. Even though I've been teaching these tools for over ten years (and I'm a badass at getting things done under normal circumstances), I was reminded just how nerve-racking a blank slate can be.

And that, my friend, is one of the biggest reasons why we (often unconsciously) keep our plates full. Without even realizing it, most of us are terrified of having empty space in our calendars. It's just too much ambiguity, with no guarantee of a successful outcome. What if it doesn't work out? Why should I take the risk? Sounds crazy, right? But *uncertainty* can lead to *failure* . . . and *that* would be unacceptable.

Of course, there's another way of looking at it, isn't there? The way we'd *like* to approach our extra time. A blank slate. That means *empty*. A sense of possibility. Like a bowl waiting to be filled with anything wonderful. Not knowing the answers yet. Infinite potential. Opening and receiving. Magic. Trust.

In a beautiful poem called "What to Remember When Waking," poet David Whyte writes about the first moment we wake up from sleep in the morning. This is the moment just before plans, worries, future-looking goals, and to-do lists reassert themselves in your head. It's the moment just before your body dons the armor that typically keeps you safe in the day-to-day world.

THE SCIENCE: MAKING TIME FOR CONNECTION

In her book *The How of Happiness*, author Sonja Lyubomirsky describes a number of simple activities that, when practiced, can elevate your mood and support your well-being. One such exercise involves expressing gratitude. Lyubomirsky suggests keeping a journal of things for which you are grateful and adding to it on a regular basis. While it doesn't require a lot of time, the practice of gratitude can be a powerful medicine. It helps us savor positive life experiences, maintain hope in times of great stress, and boost our self-esteem. It can also have a positive impact on our interpersonal relationships. In fact, research suggests that appreciating others by writing a letter of gratitude describing how they impacted your life can both increase your level of positive emotion and help reduce depression. By connecting you with your own state of gracious receiving, feeling gratitude toward others pays dividends for your well-being.

What's more, taking the extra time to express your gratitude in person makes an even bigger difference. In a series of studies, participants were given the option to simply write a gratitude letter or to write *and hand-deliver* the letter, thanking the recipient in person. Those who delivered the letter in person experienced significantly larger mood boosts. These findings suggest that taking the time to nourish your interpersonal connections is also well worth the investment.

Sonja Lyubomirsky, *The How of Happiness: A New Approach to Getting the Life You Want* (New York: Penguin Books, 2007).

In that precious moment, you still have a choice. Do you choose to allow the rush of things to fill you up quickly and enter the day already knowing what's next? Do you assume the same stance you always take in order to cope? Or do you dare to suspend yourself in the emptiness of that first morning moment and open yourself deeply to the gifts the new day may unexpectedly send your way?

I know. It is *so* much easier said than done. The beauty is that every morning affords an opportunity to make the same choice again. What's more, every other beginning, small or large, offers an opportunity to make that same choice as well. And every time you choose emptiness, you step into the dance of the unknown. It's a different game than the game of "getting things done right" and "guaranteed ROI" that we typically play. It's a game of curiosity and receiving. It's a game where the only rule is trusting that whatever shows up next will be *enough*. And that you will be *enough* to receive it.

Years ago, when I would ask, "what's next?" a dear friend of mine would often say, "anything, everything, something, nothing . . ." Knowing him, it's probably a line from a film. Nonetheless, it stuck with me all this time. For me, it points to the paradox of emptiness and the infinite possibility that exists in the moment of awaiting. Although it may sound impossible, I believe that you can approach life as though you were empty and awaiting *anything, everything, something, and nothing* every single day. It is a choice you can make in your body. And it is a daily practice.

It's time to embrace the empty space. Let's start exploring how.

Empty: Reflection Questions

- If your day were an empty slate, what would you be happily and hopefully waiting for? And what would you be most afraid would show up?
- What are the various ways you fill up your day to the brim in order to avoid facing an empty slate? What are your favorite distractions, to-dos, shoulds, and have-tos?
- What bodily sensations let you know that you're in an overwhelmed, guarded, or contracted state rather than a spacious, empty, and receiving state?
- What would it look like to create space for yourself this week (including physical space, mental space, emotional space, and space in your calendar)?

THE MYTH OF TIME

Of course, this is still a thought exercise so far. But I hope it has been a useful one. I realize that your calendar next week is far from empty. Nonetheless, if you stay with me for just a bit longer, then we'll get down to the action plan.

Now that you've opened yourself to the possibility of living as though your days began with an empty slate, I'd like to propose some things to fill it with. So many of us are longing for a lifestyle that nourishes us: body, mind, and spirit. A thriving, sustainable lifestyle that (like a miracle!) manages to both pay the bills *and* allow time for rest. Often (especially for us women) that vision also includes a desire to satisfactorily meet the needs of those we love while at the same time caring for ourselves.

I believe we can find—or rather *create*—a state of affairs in our lives in which both of those desires are not just possible but are synergistic. I call it *authentic balance*. How, you ask? In order to explore how to do it, let's first look at how *not* to. I'll start with a critical question that harkens back to the leadership myth at the start of this chapter: *Have you bought into the widespread myth that your schedule is out of your control?*

And what if that wasn't true?

In the sales world, there is a saying, "It's never really about the money or the time." In my past fourteen years of coaching executives, I've come to understand the depth and power in that simple statement. It's easy, and incredibly believable, to think that an executive at a Fortune 500 company is just too busy to get on the phone. But time after time I've found that he or she will create an hour in an already jam-packed day if the topic of your conversation is something important enough to warrant it.

Having the audacity to believe something different—to believe that time is malleable and that both "have-tos" and "cannots" are negotiable creations of the mind—can open all kinds of interesting doors. Like a Jedi mind trick that turns the table on bosses, project leaders, and other gatekeepers (especially those who are still living as though the myth were true), this shift in frame creates options where before there were none. In other words, disbelieving that time is out of your control—and aligning your actions with your mindset—literally puts the power of time back in your hands.

So where does the time come from? That was the number one question my client Haley, an OB-GYN in private practice, was grappling with when we started working together. Not only was her calendar packed to the gills with team meetings and regular checkup appointments, but it also was subject to change on a moment's notice due to various "fire drills" and patients giving birth. For Haley, the sheer unpredictability and life-or-death nature of her work made it especially tough for her to imagine that she could take back the reins and get her schedule under control.

In order to create space, we started small. Our first experiment was to create blocks for "unplanned time" in her work week. In taking stock of her office policies and culture, we discovered that when a patient cancellation occurred, her administrative assistant would regularly call to offer the open appointment slot to other patients, even when the day was overbooked and she was running behind. Simply giving her assistant new marching orders—to *not* rebook cancellations—created some breathing room on a weekly basis. We also discovered that while Haley regularly took work home, she felt guilty about taking a personal appointment during the work week. This was particularly the case when her personal "need" seemed luxurious, like a massage or acupuncture appointment. She worked on easing the guilt by asking for her team's encouragement to take the time she needed. In turn, she invested a small dollar amount to purchase a monthly massage membership for *each* of her core staff members so that they could enjoy the same benefits, leaving her guilt-free.

Haley soon realized that taking time to rejuvenate herself, and encouraging her team to do the same, had a big impact on their office culture. Their collective level of stress went down, as did the number of mistakes they made as a team. As you can imagine, Haley's transformation took more than a single week. In fact, she revisited this lesson frequently over the six months we worked together. If your life is full, and time is one of your big challenges, I encourage you to do the same. Each subsequent chapter in this book has a connection to your physical, mental, or emotional experience of time, so there will be lots of opportunities to deepen your practice.

The very first, however, is to take the risk to change your mindset—to be *willing* to believe that time is more malleable than you think. Rather than asking, "What do I think is possible?" instead ask yourself, "What do I really want?" You will be less likely to talk yourself out of trying before the path becomes clear.

The very second step is to take a hard look at the current state of your calendar and take stock of what's most important to you. Like I said before, this chapter is about *getting real*. When we're stretched, we often just ignore the tension all together. But ignoring the problem is the fastest way to become the boiling frog—so deep in hot water that it's too late to get out. Noticing the gap between your real desires and your current choices can build genuine momentum that will help you to make a needed change.

The Myth of Time: Reflection Questions

- What is the biggest myth you currently believe about time, and why? In what way or ways do you benefit from believing it?
- If you really could choose something different for your time . . . where would you begin?
- Take a look at your actual calendar for the next three weeks. At a high level, what do you notice that isn't working? What *is* working? Why?

AUTHENTIC BALANCE

"Learn the rules like a pro, so you can break them like an artist."

—PABLO PICASSO

The third step, of course, is to make the change. Ultimately your mission this week is to put some new habits into practice that will bring you closer to the balanced, sustainable lifestyle you've been craving. Yep, it's that simple. But not easy. So let's look at what else is in the way—starting with "balance."

I know. Balance has become a buzz word in the workplace these days. Our lives are out of *balance*. We've got poor work–life *balance*. It's tough to *balance* work and play, and so forth. Lately the word has even got a bit of a bad rap—as in "there is no such thing as work–life balance." Is it true that balance is so difficult that it might as well not exist? And if so, what do we really mean by "balance"?

As I mentioned at the start of this chapter, our lack of belief in balance is symptomatic of our underlying pursuit of infinite progress. In theory, it makes sense to desire limitlessness expansion, growth, and success. But nothing in nature goes on forever. Everything sleeps. Everything dies. Everything grows up and then grows old. The sun rises and falls, giving us daylight and darkness in predictable proportions throughout the year. Cycles are everywhere. Ironically, our expectation of infinite progress has us *give up* the reins to life, handing our power of choice over to others, to chance, to fate, and to the physical limitations of our own bodies.

(Remember: when pushed to the limit, *the body always wins.*)

A conscious, sustainable leadership approach honors these cycles and moves *with* them rather than *against* them. A recent study followed investment bankers over the course of their first nine years of professional work. As you might imagine, these bankers' life choices were geared toward the pursuit of infinite progress at the quickest possible pace. They worked long work hours, experienced high stress, and often got little sleep. By year four, a large majority of study participants were showing signs of burnout. What they did next made all the difference. The bankers who ignored their bodies and "powered through" suffered a variety of health consequences, ultimately losing their capacity to perform at a high level. In fact, many of them eventually left the workforce. On the other hand, those who took their burnout as a critical sign, and adjusted their pace accordingly, were able to make a comeback and stay in the game. Listening and adjusting were the keys to their success.

Contrary to popular belief, cultivating *authentic balance* is not about following a formula that prescribes equal parts work-time and family-time. It's not about finding the right time-management system or figuring out the elusive rules of the game once and for all. It doesn't even mean feeling balanced every day, month, or week. There are no boxes to check. And there is no right way to do time management. That's why it's *so* hard to solve. Myth of time . . . busted.

The truth is, everyone's version of *authentic balance* will look a bit different. And sustaining your own version will require ongoing listening and adjustment—a form of conscious, embodied practice—in order to kept it intact over time. At its core, the real lesson is about honoring the wisdom of *your* inner cycles. These natural rhythms require you to oscillate between on-time and off-time in order to experience good physical, mental, and emotional health. They ask for both genuine rest and inspired action. A mix of work and play. Of love life and career goals. Of precision and flow. Of achieving and celebrating. Of doing and receiving. It's good for your body. And it's good business practice.

At the deeper level, this series of complements can be seen in the ancient energies of yin and yang. Neither the yin nor yang can stand alone. Yet together, they allow us to experience infinity. As a pair, they represent wholeness. One completes the other. In perfect balance, yin flows into yang, yang flows into yin, and so the circle continues on. One makes the other possible. And when you've mastered them, you can make *all kinds of* choices about your energy and time . . . without burning out.

Here's how it looks in the body: in a yoga class, the perfect balance is created through postures and counterpostures. One leads to another, inviting the body to stretch and open in complementary ways. In dance, we use contrasts like dynamic and ease—the experience of quick, powerful, energetic movement followed by soft, gentle, opening movement—demonstrating the *both-and*. Even the most basic practice like meditation requires two parts in order to be complete: in breath, out breath, in breath, out breath . . .

The same thing is true in life and in business. It's only when I allow myself to deeply rest that I have the energy and strength to risk the vulnerability of innovation. When I've driven myself to the limit in my work, there is nothing I crave more than an intimate connection with the person I love back at home. In order to keep giving, I must eventually allow myself to receive. In my mind, it all makes perfect sense. Again, simple . . . but not easy.

After years of imperfect practice, I am happy to share that I'm finally getting closer to a sense of *authentic balance*. But it started with a single choice. Over a decade ago, I took my first official full-time job with a boutique coaching and consulting firm in the San Francisco Bay Area. Having come from a self-directed pre-career in academia, I didn't adjust well to the full-time hours and quickly found myself starting to wilt. Somewhere between hyperactive overwhelm and immobile exhaustion, I knew something would have to change in order to make corporate-facing work a sustainable, healthy career path for me.

Funnily enough, the shift was set in motion when I said yes to my first Nia Technique class. Nia was taught at nine a.m., an hour after my official work hours began. It took place at the gym across from our office. "Just once a week," I thought to myself. If I could get there even just once a week, it would make a huge difference in my life. So I took a risk and made a proposal to my new boss. Could I come to work *one hour earlier*, then go across the street for the nine a.m. class, and come back to work again at the end? To my surprise, although there was no precedent of anyone else in our company doing anything like it at the time, he said "yes."

This decision had a massive impact on my energy level over the next six months, and probably saved my career. What's more, the risks I took created a new precedent for others. Soon my colleagues also began to make shifts toward healthier, more balanced lifestyles. I tell you this story not to toot my own horn but rather to suggest that we—each of us who hears the call—can be the starting point for something different. There are no right or wrong answers, only your body's unique needs and sense of pace. This week I invite you to consider the following: *What would an ideal sense of authentic balance look and feel like for you?*

As a metaphor, let's start with the body. If you have an established fitness routine, you can try *feeling* the contrast between yin and yang somatically (i.e., in your body) by varying the balance and force of energy as you move. Sprint, then settle into a slow steady gait. Embody a sense of precision, then a sense of fluidity. Turn in circles one morning. Jog in a straight line the next. In your Joy Workout practice from chapter 1, alternate between powerful, dynamic movement and gentle, easy movement as you dance. Focus on speed, then endurance. Agility, then stability. Notice if one is easier than the other for you. If so, there's a good chance that a similar imbalance will show up in your day-to-day life. Rebalancing through movement is a great way to adjust your internal default setting.

Now let's take it back to your calendar. Spend one week going through your daily life mindfully. Begin noticing what isn't working right now about the way you typically spend your time. Do you feel overwhelmed? Exhausted? Okay, but a little bit numb? Are you giving too much to the world and not allowing time for your body to rejuice? Do you spend time on useless tasks while avoiding the work needed to pursue your higher calling? Literally notice the habitual but misaligned choices you make in the moment. You can also ask yourself, "What are the fears that hold me back from making a change?"

Imagine clearing the slate completely and starting over with an empty calendar page and choosing balance first. How would you design your week if *authentic balance* was both possible and a priority? What choices would you make if you were rewriting the rules? Why?

Authentic Balance: Reflection Questions

- First, dream. What would an ideal expression of authentic balance look like in YOUR calendar? (Be specific and don't hold back. If you had a magic wand, what new structures would you create?)
- Now get grounded. What's one baby step you could take to move toward authentic balance starting TODAY?
- What are all the reasons you tell yourself about why that step is NOT possible? Or why you don't really have a choice?
- What are all the ways in which those reasons aren't 100 percent true?

THE SCIENCE: HEALTHY TRADE-OFFS

"Life is like a piano. What you get from it depends on how you play it."

—TOM LEHRER

Scientific models of well-being, like Dr. Martin Seligman's PERMA model, are designed to capture the key ingredients that make a life worth living. A number of such models can be found in science today. Each one provides its own take on what ingredients matter most. They cover domains like meaning, relationships, energy, achievement, flow, belonging, positive emotions, interpersonal connection, and self-concept. Yet all of these models offer one consistent message: no single ingredient, when pursued on its own, is enough to generate true happiness in the long run. We are whole human beings, and we require whole solutions in order to truly thrive.

In fact, like the title of this book suggests, real happiness may rely on the *intersection* of these elements. In other words, cultivating the capacity to live in the "both-and"—of meaning and achievement, of other and self, of frivolous pleasure and deeply committed engagement"—may be the key to success. For example, perseverance and passion for long-term goals are the hallmarks of the A (for Achievement) in PERMA. These qualities, when taken together, mirror the scientific literature on *grit*. Research by Angela Duckworth suggests that "gritty" people are more willing to work strenuously on their challenges and more able to maintain their interest over time. People who are higher in grit appear to value hard work for hard work's sake, and persist despite adversity, failure, or plateau. They also tend to achieve far higher levels of success than their peers (e.g., Arnold Palmer winning sixty-one PGA tours while the average for professional golfers is between zero and one).

Achievement, at its pinnacle, is about the willingness to work hard. Yet a person who is focused solely on Achievement may fail to take other important aspects of human flourishing into account. It would not suffice in the long run, for example, for you to throw out all of the important relationships in your life in order to "achieve." Nor would it suffice to muster all of your grit to pursue a meaningless goal or a goal that led to great harm. Instead, true mastery in the pursuit of well-being comes from your ability to make healthy trade-offs, moment to moment, in a way that acknowledges all of your most important goals.

The Practice

I hope this reflection has been fruitful. Like Joy and movement, I begin introducing *time* early in this book because I know it's one of the places that many of us feel frustrated—even "at the mercy of"—in our leadership. In my years of working with both corporate leaders and highly creative women, it's become abundantly clear that no new habit is likely to stick until 1) we get crystal clear about our intention and 2) we commit to addressing it *in our calendars* in a real and tangible way. The goal is not that you solve everything about your unruly schedule immediately. Rather, the goal is to start by taking stock of the big picture honestly and making a few critical changes now. You can always come back and make additional adjustments as you move through the chapters that follow.

Let's dive in. Think back on your answers to the last few journaling questions. Now that you have some clarity about what would be ideal, it's time to ask the next question—the one that brings daydreams into reality. Now it is time to ask *how*. Below I suggest practices that help you research both the physical sensations and the tactical elements that will serve as building blocks for your next-level relationship with time.

Rather than telling you *what* to do, I will walk you through how to create the vision of an *ideal* week for you. Then you will identify one difficult but doable schedule change and one supportive body-based practice that you will put into place *starting this week*. When you're ready for more, you can find lots of additional resources on the *Guts and Grace* book website.

PRACTICE 1: EMPTY SPACE

Using your own body as the canvas, practice creating a sense of empty space. First, allow your body to feel the pressure and strain of having "too much to do." Notice what locks, tightens, or holds. Notice what happens to your breath. Feel the sensations or emotions that arise. Then, make a conscious decision to create more space. Unlock something. Take a deeper breath. Let your energy field relax and expand outward. Feel, sense, or imagine that everything pressing down on you has eased up a bit. You can even envision (and intend) that your own presence is gently moving it away, freeing up more space both inside and around you.

Do this practice at least once a day for at least three days straight. One full week is even better. Of course, if you like it, you can keep it forever. Keep a record in your journal every day about what happens.

- What adjustments do you make in your body? How do you do it physically?
- What's easy? What's hard?
- What new possibilities open? What questions come up?

Changing your presence or behavior over a predetermined period of time, and carefully tracking the results, is the best way to discover unexpected doorways that may lead to your next level.

ACTIVE INGREDIENTS	embodied intelligence, choiceful intention, mindfulness
WHY IT WORKS	When your mind believes there is no space, your body responds in kind by tightening and bracing back. This can create anxiety. Choosing space in your body reverses the trend and makes different behavioral choices possible.

PRACTICE 2: YOUR IDEAL CALENDAR

Having worked carefully with a detailed, conscious calendar for the past decade, I have found that developing an intentional scheduling practice is the very best way to get more of what you really want. Ironically, while many of my clients are afraid that diligent scheduling will add more restriction to an already fully and stressed-out life, most of them find quickly that it actually paves the way to the kind of freedom they've been longing for.

How? The act of designing an ideal schedule brings to light the unconscious choices, irrational trade-offs, and impossibilities that we typically tolerate without thinking. While it takes some effort to work toward your ideal, you will immediately gain more awareness about the extent to which your overwhelm is (at least in part) self-generated. You may also realize that apparently "out of your control" commitments started with a choice that you made weeks (months, years) ago. Discovering that you hold the keys to your own sanity shines light on the path toward it. As long as you commit to start walking, things *will* change.

Two Caveats

First, if the last paragraph didn't resonate strongly with you, it may be the case that you fall on the other end of the spectrum: you are bored, not busy, slightly underextended, and feeling generally tired or drained. If that sounds like you, your focus will be to create *freedom through structure*. Develop some basic structures that will act as guardrails, protecting your passions and anchoring a few purposeful, action-oriented activities that keep your most important projects in motion.

Second, it's easy to lose consciousness and treat this type of activity like yet another to-do. This activity comes at the *end of the chapter* for a reason. Make sure you bring the realizations you've *already had* about empty space, myths, time-bending, and authentic balance to this activity. Rather than do the practice from an attitude of "should," or use it to yet again beat yourself up in ways akin to the old paradigm, I challenge you to bring as much NEW consciousness to these steps as possible.

Step 1: Make Your List. First, make a list of all the activities that would (and wouldn't) be a part of your *ideal* week, taking into account what really matters to you. For this exercise, "ideal" means ideal given your current life agreements (i.e., If you don't plan to quit your job in the next few months, *do* include your important work tasks and projects as a part of your list). Also include things like hobbies, exercise and self-care, time with family, friends, time alone. Do be realistic about your required number of work hours (e.g., you are paid for a minimum of forty hours), but don't hesitate to challenge yourself about where the boundaries actually lie (e.g., maybe you don't need or want to work that extra twenty). You can look back at the questions you answered earlier in the chapter for clues, or just start your list from scratch.

Note: If you know that you are not happy with your current job and want to leave it in the next six to twelve months, feel free to create two versions—one that is ideal given that your work hasn't changed (yet), and one that is ideal, period. This second version can serve as a guiding light as you begin exploring your options for the future.

Step 2: Create Your Template. Next, start with a blank calendar page that shows the view of an entire week. If you use a paper calendar, flip to the back, find a week where you have nothing currently scheduled, and make a photocopy. If your calendar is online, find an empty week and simply print one or two hard copies of that page to use as worksheets. Using a pencil (so that you can erase mistakes and make changes), "schedule" all the activities in your ideal week exactly where and when you'd like to do them, ideally. Consider the following:

- Which activities are most challenging? Which are most pleasurable?
- Which bring you energy? Which tend to drain your energy?
- Which are you able to do with others around and which require being in a quiet space of your own in order to tackle them?
- Which rely on your friends or family to be present?
- Are there days of the week or times of the day when you are most likely to get their buy-in to participate?

Be sure to account for the important activities you typically avoid. Consider scheduling them first thing in the morning. Or schedule them at a time when you have accountability from others who can help you stay in the game. Also, don't forget the activities you may need in order to *support* your most important activities (e.g., strategic thinking time is a big one my clients often forget). Be sure to schedule your Joy Workouts and ten-minute dance breaks from the last chapter. Envision the structure you are building as the supportive backbone and skeleton of a life that feels good, increases your energy, and helps you get more of the right things done.

Step 3: Make Adjustments. This document will serve as your first draft. While blocking time, you may realize that everything doesn't fit. That's good—it means there's a decision you'll need to make, and you can address it now. Go back and take stock of the total hours your activities require, and make some choiceful adjustments. Your first draft doesn't have be perfect. It does need to feel implementable. The goal of step 2 is to generate a living template—one that you can *learn from* and evolve over time. If you try out a structure that doesn't work, ask yourself why. What could you do differently that might get you closer to the heart of the issue?

Step 4: Implement and Learn. When you have a finished first draft, the next step is to start implementing. First, compare this ideal envisioned week to the next two weeks in your real calendar. Pick ONE new thing to implement (in addition your Joy Workouts, which you should have already scheduled) that puts you a step closer to your ideal template. Do what it takes to make that one change happen this week.

Then, look at your calendar a few weeks out and schedule in things that support you. For example, I block my exercise, family dinners and dates, strategic planning, and business development times up to a month in advance. That way when new appointments come up, I have already set aside time for what's most important.

Lastly, as you schedule new appointments in the next few weeks, keep your ideal calendar close at hand. Use it to guide your choices about how you schedule those appointments. If someone else manages your calendar, take time to walk them through the vision you have created (including an explanation of why it's so important to you). Ask for their support to help you stick with the structure going forward.

As we wrap up this segment, I want to acknowledge your dedication here. If this practice sounds like hard work to get started, I get it. It is. I want to acknowledge up front that this activity is the most labor-intensive one in the book. I promise, it's totally worth the investment.

It is also TOTALLY NORMAL if doing this exercise pushes your buttons. Most of us have irrational commitments—like sacred cows—that we must protect in order to hang onto our story that things can't get better. Often, those commitments are exactly what's between you and a greater sense of freedom. Take note of any emotions that come up in your journal—fears, frustrations, blame, finger-pointing, dissatisfaction. This is part of the process. Harvest this raw material and bring it with you into the next few chapters' activities.

ACTIVE INGREDIENTS	honest self-reflection, challenging old beliefs, concrete structure
WHY IT WORKS	This practice requires you to make tough decisions about your time and commit to those decisions, *before* you're in the moment where old habits and conflict avoidance kick in.

BONUS PRACTICE: CREATE PHYSICAL SPACE

As you do the practices in this chapter, you may realize that your home and physical space is also packed to the gills. If so, I recommend setting aside a bit of time on an evening or weekend to do the following (hopefully nourishing!) exercise:

> Create a place in your home, be it an entire room or a tiny corner of a shared space, that is just for you. It should be at least three-by-three inches—just big enough to sit down in, meditate, write in your journal, or stand in place and dance. Fill it with favorite things: a comfortable chair, cozy pillows or blankets, incense, candles, a souvenir from a favorite trip. If the space is part of a larger shared space, make an arrangement with your cohabitants to use it privately during certain times of the day or week. This activity may push your comfort zone with regards to allowing yourself to take up space. If so, take note of what arises. It's all part of the process.

ACTIVE INGREDIENTS	asking for what you want, physical space
WHY IT WORKS	This practice gives you permission to create a corner of the world where you can have things exactly your way. Who knows what can happen from there!

REFLECTIONS ON THE TIME FOR ME PRACTICES

After the first or second week, use the questions below to reflect on your practice:

- What are you learning from engaging with the ideal calendar practice this week?
- What are you seeing about the self-fulfilling prophecy of your time-management habits?
- What's one new thing you tried that's working? How?

Guts and Grace Playlist Recommendations

"Central Reservation" – Beth Orton

"Things You Don't Have to Do" – Peter Malick

"Tightrope Walker" – Ayla Nereo

"Landsailor" – Vienna Teng

"Yellow Brick Road Song" – Iyeoka

"Science of a New Time" – Goddess Alchemy Project

LEADERSHIP MYTH

What I want, desire, or long for is bad—and I should be good.

LEADERSHIP TRUTH

Your desire is a powerful built-in compass, and it's your number one doorway to greater impact.

Chapter 3

SAY YES . . . AND NO

You do not have to be good.
You do not have to walk on your knees
for a hundred miles through the desert repenting.
You only have to let the soft animal of your body
love what it loves.

—MARY OLIVER

YOUR FORGOTTEN SUPERPOWER

Leave it to a female poet to write a single phrase that has the potency to echo around the world. If you've heard the lines above before, it's no surprise. Mary Oliver's "Wild Geese" may be one of the most widely read poems in the personal development arena—and for good reason. The kind of permission she grants when she says "you do not have to be good . . . you only have to let the soft animal of your body love what it loves," reveals one of the core falsehoods upon which modern society is built: that there *exists* a form of "good," which runs counter to our deeper embodied longings, and that we can and should honor "good" instead of ourselves.

In other words, whether we're fully aware of it or not, many of us believe that it's good, right, or responsible not to feel what we really feel or love what we really love. It's another leadership myth: ***What I want, desire, or long for is bad—and I should be good.*** This widely shared (and embodied) belief is pervasive. It's stifling. It can be held by even the most powerful women in subtly debilitating ways. And it simply isn't true. In my years of supporting female leaders of every age, shape, color, and creed, I've seen again and again the havoc this myth can wreak. It puts an unbreakable ceiling on the level of power—and joy—we can access. It stifles both our careers and our intimate relationships alike. And when it begins to change, *worlds* of untapped potential begin to open. The truth is: ***your desire is a powerful built-in compass, and it's your number one doorway to greater impact.***

This book is based on the curriculum of a leadership program originally called *Permission to Thrive.* The title was my best attempt at naming this tension and attracting clients who were hungry to resolve it. Almost universally, my female clients' reaction to the title would be "Ha! That sounds like *exactly* what I need!" In contrast, my male clients and business advisors would either stand, scratching their heads, or tell me they didn't think the word "permission" was good for my brand. Like a well-kept secret, I was referred from woman to woman, billed as the antidote to that unexplainable feeling that "despite my outward success, something was just missing in my life."

Think for a moment about why you decided to pick up this book in the first place. *What were you longing for*? This chapter offers an invitation, a how-to guide, and (if you need it) a permission slip to start taking those longings seriously—both large and small. My promise to you is that learning this foundational skill will unlock the power, potential, and purpose that hold the keys to your next level of impact—in leadership and in life.

Have you ever heard the expression "If it's not a 'hell, yeah!' it's a 'no'"? I'd heard the phrase a hundred times before, but recently it really sunk in. Seriously! Just how many times have we said "yes" when we really meant "no"? Just how often have we made choices out of duty, concern, fear, or resentment—choices that reflect *anything but* our truest and deepest desires? It's in these tiny moments that we unconsciously build the foundations for work (or a life!) we don't love.

In the first two chapters you laid some basic groundwork for a thriving, conscious, and truly sustainable approach to leadership. We reintroduced your body to Joy and looked at the macrocosm of your weekly schedule. This chapter offers a complementary practice: the opportunity to start tracking your unconscious daily choices in *much* greater detail. Through observation and intentional practice, you will take real action to create the lifestyle you desire. You will also have the chance to break through anything you've been avoiding.

Before we dive in, I want to add one caveat here: if you are one of those women who spends a lot of time doing everything for everybody else, and running out of time for yourself, this chapter may scare the pants off of you. It's funny—in theory. But in practice, it's no laughing matter. Getting serious about the real costs and consequences of your habits at this stage will pay big dividends in the long run. It may not be easy. You will need your conviction to stay in the game. In this chapter, taking a stand for *yourself* will require you to say YES to things you love . . . and really learn how to say NO in the moments that count.

LIVING YOUR "I WANTS"

Do you ever deny yourself the small pleasures in life?

Yes, I really just asked you that. So often, despite our best intentions, many of us fall prey to the belief that we need to have a "good reason" to give ourselves what we want. It has to be practical, useful, on sale, or otherwise rationalizable to the outside world. We have to be able to explain why it was the right choice. And (we secretly believe) "for the sake of pleasure" does NOT count as a REAL reason. Some of us hold back in order to be the "good girl." For others, it's about being "strong." Some of us stifle our own desires before they're even fully formed. And, as if it were a competition, we praise ourselves (and one another) for doing so.

If you are 100 percent sure this discussion doesn't apply to you, you can move on to the next chapter. But if you have even the tiniest hunch that there may be some juice here, I challenge you to look deeper. Perhaps you're a woman who can happily set and meet financial goals . . . but spending that money on a frivolous, celebratory treat is another story altogether. Or perhaps you're happy to engage in a retail therapy spree, but when it comes to fully receiving a compliment . . . well that's a no go. For the majority of my female clients, there are some pleasures that are much harder to enjoy than others. It's my pleasure (wink!) to help you challenge your own status quo. Just what terrible and unspeakable things would happen, *really,* if you went against the grain and let yourself have it?

In her book *The Artist's Way,*[11] writer and creativity coach Julia Cameron tells the story of a client who finally decided to allow herself a simple pleasure that made a big difference in her life. The woman in question had a love for juicy red raspberries. On most of her grocery shopping trips, however, she would decide not to purchase them. "They're so expensive . . . and not really necessary . . ." her inner voice would argue. And she would go home without. Then, one miraculous day, she had a good laugh at herself. In that moment she realized that even at $6 per package, it was a very small price to pay for a tiny pleasure that could spread a feeling of Joy over the rest of her day. In honor of her story, I eat more raspberries these days.

I also dance more. As I mentioned in chapter 1, my favorite thing about dance is that it invites people feel more Joy. Choosing Joy—in dance and in life—can be an intentional practice. For example, rather than exercising for the sake of building the perfect bicep, what if we moved with an intention to reduce pain and seek pleasure? What if we moved for the sake of *feeling good*?

Funnily enough, the first time I wrote the sentence above, it came out "what if we JUST moved for the sake of feeling good?" Caught in the act. When I read what I wrote, I realized that "JUST" is a symptom of the dilemma we are facing. "*Just* to feel good?" says my own inner voice. But there's no time for that! I've got bills to pay, clients to tend to, the dog to walk, relationships to nurture . . . Whatever I do, it's got to have a point. An end goal. It's got to get me somewhere, right?

My friend and former client, Marta, is an HR executive at a Fortune 500 company. When we started working together, she told me she was bad at time management. Through our conversations, however, we realized that she was pretty much a badass at getting things done. Her new job was larger and more complex than ever before, and she was seen as an asset in her organization. The real problem was that she had a hard time saying yes to the things that mattered. Because her job was stressful, her health and her sanity were largely dependent upon her weekend yoga practice—which she'd been skimping on since the expansion of her role. She also confessed that she hadn't taken a spontaneous vacation for nearly ten years.

While taking part in my women's course, Marta had an epiphany that sparked a spontaneous act of self-care and served as an inspiration for the rest of her cohort. She'd been grappling with the idea of going on a weekend ski vacation in Colorado with a group of friends. Unfortunately, their planning efforts were a bit haphazard, and the dates kept changing, making it impossible for her to schedule the time off. She had all but let go of her dream and buried her nose back in her work when a single question reignited the flame of her desire: "*What pleasures have you been denying yourself?*" A small voice inside piped up: "You've been denying yourself the pleasure of skiing!" Marta realized the dance of *yes, maybe, no, maybe* was part of the pattern that kept her stuck. She decided on the spot that she was ready to break free.

Within twenty-four hours, she had called her boss to request vacation time, contacted some former colleagues in Europe, and booked a flight to Switzerland for an impromptu ski weekend in the Alps. Her inner child jumped for Joy at her own audacity, and she had a blast. What's more, nothing at the office blew up without her (imagine that!). Marta came back with a renewed vigor and a lot more trust in her own ability to make the choices that would help her refuel when needed.

This story offers a fun and courageous example of what's possible when we stop believing the stories we typically tell ourselves. But frankly, any small and empowering "yes!" will do. As women, it's easy to forget that our own needs matter. Instead we make our to-do list and check it twice. We ask, "Will they be okay without me?" And because we are *clearly* indispensable, we decide that unless it's absolutely critical, our pleasure will just have to wait until tomorrow. (Then we take a course on resilience, in the desperate hope that it will reduce our stress and help us get our energy back.)

Again, I tease. But am I far off? I know because I've been on the same journey with you. Even after years of practice, my own mind still diminishes *seeking pleasure* as an end goal. It's simply not something that comes easily or naturally to me. Through trial and error, I've come to learn that giving myself *permission to enjoy* is no small feat. And I laugh to myself when I remember that so many of the other things I do—like working and making money—actually have the end goal of being happy and fulfilled!

While *taking pleasure* may seem to be the farthest thing from a practical leadership skill, I invite you to consider this: have you ever tried to lead an initiative when you were feeling irritated, depleted, or resentful? And if so, how would you rate your effectiveness, as compared to your *potential effectiveness*, on a scale from 1–10? Or this: have you ever looked around the office and thought your team seemed a bit disengaged? What if your capacity to savor the good stuff had a direct impact on the daily mood of the people that work for you?

What I've found is that saying "Yes!" is a practice. Letting myself feel good is a practice. Embracing the successful feeling that goes with getting what I want is a practice. Staying open and receiving is a practice. And each of these practices increases my believability, magnetism, and compellingness as a leader.

On good days, when I fully engage in these practices, I'm able to let the critical voices go for a while and taste the positive sensations in my own body like ripe juicy raspberries. I can reconnect with my inner child who took a simple approach to life: if it feels good, it's good; if it feels bad, it's bad. On good days, I can listen to my body as it speaks to me.

On other days, I forget. I drift. I get caught up in the practical. I focus on the shoulds. I give the reins over to the task-master side of me, who worries it's all much more complicated than that. And that's why I continue to say YES, joyfully returning to this practice again and again.

Living Your "I Wants": Reflection Questions

- Beyond your Joy Workouts, what else brings you Joy? What would it look like to allow yourself 5 percent more of that this week?
- Make a list of all the pleasures you deny yourself that you "wish" you could enjoy. Include pleasures both at home and at work.
- Recall the Bonus Practice from chapter 1: to take yourself on a "me-date" to celebrate your decision to embark on this journey. Have you gone on that date yet? If yes, what did you enjoy? If not, why not?
- If I told you I'd pay for that date, provide childcare, and explain your absence to your friends, family, and colleagues, what kind of date would you go on?

THE GAME OF DESIRE

Of course, it would be easy if all of the things we wanted just dropped into our lap. Then all we'd have to do is learn to enjoy them. But you and I both know that in reality, there's often some work involved when it comes to getting what we want. So let's talk about the games we play—and how they're working for us.

Let me start with a slightly provocative example that I believe illustrates the challenge well. A few years ago, I enrolled in a class about female orgasm. Sitting in a well-lit classroom with about fifty women and men, we discussed the challenges that couples face when it comes to pleasuring a woman. It turns out that one of the biggest roadblocks that thwart *most* women's orgasmic potential is the inability to simply, clearly, and directly ask for what they want.

What do you want to eat for dinner? I don't know.

Do you want to go dancing or see a movie? I don't know.

Do you prefer chicken or pasta? Mmm . . . Whatever.

Do you want me to move my finger a little to the left or the right? Er . . . um . . . you decide. Yikes!

You get the idea, right? But have you ever stopped to wonder: is it really that we have no preference, or is something else going on here?

As we move through life, there are a hundred small choices we make every single day. Yet frequently, we defer those choices to somebody else. Without a second thought, we pass the decision off to our husbands, our parents, our friends, our lovers, our doctors, lawyers, dental hygienists, and massage therapists. We say things like "I don't know" or "it doesn't really matter to me" or "it's not important." Even the boldest women often have domains in which they're less likely to take a clear stand than to say, "I don't know."

Personally, I would do it without even noticing. I would do it instead of proactively asking for what I wanted—even when the invitation was on the table. At least, that was true in my past. A number of years ago, I started to notice an unconscious game I was playing with my body and mind. If I were to give the game a name, I would have called it something like "What they think matters more than what I want." In this game I would place my attention on the other people in the room—their thoughts, feelings, needs, and judgments—rather than focus inward and really give myself the time and space to assess what my true preferences were.

When I shared this reflection with my client Cara, she laughed out loud. "Yeah, I know that one. I do it a lot at work. But to tell you the truth, I do it most with my husband." Cara is the executive director of a nonprofit law firm outside of New York City that focuses on serving victims of domestic violence. She herself had been in a healthy, loving marriage for over twenty years. Yet she could instantly relate to the idea of subtly giving her own power away at home.

Cara had hired me to work on her confidence. Having recently accepted the role of executive director, she was committed to taking the organization to the next level. She had a big vision, and she was great at her job. At the same time, she was also a humble woman who uplifted others while secretly doubting herself. Cara noticed that at times, her team seemed to believe in ability more than she did. While we hadn't come together to improve her love life, we had a hunch that putting some attention on her relationship with desire could pay big dividends. We were right.

Cara decided to take on a simple—but not easy—homework assignment. Rather than say "I don't know" when her husband asked her what she wanted, she would give him a real answer. Mostly, Cara practiced in the small moments—choices about food, seeing friends or seeing a movie, staying home or going out. She soon started having more fun at home, and her husband did too. Yet it wasn't long before the kind of conversations we were having about her leadership *also* started to change. At the start of our engagement, I would ask Cara her about her vision and she would hedge. "Well . . . maybe . . . I sort of have this idea, but . . ." she would say. Just a few weeks into her new practice, she confessed to me that she saw the possibility to open a new center in partnership with a local university, and that she was ready to approach the dean for a conversation.

Eighteen months later, Cara's new center is flourishing. She has added several team members, and the number of women they are able to serve has grown tremendously. Cara's intentions were noble, and she was able to put her own desire to work for an entire community. In our most recent coaching conversation, I asked her about a fundraising initiative. Without missing a beat, she said with confidence, "I want to ask them to give me a million dollars." I knew that her willingness to trust—and speak—her desire was truly paying off.

If the potential for reward is so great, why do we work so hard to keep our desires under wrap? The biggest problem with the "I don't know what I want" strategy is that it works *really well.* The benefits *in the moment* are massive. On the surface, I get to look like the good guy (or gal). I'm easygoing. I don't push anyone's buttons. I'm flexible. I'm definitely not a burden. Sometimes I'm even the martyr (yes, this is a big one—see how much I suffer for you? You laugh . . . but it's real.) When I use this strategy, everybody else is pretty much happy, and I don't make any waves. And as long as I don't really *know* what I want, it's easy enough to believe that not asking is working for me.

Underneath the surface, though, there are costs—both opportunity costs and good old-fashioned physical and emotional consequences. And there are costs for relationships. When I ignore my deeper "I wants" and say "I don't know" by default, I often find myself feeling frustrated or resentful, and blaming the other person for my mood. I feel like crap, and over time this can take quite a toll. For example, one evening I go out with a friend. He asks, "Do you want to have dinner at this Italian restaurant?" I don't even realize it at the time, but somewhere inside I am thinking, "Yes! I'd *love* to!" But I'm also thinking, "It's expensive. What if he doesn't want to spend that much money? I don't want him to think I'm a high-maintenance woman." What comes out is, "Well, I don't know . . ."

We walk a long way to eat at a different restaurant. The food isn't good, the atmosphere makes me uncomfortable, and I don't look him in the eyes the entire evening. We both go home unsatisfied, though neither of us can really quite put our finger on why. I sleep less well that night and wake up still ruminating about it. The next time I think about spending time with this person, I feel that same uneasy feeling and decide against it. Even though I like him a lot, we begin to drift apart. While that one decision seems inconsequential, it's in these tiny moments of self-betrayal that I am the one responsible for creating a life that I don't really enjoy.

I hope these stories have provided some real food for thought—both about the costs of "I don't know" and the potential upside of making friends with your real desire. This week I challenge you to tune into your body and genuinely listen to what it wants. Try playing a different game. Let's call it "I say what I want, even if in the end, I can't have it." This game has no winner or loser. If your mind comes up blank, great! Take your time and keep tuning in. If the voice inside says, "I don't know," ask it, "And what if you did know?" Be as patient and nurturing with your desire as you would with a child, coaxing her out from under her blanket into the light. Let her know it's safe to come out and play.

The goal is simply to build a new muscle. The payoff is knowing and honoring what you deeply want.

The Game of Desire: Reflection Questions

- What are the moments, situations, and relationships in which you typically ignore your own desires? What would it look like to honor them?
- What's one thing you would *want* to do, if only it weren't so silly and frivolous? What would you give yourself permission to do if you could be *sure* it wouldn't be a "waste of time"?
- If you could ask your husband/lover/partner/best friend to do ONE thing for you, with a guarantee they'd say yes with compassion and empathy, what would you ask?

AND . . . NO

You may be thinking, *What happens when what I want doesn't jive with what* THEY *want?*

"They" are your husband, lover, children, parents, colleagues, bosses, and friends. Aren't "they" the ones who—for so many years—have reaped the benefit of your indifference? They have chosen the restaurant, lead the initiative, or spent the money on what they thought was most important at the time. When you start to have desires, they might not always get their way anymore. You might start saying no. And then things might start to get a little bit messy.

Yep. I'm here to tell you that 1) it's going to happen, and 2) it's going to be okay. Uncomfortable, yes. But ultimately okay.

Remember Mary Oliver's poem? "You don't have to be good . . ." And thank God for that. If you are a woman living in this time, I'd be willing to bet that *some* portion of your body-mind system, large or small, is built to make sure that you behave yourself. I will be good. I will do the right thing. I won't talk too loudly or make too many waves. I will be really smart, so that the boys take me seriously. I will make do. I will make it work. I will avoid conflict at all costs. I will control everything so that any conflict that does happen, happens on my terms. I will be seen and not heard. Unless I explode, in which case it wasn't my fault, and I'll put it away again immediately. I will remain under control, keep calm . . . and carry on.

Many of us have embodied the shape and mood of being "polite" (even, by the way, those of us who come across as "tough" on the outside). We bite our tongues rather than clearly, simply, and unguardedly saying, "No, that doesn't work for me." Oh, and *anger*? That's like defiance. That's really not good. Even the word itself can seem taboo. For example, my corporate clients use phrases like "she started getting a little bit passionate" as an apologetic blanket statement for the moment when a colleague loses her temper or takes a stand against an injustice that is meaningful to her.

Again, if you're not sure this section applies to you, it may not. This chapter teaches two skills at the opposite ends of a spectrum—yes and no. Broadly, there are also some cultural differences that can play out here. Nonetheless, I invite you to slow down and take a closer look. While you may think you're good at one and bad at the other (e.g., "no" is easy, "yes" is hard), the truth is often much more complex. Some of my toughest clients—when really honest with themselves—have discovered that their anger and pseudo-strength were built to mask a deeper layer—one that can't stand the vulnerability of setting a simple boundary and risking betrayal.

I can say without hesitation that if you picked up this book to help you with burnout, overwhelm, energy depletion, or resilience, this section has the power to change your life. If this is you, I suppose what I'm suggesting also doesn't sound new. "I know, I know . . . I just have to say 'no' more often." What *will* be new, however, is you deciding to take on "no" as a committed practice. There's no amount of science or strategy that can make this change for you. Your next move—like, literally after you put down the book TODAY—is to begin.

I can also say without hesitation that if this *is* your thing (you know who you are) and you *don't* take this practice on, you will be disappointed with your results. And if you're anything like me, you'll be flipping through the next self-help book a month, a year, or ten years from now, still looking for the silver bullet. I stand firmly behind what I said in the prologue: it's in the *embodied practice* that the magic happens. And it's time.

As part of your research this week, I hereby give you full permission to practice saying "no." Of course, you already have it. But in case you need the permission slip, here it is. You don't have to be good. Try it on. Make "I don't have to" your mantra, just for a while. Set a simple, clear boundary and practice tolerating the sensation of standing behind it with silent and bold commitment.

They—the people you love who are accustomed to your usual compliance (or bullying!)—might be a bit surprised at first. But keep in mind that THEY are also the ones who have felt sad when you suffered in silence, have faced your resentment, and have struggled to figure out how to make you happy. While they have some things to lose, they also have a lot to gain from your sovereignty. Perhaps with practice, they will be grateful to know how you really feel . . . and willing to work out a compromise that genuinely works for both of you.

To kick off your practice, I invite you to consider what honest boundaries you avoid that you might want to express this week? What demands are tugging at your heels that you could choose to decline? What would you stop doing by yourself? What would you cease to tolerate?

Then practice saying "no." This week . . . *you don't have to be good!*

And . . . No: Reflection Questions

- What is one outstanding invitation that you want to decline but haven't yet?
- What is one thing you said "yes" to recently, but would rather have said "no"? Why didn't you say "no"? Is there room to renegotiate?
- What is one task that you need to take off your to-do list immediately?
- Who are three people in your life with whom you could practice saying "no" to more often? What will be challenging about that?

THE SCIENCE: ONLY THE ESSENTIAL

Greg McKeown, bestselling author and founder of THIS, Inc., has dedicated his life to helping people do less, but better. He calls this practice *essentialism*. In his book by the same title, he questions the pervasive belief that a person or organization can legitimately have more than one priority at a time. According to McKeown, one of the most critical tools in the essentialist's toolbox is *choice*. Yet he acknowledges that many of us have practically given up on our capacity to choose. In the face of a hundred competing commitments per day, we feel our time is out of our control. The requests of our bosses, employees, spouses, children, clients, and other stakeholders tug at our heartstrings, producing a fog that makes it difficult to see the truth: we *still* have a choice.

McKeown writes, "The ability to choose cannot be taken away or even given away—it can only be forgotten." In his model, exercising the right to choose is the first place to look when it comes to taking your out-of-control calendar back. Failure to execute our right to choose produces a sense of helplessness. This leads to a self-fulfilling downward spiral, in which we let go of what we care about most, because we believe that we must. In order to turn that spiral on its head, you must exercise a healthy disbelief in your own helplessness. When you take stock of where your real choices lie, you can start exercising that muscle again.

Greg McKeown, *Essentialism: The Disciplined Pursuit of Less* (New York: Crown Business, 2014).

The Practice

As you may have guessed, the practices for this chapter are simple . . . but not easy. In fact, they may turn out to be incredibly hard. But the potential payoff is also great. If you've identified personal or professional growth areas that include things like confidence, powerful communication, executive presence, resilience, energy management, work–life balance, or a greater sense of purpose, your path starts here. The practices that follow are the foundational building blocks that help make those elusive goals truly possible. Rather than "put on" look-alikes of those desirable leadership qualities, I invite you to start here—from the ground up—and literally grow into them.

In summary, your mission is to *practice the art of intentional creation.* The practice will involve making clear and honest choices, by *saying yes, asking for what you want,* and *saying no* in the right moments, on a regular basis. Your initial actions will depend on which segment of this chapter spoke most loudly to you. But the overall intention is the same—become a master truth-teller when it comes to your real desire.

PRACTICE 1: YES, NO, AND I WANT

This practice is designed to help you learn more about your current habits. It can also serve as the springboard for change. Take a moment to look back over your notes from this chapter. If you listen to your gut, which of the three sections seemed juiciest, scariest, or most on point with the way you need and want to evolve?

Based on your honest assessment of yourself, I invite you to choose one of the three practices below and commit to doing it for a definitive period of time. It takes about thirty days to change a habit. That said, when we choose a time frame for our commitments that feels too daunting, we're *much* more likely to give up a few days in, when the going gets hard. Therefore, I recommend starting with *one full week* (ideally, beginning the moment you put the book down today). Then, if you find yourself learning from the practice (i.e., Either you're doing it and it's helping, or you're struggling and it's showing you how difficult and important it is for you), you can choose to continue for another week or two.

One more thing—I want to offer a word of advice about *commitment* before you begin. Many of us hold commitments like fad diets. We start with good intentions, but as soon as we "break" the commitment, we give up. In fact, it's when you fail that you *actually need the commitment most!* Counterintuitive but true. Only by *keeping* the commitment for the full week will you learn about the true size of the challenge and fully understand where your real growth opportunity lies. Therefore, I challenge you to keep saying, "I am committed to X (e.g., saying 'no' once a day)," every day until your elected time frame ends. This will tell your brain that 1) you're still on the path and 2) it's okay to be imperfect and still be committed. This will be helpful, since perfect it isn't actually possible anyhow. Good luck . . . and have fun!

Here are the three practices, ordered by section:

Option 1: Say a Full-Bodied "Yes." Allow yourself to do or have *one thing each day* for the sheer pleasure of it. And, allow yourself to enjoy it. (I'm serious: *Enjoy* it.)

Option 2: Take "I Don't Know" Out of Your Vocabulary. Just stop saying it. When somebody asks your preference, give them an answer! Even if you're not sure, try making a request and see how it feels. And if you do hear yourself saying "I don't know," quickly and graciously correct yourself—out loud—to the person you're speaking with. "Well, actually, let me think about that for a minute . . ." is a great way to buy a few seconds while you recover. Then pick something. Anything is better than giving your choice away.

Option 3: Say a Full-Bodied "No." Once a day, decline something that you really don't want to have or to do. Notice what fears, anxieties, or resistance come up. Take note of those, and practice standing in your truth. It's not essential that you get your way in the end. Sometimes we do have to negotiate. The main point is to say the "no" you typically avoid. The secondary point is to *observe* what happens next. For example, do people say, "Okay, no problem," and shock you that it's not a big deal? Do they push back, and you finally cave—even when you really shouldn't? All of this is useful information. Rather than judge yourself, let it be a puzzle piece that adds to your self-awareness.

Ultimately, a conscious leader will need to have some mastery with each of three of these practices. But it doesn't have to happen overnight. Most likely, you're already better at one than the others. Again, I dare you to start with the one that is hardest for you. Take note in your journal about your breakthroughs, your failures, and also what you learn. Good luck—and have fun!

ACTIVE INGREDIENTS	commitment, body listening, empowered choice
WHY IT WORKS	This practice relies on your clarity and decision *before the moment* to help interrupt your old, habitual pattern *in the moment*. As you rack up small wins, you will "learn-by-doing" how to make a new move.

PRACTICE 2: FEEL YOUR DESIRES

How do we know when we need to say yes or no? Typically, our gut-level knowing comes with a bodily sensation or emotional feeling that gives us a clue. This practice will help you get familiar with those embodied clues, so that you can recognize them in the moment.

Setup: Find or create about ten minutes in your day, in a quiet place, where you can do the practice uninterrupted. Close your eyes and take a few deep breaths. Allow your body to settle into a more neutral state. Then feel the sensations in your body.

Research Yes: Imagine something you want—or want to do. In your mind's eye, see it coming toward you, while feeling the sensations in your body. You might notice your stomach, chest, hands, shoulders, neck, jaw, or eyes. See if you can increase what's happening. Let yourself want it. Allow it to come in. Take note of the sensation.

Research No: Now call to mind something you don't want—or don't want to do. In your mind's eye, see it coming toward you, while feeling the sensations in your body. You might notice your stomach, chest, hands, shoulders, neck, jaw, or eyes. See if you can increase what's happening. Let yourself want to repel that thing. Create a boundary. Take note of the sensation.

Capture Your Learning

When you finish the practice, open your eyes and take a few notes about the emotional feelings and bodily sensations you experienced. Bonus: You can do this practice again any time you're considering a big decision, like taking on a new project or going on a second date.

ACTIVE INGREDIENTS	meditative presence, mindful body scanning, imagination
WHY IT WORKS	By creating a scenario in your mind and feeling your body, you can learn about your somatic (embodied) responses without the same distractions that happen in life.

REFLECTIONS ON THE SAY YES . . . AND NO PRACTICES

- What are you learning from engaging with the topic of desire this week?
- Did you choose to work with Yes, No, or I Don't Know? Why did you choose it? What, if anything, opened for you in trying something new?
- If you haven't done *any* of the practices, or seem to be avoiding them . . . why? What's in the way of you diving in?

Guts and Grace Playlist Recommendations

"Video" – India Arie

"Follow the Sun" – Xavier Rudd

"Go Your Own Way" – Fleetwood Mac

"Nobody's Alone" – The Polish Ambassador (feat. Yarah Bravo)

"Price Tag" – Jessie J

"Just Like Heaven" – The Cure

Empower

"You are the sky. Everything else—it's just the weather."

—PEMA CHÖDRÖN

Empowerment is the capacity to take effective action at all times—especially in moments when the going gets tough. Contrary to popular belief, this doesn't mean looking like you're okay all the time. Nor does it mean swallowing the stuff that's hard and "just dealing with it" internally. Rather, it's about taking responsibility for your triggers, your emotions, and your thoughts, and using them in a productive way. In this section, I introduce practices that teach you how to re-center under pressure, navigate difficult emotions with grace, and stop the cycle of self-sabotaging behavior that unconsciously creates the very failure it aims to prevent.

LEADERSHIP MYTH

It's useful to worry, plan, blame, and complain.

LEADERSHIP TRUTH

Most runaway-train thought patterns are actually unconscious strategies to avoid the fear of failure and chase the high of success.

Chapter 4

LASSO YOUR BRAIN

Within each of us there is a silence—a silence as vast
as a universe. We are afraid of it—and we long for it.
When we experience that silence, we remember who we are . . .
I believe that each of us can make a tremendous difference.
Politicians and visionaries will not return us to the sacredness of life.
That will be done by ordinary men and women who gather
neighbors and friends together and say, "Remember to breathe,
remember to feel, remember to care, remember life . . ."

—GUNILLA NORRIS

COMING BACK FROM GONE

Welcome to the territory of the mind.

If you've ever experienced your mind running off the rails like a runaway train, only to sabotage your best intentions, I invite you to pay special attention in this chapter. We'll have some important work to do here. The good news is, compared to when I started teaching this curriculum over a decade ago, there are far more resources (and far more empirical evidence) available to help you create effective, new habits in this arena of your leadership.

On the scientific side, we now have proof from the field of neuroscience that mindful meditation (a.k.a. "mindfulness") can have a massive impact on our psychological and physiological well-being. Workplaces that have encouraged their employees to practice these tools regularly have seen reductions in variables like stress and sick leave, and upswings in engagement, productivity, and work satisfaction.

The growing field of positive psychology suggests that simple shifts in thought (like focusing on gratitude over frustration, or recalling "three good things" from your day before going to bed at night) can improve both our mood and our effectiveness. Leaders in the pop-psychology and self-help industries argue that mindset matters—a lot. Philosophies like the Law of Attraction (i.e., you will manifest what you think about) and works like Napoleon Hill's *Think and Grow Rich* (title = self-explanatory) have been passed around in these circles for decades.

Can these simple thinking strategies *really* make a reliable difference when you're pursuing a leadership upgrade? And—perhaps more importantly—are they *actually* useful when the going gets tough? The short answer is yes . . . and no.

Bad things (or at least challenging things) do happen. We need good coping strategies. And while mindfulness and positive thinking can be incredibly effective, they are not necessarily easy to implement. Why? Because—simply put—it's hard to let go of the stuff we're worried about. Deep down in our psyches, despite what our yoga teachers might say, many of us still subconsciously believe this leadership myth: ***It's useful to worry, plan, blame, and complain.*** Worrying thwarts failure. Planning prevents things from going awry. Blame sets the record straight, and complaining makes sure it gets fixed.

Of course, these repetitive thought and language habits aren't actually effective solutions. The truth is: ***most runaway-train thought patterns are actually unconscious strategies to avoid the fear of failure and chase the high of success.*** But they also *sabotage* success by depleting our energy, leading us to make ineffective choices and keeping our vision small. In fact, worrying operates similarly to a chemical or emotional addiction, at the level of our physiology. To put it more bluntly, we may actually be addicted to the drama. And it makes sense—for better or worse, the habit of incessant thinking has real (if fleeting) benefits. If you do it often, it has probably served you—at some time, in some way, or with somebody. *That*'s why it can be so hard to change.

Your mind is a powerful thing. When it's off on a ride, it can be hard to focus on anything else. So, as a blossoming conscious leader, it's critically important for you to develop some mastery in this arena. In this chapter you will learn how. The practices in chapter 4 are designed to help you *take back your brain* and create a strong habit that keeps you in the game. This doesn't mean never contacting your own hurt or pain (we'll come back to that in a later lesson). However, it *may* mean putting some limits on your language and thoughts for the sake of your present-tense well-being.

I want to acknowledge that you may already have some resources on this topic. Maybe you have done the work to establish a regular meditation routine, or you have some practices that help you emotionally re-center in the face of stress. If so, that's great. This chapter will offer a number of nuances that will help you hone and deepen your practice. On the other hand, you may be entirely new to practices like managing your attention and effectively corralling your emotions. Or you may have some strategies that *should* work in theory . . . but have generally failed you in the trenches. That's totally fine. The tools I offer here are appropriate for beginners as well. If you're just starting out, you have the benefit of not having to *unlearn* habits that don't really work.

As a side note, some of the content in this chapter will have the most powerful impact when you're tackling big challenges or swimming in the deeper end of the pool, so to speak. If you're currently experiencing a lot of stress and overwhelm, or are faced with a concrete psychological, physical, or emotional challenge, you may find yourself thinking "yes! This is totally what I need right now." If so, dive in. The tools will be helpful—though possibly tough to learn.

If the themes don't "jump off the page for you" immediately, it may be that you're going through a pretty stable phase in life right now. In that case, I challenge you to look for smaller, more nuanced ways to apply the tools. Practice what make sense to you today. Then tuck the rest in your back pocket to come back to later, as needed. It's actually *much* easier to develop a baseline practice when you're not under stress, even if it seems less useful at the time. Trust me, you'll thank me later.

THOUGHTS, EMOTIONS, AND PAIN

Now that we've laid some foundation and offered a nod to the mindfulness movement, I want to bring us back to the body. Here's why: when I started my journey to become a conscious leader, *dealing with my fearful thoughts and negative emotions* was probably the toughest thing for me to change. In fact, it was part of my core self-sabotage strategy (we'll come back to *that* in chapter 6). It was so hard for me to believe I could do anything about this part of myself that I virtually avoided trying. Until it started to make me sick.

As I mentioned in the introduction, I discovered a lump in my breast when I was twenty-eight years old. Before then, however, I had experienced a number of other physical symptoms at various stressful moments in my life. I now know that my body was talking to me. It was raising a red flag in an attempt to pull me out of a mental and emotional spiral that I was willing to tolerate at the time but that had truthfully gotten out of control. Our bodies do this all the time, in both large and small ways.

Have you noticed that thoughts, emotions, and pain often go hand in hand? For example, when was the last time you were under emotional stress and found yourself burdened with tense, aching shoulders? Or you were thinking about a challenging conversation you needed to have and experienced an upset stomach or pounding headache? Today, both scientific researchers and pop science gurus are weighing in on the connection between thoughts, feelings, and actions. The notion that emotional trauma can lead to physical responses in the body is also now widely accepted. What I've found, through my own practice and that of my clients, is that our bodies can serve as the messenger, letting us know when we urgently need to change our thinking. It can also be the location where we experience the greatest cost when we don't make a change.

In the spirit of exploration, this week I invite you to get curious about the unique cause-and-effect relationships inside of *your body* when it comes to your thoughts, emotions, and pain. For each person, the circuitry may work a bit differently. To date there is not a unified scientific theory that can reliably predict specific relationships between our thoughts and our health. Yet a multitude of case studies exist—from tiny shifts to miraculous recoveries—documenting people who found their own answers. Here are a few examples to spark your reflection.

A few years back, in a Nia Technique training I attended, founder Debbie Rosas called out a student who complained that the process was difficult because of her "bad knee." "How do you think your knee feels when you're constantly calling it bad?" Debbie wanted to know. Of course, the student looked dumbfounded and was taken aback. We commonly use that kind of language to talk about our pains, injuries, and compromised body parts. Yet Debbie had made an important point: the negative language we use has an impact on our brains, our beliefs, and our emotions. But what about the body itself?

If you set an intention to heal or thrive, but stay negative in your thoughts and language, it's equivalent to sending mixed messages to your body. And—recalling Donald Yance's cancer treatment work from chapter 1—the negative emotions you experience while thinking about your "bad knee" (or fill in your own story) create a harsher and more hostile internal context that makes it harder for the body to heal.

A while back, I found my upper body in intense physical pain. It began in my shoulders and crept its way up my neck to the base of my skull. It came as a surprise. The movement forms I teach are designed to naturally reset the body's alignment, so I typically don't experience a lot of skeletal or muscular pain. This unexpected pain gave me the opportunity to consider the mechanism behind my physical sensations.

In my case, I could trace the pain back to a tough conversation that I'd unintentionally stuffed down over the prior weekend. Combined with working at the ergonomically unsupportive desk of my much taller colleague, and a few poor movement choices in my weekly yoga class, the situation left me nearly unable to look to the side, up, or down. I also noticed that as the week went on and my pain increased, *I became increasingly more negative in my language and thoughts*. My positive disposition was lost to nagging, complaints, and disappointed expectations (including the realization that the chiropractor I'd hoped to see was out of town). The pain continued to get worse.

As an experiment, I decided to take charge of the one thing I could control—my language. I made a commitment to stop saying anything negative for the rest of the week, and asked my roommate to support me by pointing it out when I slipped up. Within a few hours, I began to relax. Although I still felt pain, the sum total of my negative experience of the pain was far less. I started to enjoy my life again.

In fact, a couple days later a healing practitioner came to visit a class I was taking. She offered to do some free work on my neck and shoulder on the spot. When she did, the pain lessened dramatically. Had I been stuck in my negative thoughts, I likely would have met her offer with skepticism and declined her gift outright.

This week, I invite you to take stock of your relationship with pain and other uneasy sensations—including the role your thoughts, feelings, and emotions may play. For example, as you do your Joy Workouts (yes, you are still doing them!), you might try holding any pain you experience as *useful information* (rather than a "problem"). It's easy to decide not to exercise in order to avoid pain or, inversely, decide to push through any physical pain while exercising (sometimes creating a further injury). Instead, can you hold your "bad knee" as a "knee that is healing" and adopt a healthy curiosity about what message that particular pain at that particular moment is trying to give you?

If you don't tend to experience a lot of pain, you can instead home in on other feelings and sensations that you think may have value to explore. Something minor, like a slightly queasy stomach going into a difficult conversation, can still teach you a lot about the quality of your thoughts.

I also challenge you to consider whether you receive any *benefits* from your pain. What do I mean by benefits? O. Carl Simonton,[12] oncologist, cancer survivor, and pioneer of many current-day visualization techniques for self-healing, discovered that many people receive unintended but juicy benefits when they are sick or emotionally unwell. For example: people take care of me and reassure me; I get sympathy; I finally get to rest; my daughter stops her teenage crisis; my husband actually cleans the house and makes me dinner; I get to put off doing that difficult and scary project at work; I can act like a bitch and people are still nice to me . . . you see the point. Unfortunately, these benefits aren't actually helping them to heal.

Harsh as it may sound, Dr. Simonton took this point of view seriously. He prescribed *limiting the benefits of pain* as a key ingredient in his cancer treatment programs, and it led to great success. According to Simonton, if you are going to get well, you must find out what needs you are unconsciously satisfying by attaching to your pain. Then, you must find different ways those needs would be sustainable even if your health were at 100 percent.

If this resonates, you might include some self-observation on "unconscious benefits" as part of your research this week. In addition to taking stock of the ways your physical experience may be impacted by your thoughts, also consider what it would look like for you to *limit* the benefits of your pain and other uneasy sensations. Use the reflection questions below, paired with mindful observation, to explore where, when, and why a change may be in order.

Thoughts, Emotions, and Pain: Reflection Questions

- What kind of thoughts, judgments, or language do you use in relation to your body that could be making it harder for you to thrive?
- What do you talk yourself out of doing that might actually help?
- How do you let yourself behave when you are in pain or feeling uneasy that you might not stand for if you were feeling better?
- What are the ways you let yourself off the hook when you are in pain or feeling uneasy? How does that get in the way of creating the life or work you most desire?
- What do you give yourself when you're sick or hurt that you never let yourself have at other times? Why?
- What messages do you think your pain or uneasy feelings may have for you? What else might you learn from your body on this subject if you were willing to listen?

THE SCIENCE: ABCS OF RESILIENCE

Is it possible to bring your mind back when your thoughts seem so *real and compelling*? According to University of Pennsylvania psychologist Karen Reivich, coauthor of *The Resilience Factor*, this skill is absolutely necessary if you want to build a strong foundation of emotional resilience. Reivich teaches cognitive interventions that help people corral their minds and re-center in times of stress. Her tools have helped thousands of people, from Fortune 100 executives, to war veterans, to Ivy League graduate students, to the spouses of soldiers who died in combat.

Reivich explains that most people tend to fall into the same unconscious, unhelpful thought patterns—called *thinking traps*—again and again. Reivich teaches her clients how to consciously track their "ABCs" in order to step out of these patterns. A is for adversities—the situations that typically push your buttons and cause you to react. B is for beliefs—the thought patterns you generate as a result. C represents the consequences—the feelings you feel and the behaviors you then enact. Since the *adversities you face* may be out of your control, Reivich argues that changing your *beliefs* is the most effective way to change your overall experience.

Here's how. First, note your ABCs. What's the adversity? What are you believing about it? And what are the current consequences? Then, challenge your own thinking. Could your thoughts be more flexible? More accurate? Come up with some alternative possibilities for what may be going on *other than* the belief that pushed your buttons. Look for less painful beliefs that are may also be truer. You can even look for evidence *against* your thinking-trap beliefs. The goal is to build resilience. When you practice tools like the ABCs, you'll feel more optimistic and have the ability to be more present with the people you love and serve.

Karen Reivich and A. Shatté, *The Resilience Factor: 7 Keys to Finding Your Inner Strength and Overcoming Life's Hurdles* (New York: Three Rivers Press, 2002).

THE LASSO

While it's easy to talk about changing the quality of your thoughts, I want to acknowledge that may *not* be easy to do. (Detecting a theme here?) The reflection questions in the last section may have helped you clarify some things that need changing—and why they matter. That said, if the topic of *pain* doesn't resonate, you may have some skepticism. Below are a few more questions to help you get clear about how, when, and where the next set of tools may be helpful. You can answer them in your journal or simply consider your answers as you read.

- What do you worry about most?
- When something goes wrong with a colleague, partner, or friend, what do you do?
- What happens before (or after) a difficult conversation?
- Do you ever second-guess yourself or feel guilty after making a decision?
- Do you ever get frustrated with other people for how they're behaving?
- All in all, how many hours do you typically spend worrying, ruminating, gossiping, running worst-case scenarios, rehashing, regretting, planning, figuring things out?
- How does that impact your mood?
- How does it impact your overall effectiveness?

Even as a long-time practitioner of these tools, I must admit that I had something to say for *most* of those questions. It's pretty normal. The truth is, our human operating systems come equipped to think and think and think. Our brains are built to run scenarios and keep us safe. We do it often, and we do it automatically. You might say that needing to manage your attention and corral your thoughts is a part being of an effective adult. Certainly, it's part of being a fully conscious and thriving leader.

Most of the time we're running these troublesome programs behind the scenes. We keep quiet about the chaos in our heads and go through our days looking relatively normal. But, in my experience, it can sometimes get *a lot* worse in there than we'd like to admit.

What happens on the days when you get *so stuck* that you feel like you're suffocating? What happens when the anxiety is *so bad* that you have *no idea* how to recover your balance and reenter your life? What happens when you lose more than twenty-four hours of productivity rehashing a single conversation again and again in your mind?

I hear you.

Sometimes my mind goes out of control like a runaway train. It spins and spirals, taking me for a ride. Although I may appear to be in the world, I have left my body and I'm somewhere far away. Often the same old tape-recorded message plays itself out over and over again. Did I make the right decision? Should I have done it differently? How will I prepare for . . . ? Is this really the right job? The right doctor? The right man? The right approach? What if I can do better?

Can you relate to this experience at all?

Depending on your personality, these statements may seem dramatic.

Or perhaps they are beyond your experience. If so, it's fine to put yourself in someone else's shoes for a moment. Think about the people you love who may be feeling that way. Or, if it's helpful to put it in a specific work context, you can also think about the hurricane of thoughts that ran through your mind before a recent presentation or after a big failure at work. If you do relate to sometimes feeling overwhelmingly stuck, anxious, or afraid, please know that that you're not the least bit alone. And it's possible to do something about it.

When I first met my client Veena, she seemed like a successful woman who had it all together. She had a cheery disposition, and I instantly liked her. Not long after, however, I came to understand that her inner world was strikingly different than the face she showed to the outside. Veena reached out to me for support with her leadership. She quickly confessed that she'd recently "burned out" in a high-profile job and had taken a much less exciting (and less well-paying) role in order to recover. Through our work together, we identified the root cause of her burnout: a constant, nagging, and sometimes debilitating worry that she wasn't good enough.

This fear took up a ton of emotional and mental space. It produced a high level of stress that took a toll on her body. It kept her mind on high alert and made it hard for her to focus on what really mattered. According to Veena, she spent so much time running future scenarios and rehashing the past that she was rarely present with her daughter at home. Meanwhile, she was getting great feedback at work, but could rarely let the compliments in. Because she was so concerned about not being good enough, she would say yes to projects that she didn't have time for, then scramble to get everything done. This pattern of behaviors had culminated in her "burnout" episode, when a project went awry at her former job.

Veena felt both embarrassed and sad about this. She also felt frustrated. While we were working together, she took on a more senior position at a national consulting firm, and was invited to serve as a mentor and role model for other women in her organization. In theory, the promotion could have quelled her fears. It actually made her more anxious—at first. But Veena was also a woman who knew how to dedicate herself to a practice. When we first spoke about the Lasso (a practice I'll introduce shortly), she got excited and took it on with delight. She loved the idea that she could truly be the master of her own thoughts. And she *deeply wanted* to be more present for her daughter and the women she mentored at work.

Veena practiced every day. In addition to my initial recommendations, she developed a playlist of podcasts on mindfulness, positive psychology, and self-empowerment. She chose to put her powerful mind to work doing something more productive: focusing on the right stuff, building her self-esteem, and hanging out in the here and now. Her career began to skyrocket, and she felt better than ever. What's more, when she received a challenging physical diagnosis a few months later, she was able to make powerful, centered decisions and go through the treatment process with dignity and grace. Through intentional daily practice, Veena had turned her biggest challenge around, developing mastery of her thoughts, feelings, and emotions.

Without further ado, I want to share with you the next practice of *Lassoing your brain*. It isn't easy, but it works. I sometimes liken this practice to riding a wild horse in the rodeo. The goal of the practice is to take back your mind, so that you dedicate it, as often as possible, to the things that really matter.

When given free rein, regrets from the past and fears about the future can quickly take up nearly 100 percent of your thinking. When the anxiety creeps in, it's easy to go on its ride. Like Veena, you may find yourself worrying, regretting, strategizing your revenge, formulating a battle plan, or guilt-tripping in the unstructured moments of your day. That doesn't leave much space for being aware of what's happening—or what's most needed—in the present. It also doesn't leave much time for visioning, creativity, or even centered problem-solving. The act of corralling your thoughts and bringing yourself back to now can take a Herculean effort on some days. Yet, when you consider the number hours, days, and even weeks you may be losing, you understand what's at stake. It's the quality of your life.

I can relate. Today, I come across to the outside world as a healthy, stable woman who has generally got her shit together. And more and more often, it's true. But for years my dirty little secret was my ongoing love affair with self-destructive and self-sabotaging mental spirals that would leave me utterly helpless and depressed. For me, the addiction was the equivalent of knowingly drinking poison that wrecked my body and destroyed my soul. But I just couldn't stop.

Over the years I discovered just ONE excellent tool that effectively supported me to shift: *an inescapable commitment to stop*. End of story. Period.

My breakthrough in this arena doesn't mean that I never wallow. I have yet to master the perfect execution of my commitment. But when I do fall into a mental spiral, I have learned to use that commitment—like a Lasso around my brain—to bring me back more and more quickly to the life I know I'm not ready to give up on. Without this tool, I can honestly say I would not be here to share these lessons with you.

This may all sound a bit dramatic, and I agree that it is. Every woman is different when it comes to her vices. For some of us, our nagging thoughts are simply a nuisance. Without them, we'd be more effective, more of the time. For others—maybe even you or someone you know—they are utterly self-destructive. I am reminded of the surprising and tragic death of fashion icon Kate Spade. When I think about how little we actually know about one another's inner lives, I feel strongly that bringing a certain amount of fierceness to this discussion is worth it. One of the challenges that comes with being a powerful, public female leader is that pressure to be "okay" all the time *increases* as your visibility, success, and impact grow. Between myself and my work with clients, I've seen again and again how this type of pressure can lead us to travel down our spiral in silence, rather than get the support we need.

I've also seen how the spiral itself can become our greatest adversary. As our success (or the potential for success) grows—when we've apparently beaten (or are in the process of beating) the game of the external ladder—what's left to hold us back from our greatness but our own monkey mind? We'll come back to self-sabotage in chapter 6. For now, I want to invite you to do a quick gut check: are the things your mind "spins" on always real? Are they always as big of a problem as they seem in your head? Or is it possible that *sometimes* you blow them out of proportion—that you unconsciously make it harder for yourself because underneath it all, you're scared of your own success?

Whether you can relate to the paragraphs about drama and self-sabotage above, or you simply want to increase the amount of time your mind is working powerfully for your benefit, I offer you this chapter's core practice: *Lassoing your brain* (a.k.a. the Lasso). In short, I challenge you to make a commitment to stop the train. There's too much potential in the present moment to keep letting it go by.

Here's how it works. First, you commit. You do this in advance, *before you need it*, so that your body-mind system already knows what to do when the moment of need arises. (Picture a cowgirl saddling up for the day, pausing, reaching for the nail on the wall where her trusty lasso hangs, and making the conscious decision to throw it in her pack.) Then, when you need it, you use the Lasso to bring you back. This works best if you've done some work in advance to define "back to what." It also works best if you stick with your decision. I describe how to do this in more detail in the practice section of the chapter.

You can build your Lasso muscle by simply bringing your awareness back to your body each time you notice your mind starting to wander. For example, practice while doing your Joy Workouts (or just walking to and from your car). Feeling your own body sensations is a quick and immediate way to get into present time.

You can also practice at work. When you notice yourself going into a downward mental spiral, try putting a limit on it. Allow yourself no more than fifteen minutes of obsessing, then stop. Close the book and get on with your life. Ask yourself, "What's the next action I need to take that has nothing to do with my mind chatter?" Do that. It may take time to make the transition. Stick with your decision. When you reengage the creative, adult parts of your brain, your entire system can (and will) eventually come along.

THE SCIENCE: WANDERING MINDS

Think you're happier when you're multitasking? A recent Harvard research study suggests that a *wandering mind is not a happy mind.* According to this study, the average person spends about 49.6 percent of their time thinking about something other than what they're doing at that time. And, when people's minds are wandering, they're *less* likely to be feeling happy. The research, conducted by Matthew Killingsworth and Daniel Gilbert, used an iPhone app to ask 2,250 volunteers aged eighteen to eighty-eight to report on their happiness at random intervals throughout the day. They were also asked what they were doing, and whether they were thinking about their current activity or something else. The volunteers' minds were wandering during every kind of activity they studied—including making love.

They also found that mind-wandering was a stronger predictor of unhappiness than the type of activity the volunteers were engaged in. People were happier when they were fully present, irrespective of what they were doing. Importantly, the data suggested that mind-wandering was more likely to be the *cause*—rather than the *consequence*—of unhappiness. The researchers note that human beings are one of the only animals who have the ability to think about something other than what they're doing at a given moment. While evolutionarily, this is considered a cognitive achievement, it appears that it comes with a pretty big cost.

M. A. Killingsworth and D. T. Gilbert, "A Wandering Mind is an Unhappy Mind," *Science* 330, no. 606 (2010): 932.

If the practice sounds a bit fierce, I want you to know that it's coming from tough love. This practice has been the only Lasso I've found powerful enough to pull me out of my own addictions to overwhelm, victimhood, anxiety, and fear. Having access to a tool that would help me come back enabled me to take on massive challenges in my leadership and walk on the edge of necessary emotional extremes, without getting lost or drowning along the way. Building a strong relationship with this tool will make it possible to do some of the tougher work on self-sabotage that you will need to do, in order to effectively lead, create, and innovate on the cutting edge.

I also want to assure you that the Lasso practice is not in conflict with "feeling your feelings." I am absolutely *not* a proponent of numbing or "stuffing emotion." Quite the contrary, I believe that our authentic emotions are one of our greatest superpowers. They hold important keys to both personal transformation and intuitive leadership. I've dedicated the entire next chapter to this topic. For now, my goal is to give you a critical tool that builds your resilience so that when we do dive deep, you know how to come back to the surface.

Typically, some women will find chapter 4 tougher, and some will feel that way about chapter 5. These tools are like two sides of a coin that *most* of us have been living only half of. Some teachers will relate this pair of opposites to the principles of masculine and feminine. I hold them as necessary parts of wholeness, and I've succeeded in supporting clients on both sides of the equation, because I understand that—contrary to popular belief—they cannot work alone. When you're *both* able to Lasso *and* to feel deeply, you have access to a range of choices that significantly expand your leadership potential.

As a teacher of mine once said, she who has the least rules (and the most tools!) wins.

The Lasso: Reflection Questions

- On what topic do you most often get sucked into a downward emotional spiral? Where, when, and how?
- What are your considerations about committing to stop?
- What is at stake? If you don't stop, what are the potential costs (for you, for others, and for your life)?
- Are you better at feeling your feelings or at stopping your feelings and moving on? Where (or from whom) do you suppose you learned that strategy?

The Practice

Your mission for chapter 4 is to build a strong relationship with the Lasso practice. I've given you a few examples in the previous sections. I hope these helped to illustrate the goal, the payoff, and the practice itself. Since the Lasso practice can be used in a wide variety of ways, I invite you to choose the examples that resonated most strongly with you. Do you identify as an emotional drama queen who could benefit from pulling herself together in order to get things done? Are you like Veena—highly successful and emotionally calm on the outside, but worried and struggling with incessant thoughts when nobody is looking? Do you distract yourself with unrelated thoughts when it's time to work on an important goal that you're afraid to achieve? Do you experience pain that takes you out of the game, coupled with unhelpful thoughts that either create it in the first place or contribute to making it worse?

Look back at the answers to your reflection questions for help designing the right commitment—and practice—for you. The Lasso works best when you personalize it. I recommend limiting your practice to one key topic or theme. Choose the domain that you believe will help you get the most leverage in your leadership or your life.

PRACTICE 1: IF IT DOESN'T FEEL GOOD

According to one of my favorite mindset teachers, "if it doesn't feel good, it probably isn't true." In this simple, body-based practice, you will leverage the sensations in your body to initiate a pattern interrupt, stopping the downward spiral in its tracks.

First: Begin tracking the embodied feelings and sensations that show up when you're worrying, planning, complaining, or blaming. Take note of the primary thought patterns that go with them (e.g., "I messed up again . . ."). Then, practice running those repetitive thoughts through your mind on purpose while sitting, standing, or walking around the room. Notice your bodily sensations and mood. Anchor these feelings.

Second: Do the opposite. Spend a few minutes thinking positive, empowered, and productive thoughts that locate you in the present tense. Sit, stand, or walk around the room. Notice the difference in your bodily sensations and mood. Anchor these feelings.

Third: Take note of both in your journal. Then, use this information to mindfully track when you're off the rails throughout your day. When you notice "I'm feeling awful!" pause and ask yourself, "What am I thinking that may not be true?" Challenge yourself to find a new thought that seems *even truer* and also makes you feel better in your own skin.

ACTIVE INGREDIENTS	mindful awareness, body scanning, the pause
WHY IT WORKS	When we're lost in thought, we may need to be reminded to come back. When you're aware of your unpleasant body sensations, they can serve as strong and useful signals.

PRACTICE 2: THE LASSO

The Lasso practice begins with making a commitment. It's critical to stick with that commitment, even if you fail to use the Lasso every time you feel that you should. Trust that you don't have to do it perfectly. Contrary to popular belief, you *can* still reap the benefits by practicing "too little" or "too late."

One of my most powerful moments with the Lasso came in the middle of a fight with my ex-fiancé. I was standing in the hallway with my cell phone in my hand, debating whether I should fling it at the wall behind his head (yes, sometimes it gets that bad). I remembered my commitment and caught my breath. Truth be told, I'd missed the "right" time to start Lassoing about forty-five minutes earlier. But I decided to stop, and it worked. I leaned back against the wall and slid slowly to the ground. All I could think was "I just don't want to go down this road anymore." I had no idea what to do next, but I had what I needed—a different starting point.

Let's get started. You can follow these steps to create your custom Lasso practice:

Step 1: Take stock. Identify where, when, and how you most often let yourself spin, run, or wallow mentally (e.g., after our morning meeting, I always beat myself up for the things I wanted to say but didn't). Choose one domain, topic, relationship, or situation in which to practice. Be specific. Name the who, what, where, and when. Then, make an inescapable commitment to limit or stop the thoughts and actions that drive the spiral cold turkey this week. *I commit to stop.*

Step 2: Define your parameters. What reasonable container are you willing to give yourself in order to help you stop? For example, make an agreement with yourself that you can have a maximum of fifteen minutes to derail (e.g., wallow in self-pity, cry, dump words in your journal, call a friend and vent, lose your temper—whatever makes sense, given your current habit). *Note:* For most commitments, it's safe, useful, and healthy to do this. In *some* commitments with high costs, however, it makes sense not to (e.g., if you're using the Lasso to stop yelling at your four-year-old daughter, it's best to allow zero minutes of release in the moment).

Step 3: Define what you will do *instead*. For example, after your fifteen-minute vent, decide that you will *Lasso* your body, mind, and emotions, sit yourself down, and spend one hour working on a meaningful and important project that you care about even more than the spin. This step is key—and we often miss it. In order to change a habit effectively, you must also decide what to replace your old behaviors with. Otherwise, you've left a vacuum, and the old habit will be tempted to creep in. When you move into creative action, or rally your mental resources for something more productive, you engage the more evolved parts of your brain. This releases a different set of neurochemicals, literally weaning you off of the mental addiction.

Bonus

Decide *which* specific project you'll tackle after you use the Lasso. Choose it now. Ideally, choose something *unrelated* to the topic you typically derail over (e.g., learning to paint, dating online, building your website). If you're working on a big initiative right now, choosing that project may help limit any unconscious self-sabotage.

ACTIVE INGREDIENTS	fierceness, commitment to a predetermined action, self-awareness
WHY IT WORKS	When you want to replace an unhealthy behavior, it's most effective when you decide in advance what you plan to replace it with.

PRACTICE 3: CENTERING IN THE BODY

A structured re-centering practice is also worth adding to your bag of tools. This practice, often called centering, sits at the foundation of my lineage in somatic coaching and embodied leadership. When I work with clients, I teach a simple practice that comes from my coaching alma mater, the Strozzi Institute. This practice can be done in seconds or can be extended over five to ten minutes, and it offers deep grounding in the physical body. It's designed to help you come back to the present and take more effective action under stress.

Here's How: Sit or stand with your spine upright. Breathe deeply as you bring your attention to your body. Take a moment to notice any sensations that are present. Connect with your center of gravity, just below your belly button. Center in *length* by extending through the length of your spine. First feel your feet, and let your weight settle down in gravity. Then become more upright at the same time. Center in your *width* by feeling and filling yourself out sideways, from your spine to the sides of your arms, legs, torso, and beyond. Center in your *depth* by feeling and filling yourself out from front to back. Include your back and the space behind you, your organs and the space inside of you, and your front and the space ahead of you. Finally, center in your *purpose*. Return your attention to the center of gravity in your belly. Call to mind something you deeply care about. Let it shape your physical and emotional presence. To complete, take note of your current mood. Now, you're ready for effective action.

ACTIVE INGREDIENTS	bodily observation, mindfulness, breath, slowing down
WHY IT WORKS	Bringing attention to the sensations in your body is the fastest way to get present. Centering in length, width, and depth counteracts our stress-related contractions.

The practices above are a few of my favorites. These are the tools I come back to with my clients again and again. You can find even more Lasso and mindset tools, guided versions of my meditations and practices, on the *Guts and Grace* book website (www.gutsandgrace.com/book-resources/).

Here are a few others I recommend: Karen Reivich's The ABC's in the book *The Resilience Factor*,[13] Regena Thomashauer's Spring Cleaning in the book *Mama Gena's School of Womanly Arts*,[14] Byron Katie's The Work in the book *Loving What Is*,[15] and Carl Simonton's visualization techniques in the book *Getting Well Again*.[16]

REFLECTIONS ON THE LASSO YOUR BRAIN PRACTICES

- What are you learning from engaging with the Lasso practices this week?
- What topic, situation, or relationship did you apply your Lasso practice to? Why did you choose it?
- How did it go? What, if anything, opened for you in trying something new?
- If you haven't done *any* of these practices, what's in the way of you diving in?

Guts and Grace Playlist Recommendations

"Kiss the Sky" – Shawn Lee's Ping Pong Orchestra (feat. Nino Moschella)

"Eye of the Storm" – Bliss n Eso

"Free" – Thievery Corporation

"Sober" – Pink

"Live Like a Warrior" – Matisyahu

"Release Your Problems" – Chet Faker

LEADERSHIP MYTH

It's better not to feel your feelings. It's useful—even essential—to hide them or stuff them down in order to succeed.

LEADERSHIP TRUTH

Emotions are the body's natural guidance system, without which we end up missing huge pieces of information about our needs, circumstances, and surroundings.

Chapter 5

INTO THE WELL

Quiet friend who has come so far,
feel how your breathing makes more space around you.
Let this darkness be a bell tower
and you the bell. As you ring,
what batters you becomes your strength.

—RAINER MARIA RILKE

THE ONLY WAY OUT IS THROUGH

Heads up. This chapter may be one of the juiciest on your journey.

While the Lasso practice is designed to help you get out of mental and emotional drama, and help you take action more effectively in times of stress, chapter 5's core practice, going *Into the Well*, is its counterpoint. Because we are sensing, feeling, and caring human beings, we are bound to get hurt sometimes. People say unconscious (and conscious!) things that cause us pain. They push our buttons, betray our trust, and take actions that enrage us. They make mistakes, they tell untruths, and sometimes they even die. This is true whether you're a starving artist or the CEO of a Fortune 500 company. It's part of being human, and it doesn't go away.

Simply put, *emotions* are our bodies' natural responses to this wide variety of human experiences. They are normal, healthy reactions that, if left alone, will eventually run their course and play themselves out to completion. Yet many of us, for one reason or another, learned at an early age that we should do our best to keep them under wraps. Leading to another widespread leadership myth: ***It's better not to feel your feelings. It's useful—even essential—to hide them or stuff them down in order to succeed.***

It can be a good short-term strategy. For some of us, it may have even saved our lives in our younger years. But in the long run, it leads to a buildup of toxins in the body that warp our judgment and eventually end up making us sick. The truth is: ***emotions are the body's natural guidance system, without which we end up missing huge pieces of information about our needs, circumstances, and surroundings.*** They are also a potent source of raw and renewable energy that can fuel our work and enhance our impact as leaders.

Today there is a *wide variety* of research, fully scientific and otherwise, that demonstrates why feeling your emotions is a natural, healthy, and helpful thing to do. You can find some data in the science sections of this chapter. What I'd like to do first, however, is have a conversation with the less rational parts of yourself—tell some stories, connect with your longings, and begin to build a case for going Into the Well of your own emotions, as a core strategy for conscious, thriving, and sustainable leadership.

In this chapter, we will continue to explore the connection between your mind, body, and emotions. For the sake of unlocking greater personal power, we will take the leap to "thaw out" the old passions and old pains that make up the fabric of who you are. It has been said that only by deeply *feeling* ourselves can we truly *heal*. It's also true that deeply feeling ourselves is the doorway to the kind of radiance, passion, and charisma that compels others to get behind our big visions and follow us to the moon. This week is about setting aside fear and reconnecting with the parts of yourselves that you may be used to silencing.

To support your practice, I will introduce several ways to stop numbing emotion and safely explore the process of emotional release. We will work with movement, sound, or visualization to move through emotions like grief, anger, fear, and pain, and move into greater joy, clarity, compassion, and serenity. This work may not be easy. It may not even be appealing. But I promise you that it can be an incredibly rewarding part of the journey.

As I set this context, I'm fully aware that you *might* be thinking this is a bit strange. You might also be considering closing the book all together and going back to the business of getting things done. Depending on your beliefs, and your personal story, going Into the Well might seem like an odd practice for a leader. But when tough, traumatic, or shocking things happen in life—and believe me, they do—it's incredibly useful to have access to tools that can help you cope in a genuinely healthy way.

Personally, I believe that any conscious female leader should have a basic mastery of these tools, for the sake of her personal emotional hygiene, and for the sake of increasing her capacity to be with others who are experiencing charged or difficult emotional states without over-containing or running away. As my clients develop competence in this arena, they reliably become better supervisors, better mentors, better partners, and better lovers. They are able to move more quickly through painful challenges and take more effective actions in the face of workplace chaos.

Here's the truth: when it comes to navigating big emotions . . . the only real way out is through.

BOTTLED UP EMOTIONS

It's useful—even essential—to hide our feelings or stuff them down in order to succeed.

As a result of this widespread belief, many of us women have become masterful at making our real selves invisible at work. We know how to sit down, shut up, and do our jobs. We do this at work, or we do it at home. If we feel something, we keep it under wraps for fear that it might create an unexpected mess or otherwise get us in trouble. In other words, our modern-day female bodies have been trained to *contain*.

The image that comes to mind is one of a corked bottle. Even when shaken up, the cork rarely pops. Rather, the pressure just builds and builds and builds inside. My body, for example, was trained to hold in energy for a very long time. As a small person who was the recipient of frequent childhood bullying, this was a safe and effective strategy. If I didn't let them know it was hurting, eventually they would stop. And if I didn't lash out, I wasn't at risk of getting into a fight I couldn't physically win.

As I got older, I came to believe that the antidote was getting *very* visible: when I couldn't take it any longer, I'd find myself taking an angry stand or righteously speaking out. I'd blow past my own tender emotions and go to bat verbally for myself and for the proverbial "little guy" at every chance I got. *If I don't take this on, who will?* Sometimes my reactions came across as sharp, cold, and intellectual. But most of the time, I'd wait until my outrage was so strong that I had no ability to channel it in effective or healthy ways. In both cases, my battle cries were typically ineffective.

More recently, I've come to see that healthier, more effective alternatives are within reach. *If I allow myself to relax more and face each emotion in the present tense . . . the energy flows forth in smaller waves, all on its own.* It doesn't get stuck. This approach is both more vulnerable and stronger at the same time. Over time I've developed the capacity to trust what I feel. I use it to forward important conversations. My emotions have become a huge part of the intuitive compass that guides my life, work, and relationships. But the first step was to actually *feel* them.

In chapter four we developed the muscle to Lasso the mind, body, and emotions. We did this because you will need the Lasso tool in order to trust yourself enough to take the cork off the bottle and really take a look inside. In this chapter, we will *go Into the Well*. In other words, this week I will encourage you to practice *not containing*.

You may be wondering, *What will happen? Will I get angry? Burst into tears?* Maybe. Or you may feel the joy that's been bubbling just under the surface for years. Maybe you will sing out loud. It's hard to say, in fact. But you'll only know if you try it.

Truth be told, you may already have a hunch. Often our bodies have a felt sense of what's available under the surface, if we take a pause and listen. Let's do that now. In life, what do you suppose *not containing* would allow you to say, do, or feel? What emotions do you suspect you've been bottling up, if any?

Here are a few ideas of how it might look to put a hold on emotional containment this week. In your Joy Workouts practice, you might try relaxing and letting more of your spirit flow forth. Dance like nobody's watching. Feel the rush of adrenaline as you move with greater speed or abandon. Sing as you vacuum the bedroom and make the bed. Sprint the last ten yards of your morning stroll just because you can and because it feels good to get your life-force energy flowing again.

Or, if you've been containing anger, frustration, or grief, you might stop holding back the tears in your weekly spin class. Let them run with the rest of your physical energy until they are equally spent. When a sad song plays on the radio, let yourself dwell a little in its haunting chords and allow your body to speak. When an angry song comes on the radio, do a "f*#k this" dance.

There are no strict rules for this practice, and frankly there is no way to do it wrong. Some of us tend to contain all the "bad" stuff. For others, it's the "good" stuff that we run away from. Some of us are equal-opportunity containers. Still others (like me) claim to *feel everything*—but in reality, we quickly blow past the more vulnerable emotions that hold the keys to our freedom and linger in the heavy or dramatic ones that serve as an effective and believable smoke screen.

Whichever is true for you, I invite you to consider both the upside and the potential downside of all that containing. In the Practice section of this chapter, I provide more detailed instructions on *how* to do the official going Into the Well practice. For now, take a few moments to take stock of *when* and *why* it matters.

By the way, at this stage, I'm not even suggesting you do this practice with others present (though you may be ripe and ready, and now may be just the right time). At first, your journey Into the Well may simply happen between you and you. Primarily, I'm proposing that you practice in the solitary moments when nobody is holding you to these "be good" expectations but the ghosts from your own past.

Bottled Up Emotions: Reflection Questions

- In what kinds of situations do you find yourself containing or stuffing your feelings (both good and bad)? What's the benefit? What's the cost?
- Which emotions are you most likely to bottle up? When and why? Or, if you are the type of person who shows *certain* emotions easily, what do you suspect might be under *those* emotions?
- What could be the greater benefit of letting yourself feel them more?
- What are your fears or considerations about doing so?

TO FEEL ALIVE

Sometimes my clients want more evidence on why it's worth it to feel emotions in their daily life. "Why do you do it, if it's *so* uncomfortable?" they wonder.

Personally, I do it because *I want to feel fully alive.*

But what does that mean, to feel alive? It's such a simple thing, yet we often take it for granted. To look into a lover's eyes and feel a rush of warmth. To sense your atoms buzzing after a long soak in a hot tub. To feel the adrenaline pumping though your limbs as you near the finish line. To feel the bass pulsing through your body as you dance to your favorite song. Without naming it, we know these peak experiences are connected to a sense of aliveness. Their hallmark is the glow. It just feels a little bit more remarkable than the sensation of ordinary life.

When we taste these moments, we want more. Yet they can seem elusive. *How did I get there? Wow! What was that?* Most of us can name them, but few of us feel that we have complete control over their presence. And even fewer of us have mastered the art of accessing them *at will.*

In her book, *Positivity,*[17] leading emotion researcher Barbara Fredrickson describes the benefits positive emotions can have on the body and mind. They help us broaden our perspectives and build resilience to face the challenges that inevitably come toward us in life. According to Fredrickson's

THE SCIENCE: BODY, MIND, AND EMOTIONS

Anna Halprin, founder of the Tamalpa Institute, is a pioneer in the dance therapy movement—and a cancer survivor of over forty-five years. At the time of writing this volume, Anna was ninety-eight years old and is still teaching from her studio in Northern California. In Anna's book *Returning To Health*, she describes her own healing process. She also shares the tools from dance, somatics, art, and ritual that she uses in her work. While the volume, published in 2002, does not include scientific journal references, Anna cites the work of her contemporaries, who were also engaging in pioneering body-centric healing work. These visionaries, including Ron Kurtz (founder of the Hakomi Method), Reinhard Flatischler (creator of Ta Ke Ti Na), Ida Rolf (founder of the Rolfing bodywork method), and Hawayo Takata (introducer of Reiki to the Western World), developed their work from the inside out. Their "data" included both personal experience and impressive client results.

At a time when science was only scratching the surface of the body–mind connection, Halprin "cured" her cancer by pairing traditional non-Western approaches and physical movement with standard medical support. She then spent decades developing and teaching these profound tools to cancer survivors and others seeking a comprehensive emotional and psychological approach to healing. Halprin's early work is corroborated by Dr. Kelly A. Turner in her book *Radical Remission: Surviving Cancer Against All Odds*. Turner researches *scientific anomalies*—cases of healing that defy the odds of the original medical diagnosis. By studying these outliers, she offers recommendations that *complement* medical treatments or may be used in cases when no known treatment exists. Turner recommends both *releasing suppressed emotion* and *increasing positive emotion* as part of the healing path, citing case studies of miraculous recoveries involving emotional release.

Today, fields like embodied cognition and neuroscience provide further scientific evidence for a relationship between the mind, emotions, and physical health. Researchers who study disease are more frequently including emotions as part of their agenda. These evolutions in science have the potential to add credence and nuance to the work that Halprin and her contemporaries began using: intuition, practical action, and observable results.

Anna Halprin, *Returning to Health with Dance, Movement and Intimacy* (LifeRhythm, 2002).

Kelly A. Turner, *Radical Remission: Surviving Cancer Against All Odds* (New York: HarperCollins, 2014).

R. A. Ferrer, P. G. McDonnald, and L. F. Barrett, "Affective Science Perspectives on Cancer Control: Strategically Crafting a Mutually Beneficial Research Agenda," *Perspectives on Psychological Science* 10, no. 3 (2015): 328–45.

research, positive emotions can be practiced. And when they *are*, they can begin to move us into an upward spiral, where they become easier and easier to access.

Yet, for some of us, *positive* emotions and sensations are the very things we've written off as "not for me anymore." Other people get to feel that. Me? I've got work to do, bills to pay, a family to feed. If Joy alone could pay the bills or run the business, I'd spend more time with it.

A number of years ago, I traveled to Haiti to visit my sister who was living and working there. What touched me most was that, even in the face of the extreme poverty and devastation that followed the 2010 earthquake, there is *so much* aliveness there! Nothing is suppressed. Anger smolders just below the surface of conversations about the political climate and the lack of real support the nation's people feel from the global community. Yet along with it comes joy in bucketfuls when groups of two or more people get together to make music. Rhythms, beats, melodies, voice. These things serve as a universal medicine that is available in abundance and shared freely among friends.

It reminds me that aliveness is *available to everybody.* It can be accessed in the here and now. Despite chaos. Despite busyness. Despite real oppression. It's the opposite of feeling numb, and it's a choice that is available to all people, all the time. How and when we make that choice can dictate the quality of our lives.

Which brings me to our universal human dilemma: *I want to feel all that good stuff, but I don't want to feel the bad!* I don't want to be angry. I am afraid to allow the pain. If I let myself cry, I'm afraid I'll cry forever and never stop.

I know. The thing is . . . it just isn't true.

What *is* true, according to Dr. Brené Brown's research on ordinary courage, is that "you can't selectively numb."[18] You don't get to keep joy while avoiding anger or sorrow. When you stuff your pain (with a "beer and a banana nut muffin"), you also stuff all of the pleasures that life has to offer. When the body contains, it doesn't discern. It just clamps down and holds on for dear life. In order to feel your *full aliveness*, you have to be willing to take the bad with the good. And that's what building a truly conscious, sustainable, and thriving leadership approach is all about.

If you are familiar with Brené Brown's work, you probably know that she delivered one of the most widely viewed TEDx talks of all times. Her talk was entitled "The Power of Vulnerability." It has been translated into fifty-three languages, and to date has been viewed over thirty-six million times. I believe the viral spread of this talk reflects the ubiquity of the how-to-feel-the-good-stuff-without-the-bad dilemma we grapple with as human beings in the twenty-first century. I also believe it reflects the potency of our collective longing for something more.

Are you willing to entertain the possibility that you could be feeling more alive? If so, I encourage you to spend a few minutes with the questions below. As best you can, let your body do the talking.

To Feel Alive: Reflection Questions

- What types of *aliveness* have been missing recently in your life? What do you most long for? (Hint: Think about your life at work, at home, with your family, in your community, with your partner/lover/spouse, with your children, your health, your hobbies, your creativity, your sense of vision or innovation, your sense of contribution or impact.)
- What do you imagine you'd have to face in order to have what you long for?
- What's scary about that?
- Why might it be worth it?

GOING INTO THE WELL

In the earlier sections of this chapter, I built the case for the value of *emotional release*. Yet even before delving into chapter 5, you may have already noticed your emotions starting to stir. Perhaps, over the last few weeks since you picked up this book, you've been surprised to find that under-the-surface emotions began to show. And perhaps, you've been thinking, *Where the heck did all this come from?*

The truth is, it's probably not just a coincidence. Especially if you have old wounds that have yet to fully heal, you may experience a wave of emotions as a result of setting your intention to become a more conscious, sustainable, and fully thriving leader. This kind of declaration is a powerful force (you'll learn more about *that* in chapter 7). If things have been bubbling up, it's a sign that you're on the right track. When we embark on a path of personal transformation, emotions serve as markers of the territory that will—and must—be covered in order to get to the other side. That's one of the reasons that *feeling* your emotions is such an important tool for conscious leadership. When you're numb, you literally don't see important trail markers that keep you from straying off course.

Check in with yourself for a moment. What emotions have you been feeling since you started reading this book? And what did you do with those emotions when they came up? In case you haven't already done so, this chapter provides an opportunity to consciously face them, honor them, and move through them. This week you can begin to either integrate them or let them go.

In a wonderful essay on self-compassion,[19] the poet David Whyte uses the metaphor of "going Into the Well" to describe the process of deeply facing yourself. It comes from classic literature. Just as the hero in the epic poem *Beowulf* dove deep into the lake to conquer the monster of the forest, there is an opportunity for you to dive deep into your own emotional stream and face the demons (and dolphins!) within.

Feeling some resistance here? I get it. When you're used to people relying on you—even looking up to you—for information about how they should feel about what's going on in your organization or industry, it can seem as though there's no space for a bad day, let alone a deep well of emotional turmoil. Take my client Kate, for example. Kate had just finished an assignment as the executive director of a high-profile nonprofit organization that supported women leaders. She was known for her drive, her compassion, and her positive, uplifting attitude.

One day, while in the process of scouting for her next big thing, Kate showed up to a coaching session without a smile on her face. When I asked how she was doing, she said, "To be honest, I'm just in a *bad* mood." I immediately appreciated her honesty. I'd seen Kate cover up frustrations with a nice-girl smile more than once in the past. And I had a hunch that the more vulnerable (and more powerful) truth-telling part of herself would be needed in her next level of work.

She told me about several frustrating things that happened in the past week. Yet many of them were connected to frustrations she'd been carrying for months. I could feel the fire just underneath the surface. "How do you feel about boxing?" I asked. Her eyes lit up. "I love it! I'm actually certifying to teach a fusion kickboxing class." Totally new information to me. But it made a lot of sense.

I challenged Kate to spend a week connecting more intentionally with her anger. She agreed to let it run in safe places: at the gym with a punching bag and in her kickboxing classes. On the other side of that week, Kate came back with clarity and fierceness. She was built to be a woman who tells uncomfortable truths to powerful people, and she was committed to show up fully as that woman. No longer would she begrudgingly carry her anger like a heavy and hidden burden. Instead, she had learned how to transform it into rocket fuel that would support the powerful teaching and advocacy work she was soon to begin.

Like Kate, I invite you to explore the ways in which emotions could actually be a *useful* asset that support your path and your purpose. Your official tool for this chapter, the going Into the Well practice, is about *feeling* what there is to feel right now. That's it. In the Practice section below, I guide you through a process that will help you contact and embrace your emotions. The ultimate goal is to access more aliveness and to unlock energy that can fuel your leadership vision.

The good news is, contacting your emotions doesn't mean you have to "analyze them," "process them," or "figure them out." It simply means being present with them when they come and allowing space for them to have their say. Like children, they desire to be seen and heard (and will continue to squeak and squawk until given some loving attention).

If you're currently masterful at keeping them under wraps, and this idea makes you nervous, I completely understand. From my own experience, I've found that emotions don't last nearly as long as I fear that they will. It's as though the *fear of the thing* is worse than *the thing itself.* And, keep in mind, you have already learned one tool (the Lasso) that can help you "come back" if the process gets too intense. You get to go at your own pace. Period.

On the other hand, you may already have a strong support system that *helps you* navigate your emotions regularly. In that case, you might be wondering if it makes sense to learn additional tools for self-guided exploration. The truth is, human beings have engaged in self-guided emotional clearing practices for thousands of years. Yet in modern Western society, many of these practices have fallen out of favor or been relegated to the fringe.

Today, instead of learning how to navigate our own emotions, many of us give our agency away to therapists, bodyworkers, and other healing practitioners. Of course, it's a great move to get support with emotions that ail you! But also, it's crucial to remember that emotions are part of the natural, healthy system of healing to which your body—and *every* body—has access. As you practice going Into the Well, you may discover that in many cases, your body knows how to release stuck energy and to heal old pains on its own.

Again, I invite you to recall last week's practice: Lassoing your brain. Using this tool, we practiced putting a strong container around the self-destructive side of our emotions. We took a stand in the face of fear: I WILL NOT allow myself to wallow and drown in my sadness. I WILL NOT allow myself to sit still and be the helpless victim for too long.

This is an incredibly powerful tool that can help you pull yourself up by the bootstraps in the face of a heavy or scary emotional moment. It demonstrates you can and will stand up when needed and take the next step.

But this tool alone is only half the picture. It's a self-containment practice that gives you the confidence to work with the other side of the coin: allowing emotions to run through to completion. If you haven't completed Chapter 4: Lasso Your Brain, be sure to revisit it before or after going Into the Well.

Going Into the Well: Reflection Questions

- What are the ways you currently release your emotions, consciously or unconsciously (e.g., tears, exercise, blowing up, drinking, partying, dancing, none/I don't . . .)?
- What, if anything, works well about your current practice? What, if anything, isn't working?
- How do you feel about the prospect of feeling your emotions more fully? Why?
- What ideas do you already have about how to practice going Into the Well?

The Practice

Chapter 5 has just one practice: *going Into the Well*. By now you probably have a pretty clear sense of what this means and why it matters. It may sound like fun. Or it may sound a bit confronting (or utterly terrifying!), depending on who you are. I promise it's *super* useful for moving emotions. And it's never as bad as it sounds on paper.

As with many of the tools in this book, the power comes in doing it. No amount of words describing this practice can give you the gift of its bounty. It's a gift you must give yourself. Whoever you are, there are benefits to be gained. I have taught it to super-conservative female engineers and scientists who support the US Navy. I have also taught it to spiritual groups, for whom this type of activity serves as daily healing and community-building practice. In both cases, participants reported a deeper level of self-awareness and a sense of grounded relief at the end.

Personally, I've used this practice to self-heal old fear, pain, and anger that I'd been carrying for decades. Having emptied those things out, I feel freer, more joyful, and more present in my life. It doesn't mean I never feel sad or hurt these days. But the emotions that *do* come up now are more authentic and attached to the present moment (rather than tied to years of unresolved emotional baggage). And they are easier to move through with grace.

Take a deep breath and let's get started.

PRACTICE 1: GOING INTO THE WELL (SELF-GUIDED EMOTIONAL RELEASE)

Going Into the Well is a self-guided emotional release practice. These types of practices have existed in most cultures around the world for thousands of years. While it may seem strange at first, you can trust that the deeper wisdom of your human ancestors, stored inside your body and DNA, will help you to navigate.

Below, I walk you through two versions of the practice. It is a somatic (body-based) practice that you can do on your own or with another person. One version (version A) is designed to be done in the moment, as needed. It works well with smaller stuff. The other version (version B) is designed to be done when you set aside time on your own. It works well with the bigger stuff. There is also a guided download of version B on the *Guts and Grace* book webpage.

Step 1 (Both Version A and B): Set Your Intention. Begin by setting a clear intention. Your intention can help to guide you in the moments when you don't know exactly what to do. If you believe it would be useful for you to allow yourself to feel more emotion, set an intention to do so. Include something in your intention about feeling both the good and the bad. Then, when it starts to happen, allow it. When it comes to feeling aliveness, you may not know how to get there, but you will know it when you find it, I guarantee.

You might also create a container of intention by letting the people close to you know what you are up to. You can even ask for their moral support. You might say something like, "I think I've been carrying around a lot of sadness (anger, untapped Joy) for a while now, and I want to let it out. So you might see me showing it more than usual for a while. If so, just know it isn't about you. It's something I'm doing for my own healing." If there is something specific you'd like them to do (or not do) when you're feeling that emotion, let them know.

Here are three intention-setting questions to get you started:

- What is your intention for emotional release? What emotions would you like to allow and to heal?
- Who in your life would it be beneficial to enlist for support? What will you tell them about your intention?
- When and where would you like to practice "going Into the Well" this week?

Step 2 (Version A): Let It Come. Sometimes emotional release will happen by accident when it gets triggered in your daily life. It may feel like you fell Into the Well. In these moments, all you have to do is *allow it*. Like a mother with a child, tell yourself "let it come" and practice self-compassion. Give yourself the time it takes to pause and be with it rather than shove it down and rush off to the next thing. Simple, though for many of us, not easy. As a head's up, many women feel shame, or want to apologize, the first few times they do this practice. It's totally okay. And it helps not to apologize. Just let yourself be you. It's real. And it's healthy.

Step 2 (Version B): Call It Forth. Other times, you will sense that a release is needed, but it won't happen on its own. In this case, you can make a conscious choice to go Into the Well using music, movement, or visualization. This is a very adult move—one that a conscious leader can decide to make whenever she knows she needs it. Perhaps you feel the emotion "lurking around" below the surface (e.g., I think I need a good cry). Perhaps it's been trying to get your attention in moments when there's not really space for it (e.g., in the boardroom, with your kids, with your mother-in-law, on a critical project at work). The goal of this practice is to set aside some intentional time one day (or even *each day* this week) to call it forth.

Here's How

Below I suggest a number of songs, organized by emotion, that I use for what I call "freedance healing." Feel free to use the ones I suggest or come up with your own.

- "Minor Blue" – David Darling
- "The Blower's Daughter" – Damien Rice
- "Vole" – Celine Dion
- "This Woman's Work" – Kate Bush
- "I Shall Be Free" – Kid Beyond
- "Bone Dance" – Deya Dova
- "Keep It in the Family" – Hybrid
- "Palladio" – Escala
- "Drive It Like You Stole It" – Ample Mammal

Choose three songs with a similar emotional tone and play them back-to-back (ideally, do this in a private place where you feel safe and aren't worried about receiving judgment from others). Let your body move freely. Make any movement or sound that wants to come through.

As you move, direct your awareness toward the myriad of things going on in your body at any given moment. Sense your heart beating, your muscles straining, your lungs doing their job. Turn the music up and try just letting your body go! Don't censor anything. Just see what shows up. This is a great way to allow your aliveness to flow.

You may end up moving fast and shaking everything out. Or you might move slow, squeeze, contract, and increase the feeling of being stuck. You might yell. You may stop and just cry. You might get really small and still. Every move is okay.

Try exaggerating it. Let it get bigger and stronger. Allow yourself to empty it all out. Typically, at some point your body will feel done, and a new feeling or sensation will come to the surface. To help you know when to bring yourself back, I recommend setting a timer or using the end of the music to signal that it's time to come back up to the surface.

Alternative Practice (No Movement)

If this kind of movement feels too scary as you begin, another option is to listen to the same music and freely speak out loud the imagery and emotions that come to mind as you listen. This practice is best done with a partner, who can record what you have spoken and read it back to you at the end. However, it's also possible to do it by yourself. I highly recommend using the body-based practice if possible. It will prevent you from getting "intellectual" and missing your feelings altogether. That said, if the stretch feels too big, and you're inclined to avoid it all together, this alternative practice can be a safe place to start.

Step 3: After the Release. As your practice unfolds, notice when your body's cycle of emotion is complete. This may happen in natural time, or it may happen when the time you've chosen for your practice runs out. At that moment, pause and allow yourself to be struck by the empty silence that envelopes both you and your surroundings. From that place of silence, notice if you are able to perceive any tiny bits of information—bird sounds, the temperature of the air on your skin, the sensation of relaxation, an intuition about a next step.

Can you become a receptacle for new impulses and insights that bring you closer to a sense of peace? At the end of your practice, allow yourself to drop into a stillness that invites sounds, sights, and body sensations to fully communicate with you. What else comes in when you create the space for it?

That's it. You're done. Whew!

As a general suggestion, I recommend having your journal on hand and planning a little extra time after the practice to take notes on what you are learning. If realizations came up during or after the practice, capture them. If ideas about next steps come to mind, feel free to take action on them. If other emotions come up, invite them in and hold them gently as well.

I also want to warn you about something my fellow somatics practitioners and I affectionately call "backwash." Sometimes after engaging in a big practice like this, we feel shame or guilt afterwards—"I shouldn't have let myself feel or think or say that." I encourage you to be compassionate with yourself. Emotions are normal. We human beings feel and think all kinds of things, good and bad. It doesn't mean they are true or that we will act on them. It's by letting them move that they can eventually transform into more productive impulses that will fuel your life and leadership.

That said, if you ever have a hunch that you've uncovered an emotional well that is bigger than you can handle alone, ***it's totally okay (and useful) to ask for help from a friend, therapist, doctor, or healing practitioner.*** Trust your gut here. If you're not sure, start by talking about it with the person you feel closest to and trust the most.

ACTIVE INGREDIENTS	blending with your emotions, body listening, mindfulness, surrender
WHY IT WORKS	When you allow your emotions to run their course, your body will process them naturally and eventually show you what's on the other side.

REFLECTIONS ON THE INTO THE WELL PRACTICE

- What was your intention for emotional release? What emotions did you choose to allow yourself to feel?
- Who in your life did you (or did you want to) enlist for support? What did you tell them about your intention? If you didn't tell them, why not?
- If you didn't do the practice, why not? What's holding you back from diving in?

Guts and Grace Playlist Recommendations

"Let It Go" – Michael Franti (feat. Ethan Tucker)
"Glitter in the Air" – Pink
"Let It In" – Ayla Nereo
"Within" – Daft Punk
"Laugh So You Don't Cry" – Andy Davis
"The Sea Is Rising" – Bliss n Eso

LEADERSHIP MYTH

Something other than me is getting in the way, and that's why I haven't succeeded yet.

LEADERSHIP TRUTH

Some part of you is literally designed to work against yourself. And when that part is running the show, there will always be a ceiling on your success.

Chapter 6

THE CORE DILEMMA

I walk down the street.
There is a deep hole in the sidewalk.
I fall in.
I am lost . . . I am helpless.
It isn't my fault.
It takes me forever to find a way out.

—PORTIA NELSON

YOUR UNIQUE ROAD TO SUCCESS

Well done. For many successful female leaders, Into the Well is one of the most difficult and confronting practices in the book. If you're still reading, and still doing the work, I want to appreciate your commitment. As I mentioned, chapters 4 and 5 offered complementary practices. Like two sides of a coin, the Lasso and going Into the Well are designed to work together. As a pair, these two practices have the power to round out your leadership approach and rebalance your default habits related to mindset, emotions, and behaviors.

They *also* have the power to uncover important, hidden territory that *may* hold the key to your next level of leadership and impact. Hold onto your seat, because we're about to dive into that territory now. Like descending into a valley, we'll drop one layer down into your subconscious, where your central programming is housed, and clear out the old habits that are no longer serving your leadership. Then, after the clearing is done, you'll come up the other side to the top of the next mountain, where it's possible to see the new horizon.

Here's why this deep dive is crucial to your success: most of us women who are ready to advance, or make a bigger impact, naturally think we're doing everything we can to get there. And, if that's the case, then there must be some *external reason*—a "glass ceiling," so to speak—that is responsible for holding us back. This brings us to another leadership myth: ***Something other than me is getting in the way, and that's why I haven't succeeded yet.***

While there are most certainly real constraints facing women in the workplace, these constraints result in a lasting ceiling effect primarily *when they interact with* your own behavior and mindset. The truth is, ***some part of you is literally designed to work against yourself. And when that part is running the show, there will always be a ceiling on your success.*** In chapter 6, we delve into this powerful, challenging, and ultimately freeing topic: *your unique, habitual pattern of self-sabotage.*

If, by chance, you picked up this book based on a hunch that you may be unconsciously derailing yourself, or you've developed such a hunch while reading the last few chapters, you're probably on the right track. In fact, I have yet to meet a woman (or man!) who doesn't have her fair share of unhelpful habits and "dirty little secrets" that limit her ultimate success. You may even be thinking, "I have SO many! The list is long."

Luckily, it's not that complicated. What I've found is that the ones that have the greatest negative impact *tend to cluster* in a *constellation* of behaviors. These behaviors can typically be boiled down to a single Core Dilemma—the one thing that is *most* in the way of you consciously, sustainably, and joyfully approaching your work, life, and leadership day to day.

Chapter 6 is about identifying that internal roadblock—we might call your *internal glass ceiling*—and facing it head on. The good news is, there's a decent chance you've already bumped into it while working through the first half of the book. Consider the territory we've already covered: surrender, grit, cultivating joy, physical movement, making time, saying yes and no, owning your desire, containing your emotions, taming your monkey mind, feeling your emotions, releasing old pain. Chapters 1 through 5 were full of opportunities to face yourself.

When a person commits to engage in these empowering practices, it's common that an old psychological or emotional wound will simultaneously present itself to be healed. This is good. In this chapter I'll show you how to take an honest and compassionate look at the parts of yourself you've consistently judged, stuffed, hidden, tolerated, avoided, or ignored—the parts that have plagued you, despite your best efforts to succeed. Through mindful self-awareness, you will discover pathways to greater wholeness and greater impact.

The disempowering myth that this chapter will help you bust?

"It isn't my fault."

GETTING HONEST

We all want to thrive. And it's true that we're brave, strong, smart, successful women, who know how to get s*#t done. So, what's *really* holding us back from having it all?

What I've found, over a decade of client work, is that most women who are ready to level-up *tend to focus on the wrong things*. For example, we treat the symptom instead of the root cause. "I just need to learn a better time-management system, right?" We give ourselves an unsolvable label. "I'm not confident enough." Or we focus on what we wish other people would do. "If only they would acknowledge me for all that I've done." We cover up the real problem with a Band-Aid, and often silently (or not so silently) blame others when things don't get better. It's human nature.

We don't do it because we're bad people or because we don't care about taking responsibility. It's not even because we don't *want* to face our biggest challenges. Rather, we're like the fish who can't see the water . . . we can't detect the real problem because it's as woven into the fabric of our lives as the air we breathe. We go on believing that there's nothing we can do about it, when the truth is something quite different all together.

A number of years ago, when I was going through a particularly difficult time in my life, I dared to ask myself the sobering question, *What is the one thing I need to shift in order to fully heal my body, mind, and spirit?* Though I'm known among my friends and colleagues for being "complicated" (a.k.a. sometimes indecisive, complex, or confused), the answer came through loud and clear: It was *still* my ongoing struggle with emotional addiction in intimate relationships.

How did I know? Our bodies talk to us when we're willing to listen.

When I was twenty-eight years old, I discovered a lump in my breast. By this time in my life, both my best friend from college and the founder of the company I was working for had lost their lives to cancer. I'd learned enough from their journeys to take it as a serious wake-up call. I was young and healthy, so my doctor (who had a strong preference for alternative treatments) recommended monitoring the area with ultrasound for a few months before pursuing a biopsy. But I knew in my gut that I was eating myself alive emotionally, and the potential for a physical manifestation of those intensely negative feelings seemed incredibly high.

At that time, I was choosing to stay in an intimate relationship that was toxic to my system in many ways. About two years prior, I had attempted suicide, given up my job, moved countries, and turned myself inside out in the face of an impending breakup with a man who I was sure was my soul mate and the love of my life. My efforts directly resulted in us reconnecting as a couple and moving together to California. Sort of.

My partner, though professing to love me deeply, was still consistently choosing both his work and other women over me. Even though I'd done everything I could imagine to fix things between us, I was still losing the game. The pain of feeling unwanted, combined with my family legacy of painful infidelity, led me into a cycle of self-destructive emotions. The spin gathered steam, like a cyclone that tore away at my soul. It also pushed my partner further away, creating a self-fulfilling prophecy loop between us. Intuitively, I had a hunch that the emotional turmoil was also impacting my physical body. I feared it had something to do with the impending diagnosis.

In a moment of clarity, I committed to either heal or end our toxic relationship. What happened next wasn't pretty. But in one way or another, it probably saved my life. The declaration led me on a journey that unraveled layers of fear, addiction, manipulation, betrayal, and avoidance of which I was both the victim and the perpetrator. And while I was *certain* that someone else was to blame, in the end it turned out to be a conversation between me, myself, and I. The journey asked me to take an honest look in the mirror. But it also offered a way out of the maze I'd been living inside for years.

I had discovered my Core Dilemma. And by admitting that the hell I was living in was to a great extent my own, I'd set myself free. I could choose to make some new moves. And I did.

To this day, I don't know if I had—or have—cancer. Statistics would say probably not. Statistics would also say that someday I probably will. In the meantime, I do what it takes to stay on a conscious path, one day at a time. My commitment is to practice personal reflection and radical self-care as if my life depended on it, even when I'm feeling "healthy" and continue asking the difficult questions about my own thoughts, feelings, and behavior in the realm of emotions and intimate relationships.

If you can relate to anything at all about this story, I encourage you to pause and take a deep breath. Let yourself feel the gravity of what you are thinking or feeling in this moment. You may even want to take a few notes about what's coming up in your journal, before you read on.

If on the other hand this all feels dramatic, intense, or far-fetched . . . don't worry. That's perfectly normal too. Not everyone's Core Dilemma is necessarily as dark as mine. To illustrate, here are a few examples of the Core Dilemma identified by some of my clients:

- Becoming paralyzed when faced with any mission-critical decision
- Hiding constant anxiety that runs under the surface
- Saying "whatever"—checking out early when it looks like I may not succeed
- Always being "nice" to keep the peace, instead of being honest
- Choosing relationships (both work and personal) that are not good for me
- Righteousness—constantly going to battle to protect the "little guy"
- Martyrdom—harboring long-term resentment against those who took my contributions for granted

The bottom line is that each of us has a unique, habitual form of self-sabotage, orchestrated by the structures of our ego. It shows up on the surface as a less-than-helpful behavior. And sometimes, its roots go deep. You might think of it as your Achilles heel: "If only it wasn't for X, then I could be *really* successful." But the truth is, it's actually running the show. It's both creating the problem *and* preventing you from solving it, while presenting itself as the right or (only possible) thing to do. In other words, it often creates a self-fulfilling prophecy.

In order to get out of this pattern and reach your next level of leadership, you will need to identify and stop the cycle in its tracks. And in order to do *that*, you may have some deeper healing to do.

That said, I happen to believe that this type of healing, while sometimes difficult, can also be joyful. Like growth and transformation, it is a way of life, not a destination. And you are *already* on the path. I have seen that acknowledging our part in our own stuckness can lead to great relief. There is power in proving ourselves wrong about our deepest, darkest fears. Uncovering the Core Dilemma is about looking in the mirror—without judgment and without letting yourself off the hook—and then taking a stand for the person you know you were born to be.

You may or may not agree with me on all of this, and that's okay. Though, if you haven't stopped reading yet, chances are there's at least something about my approach that intrigues you. If you feel skeptical or resistant about this chapter, that might even be a great place to look for your Core Dilemma. For example, early on in my career I had a client who was seriously doubting the process. While it's true (of course!) this process might not be right for everyone, there was something in her particular *way* of doubting that struck me.

Like a number of my clients at the time, she was facing a life-threatening illness. After several weeks of working together, she called me up and said, "Well, if it's going to be like this, it just isn't going to work for me. I mean, the other people you support don't have anything in common with me. And here's the thing: all this stuff about healing—the only thing I care about is how I'm afraid that I'm going to die. I don't think your activities can help me at all."

She told me that what she probably needed most was nutritional supplements. That made sense, so I figured I'd encourage her to follow her intuition. But when I asked her if she'd consulted anyone about it, she said had been given referrals to nutritionists a while back, but she hadn't gone to see them yet. As a way of supporting, I offered her a referral to a renowned cancer treatment specialist who works with very difficult cases, using a battery of blood work and personalized herbal supplements to complement the patient's ongoing medical treatment. I mentioned that he had saved many lives. To my surprise, she said, "Oh, but that's going to take a lot of time. It sounds really intense. I'm already doing so much right now. *I don't think that would work for me.*"

I share this story primarily to illustrate the way our minds can get the better of us in the face of a possible way out of the maze. In my former client's case, the Core Dilemma for her may have been her willingness to trust in others' help and support instead of needing to have all the answers herself. While we didn't get the chance to complete the conversation, I can imagine it may have been scary for her to embrace the possibility that someone else might have something useful to offer.

I hope these examples have got you thinking. Unfortunately, because everyone's ego structures are different, there's no cookie-cutter process to identify your Core Dilemma. Instead, I invite you to lean on your intuition where possible.

As you go about your daily tasks this week, I encourage you to observe yourself. What do you notice? What strikes you? If you had to put your finger on it, what would you say is the one thing you are being called to shift right now in order to become a fully conscious, sustainable, and thriving leader?

Don't think about it too hard. Let your body show you. Try jogging the questions. Dancing the questions. Swimming the questions. Bring them into your weekly routine and trust the wisdom of your body to provide some answers.

Getting Honest: Reflection Questions

- What would you say is *the one thing* you are being called to shift right now in order to embody a fully conscious, sustainable, and thriving leadership approach?
- If you were to name a single behavior that you're willing to admit has been your Achilles heel—either at home or at work—what would you say? (*Note:* This question will often uncover a symptom or piece of your Core Dilemma.)

KNOW THYSELF (A.K.A. GATHERING DATA)

Take a moment and think about what you read in the last segment. Does the idea of a personal self-sabotage system sound plausible? Far-fetched? Exciting? Intimidating? Is there anything that either particularly strikes you or feels important to you at this moment?

Again, my aim in teeing up this topic is not to overdramatize something that might be a pretty small deal in your life. But it is *also* not to minimize something that, for some women, may be a pretty big deal indeed. In my early career, I was blessed to work at a boutique coaching and consulting firm in the San Francisco Bay Area as a young executive coach. Our firm was known for cracking tough cases and transforming the leadership of both individuals and teams. Drawing on a combination of common professional development tools and seriously *uncommon* personal development tools, we took our clients through a capstone nine-day-long workshop called "Personal Mastery." What struck me the most about these deep-dive trainings was the fact that *everyone*—from nonprofit directors to executives at Fortune 500 companies—had a formative personal story. Everyone had faced life challenges (some of which I could only dream of making it through!)—and those challenges had an impact on their default style of leadership, both for better and for worse.

If you're tracking with me, and you're wondering how *your story* might relate to your Core Dilemma, then let's continue our reflection together. Again, I am proposing that each of us has a unique, habitual pattern of self-sabotage. You might think of it as an *internal* glass ceiling. It's the behavioral pattern that's *most* in the way of your real-time success, when you take away any factual constraints that exist. Sometimes it's completely hidden to you (though other people see it, you can be sure!). In other cases, it's literally the excuse you most often make for yourself. When you're on the verge of a big success, or tackling a next-level project, it shows up to bring you down.

That said, it also isn't a "bad" thing. The truth is, somewhere early in your life, your Core Dilemma got formed in order to keep you safe. Here's what I mean: More likely than not, the Core Dilemma was part of an early survival strategy—something you did as a very young person to get more love, feel a greater sense of belonging, or preserve your safety or dignity around others. At that time, you did it because *it worked.*

It may have been that you grew up in a pretty chaotic environment and the strategy literally helped you to survive. Or, if you grew up in a pretty normal or safe environment, it may have been the best strategy to gain approval and praise or to get noticed or to fit in. It may have helped you to compete with a sibling or to *avoid having to* compete. It may have aligned with your parents' values, or it may have been your way of safely challenging them. Regardless, it was useful at the time, and it helped you become who you are today.

However, this same strategy—when played out in a fully adult context where you actually have the power to choose, to create, and to lead—can become a repetitive loop that keeps you stuck in the past. If you've ever heard the expression "what got you here won't get you there" (or read the book with the same title[20] by Marshall Goldsmith), this is *exactly* what I'm talking about. In order to fully empower yourself—to truly lead in a conscious, sustainable, and generative way that is *relevant* to the present moment—you will need to get very familiar with this strategy and understand how it can sabotage your goals. You will need to shift your relationship with the Core Dilemma, so that it goes from being your *default strategy* to just *one option* in a diverse bag of tools. You will need to loosen its hold on you, so that you can use it *only when it's genuinely needed.*

In my own journey, getting to know my Core Dilemma went something like this. First, I uncovered the behavior I described a few moments ago: I would find myself in emotional turmoil about something bad that happened in an intimate relationship. I wouldn't have admitted this ten years ago, but I was quite good at *creating* that turmoil by finding fault, failing to trust, or just plain old picking a fight about something that didn't matter much.

This *worked* as a sabotage strategy for two reasons that had roots in my past. One, my father had cheated on my mother, so I had a good reason be vigilant for the impending dissolution of my intimate relationship. And two, tears were the most effective way I'd found to get attention from my family as a young person. I unconsciously believed that I would get more of the connection I desired when I got upset. The other person would come closer to console or appease me, which eased the tension for a while. But it had the opposite effect in the long run. My lovers became tired of putting up with the drama and *actually* started thinking about finding a partner who was less draining and more fun. Loop 1.

My bigger discovery, however, came a bit later. While I knew that this self-sabotage pattern was wreaking havoc on my dating life, I was far less aware of how it was also holding me back as a leader. As I continued to observe myself, I started to notice a pattern: the emotional drama in my intimate life *almost always* coincided in timing with a shiny new project or a high-profile challenge at work. Without realizing it, I had created a bullet-proof excuse for failure: "I'm so sorry . . . I'm a mess. You'll never believe what so-and-so did last night."

Why this pattern? Because I grew up in a family where high performance was a strong expectation. A good deal of competition existed between myself, my younger sister, and the hundreds of other young women my mother was teaching at any given time. In my ego's system, maintaining safety, belonging, and dignity meant being *the best* at all times. And if I didn't have a chance at winning, I didn't want to be part of the game. So I would crash and often take the whole game down with me. In fact, the bigger the challenge—and the *closer* I got to embracing my *true calling*—the more intense this pattern of self-sabotage became. It was only when I started calling my own BS that I was able to fully show up for my dreams.

And *that* is why I teach this work.

The problem with many women's empowerment programs is that they fail to call out the ways we are responsible for creating our own hell. They don't challenge us when we blame others for keeping us down. Please don't get me wrong—I acknowledge there are *real* constraints faced by women and minorities that make our lives more difficult every single day. But I have *also* seen that when we clear out the constraints we've created *inside* and master our self-sabotage patterns, it becomes much easier to break through our factual constraints and become the leaders we were born to be.

Here are a few more examples. Again, your unique self-sabotage pattern may be *much simpler* (or much more complex!) than these. What matters is that you identify a pattern that makes sense to you, given your story and the ways you typically get stuck.

THE SCIENCE: HEALING DEEP TRAUMA

In her book *Healing Sex: A Mind-Body Approach to Sexual Trauma*, Staci Haines describes the neurobiology of trauma and how it impacts those who have experienced childhood sexual abuse. Staci is the founder of Generative Somatics, an organization dedicated to forwarding systemic change through social and environmental justice. Her work focuses on the healing of individual and collective trauma through body-centered (somatic) approaches. These methods engage the entire psychobiology of the human being in the healing process, and are more effective than talk therapy when it comes to healing trauma.

Haines's work draws upon neuroscience, including the work of Dr. Andrew Huberman and research psychiatrist Dr. Bessel van der Kolk. According to this research, people in a traumatic situation experience an immediate physiological reaction. In fact, all animals demonstrate similar biological responses to threat—including the fight, flight, and freeze response. The body gets ready for action by pumping blood away from the neocortex and into the larger action muscles, raising the blood pressure, and shortening the breath. In ordinary circumstances, the brain and body return to balance through a process of release: shaking, trembling, yawning, sweating, crying etc. When this process is allowed to happen, long-term PTSD symptoms are limited.

Unfortunately, for a wide variety of reasons, many survivors of abuse are unable to complete the natural process of release. Instead, the experience gets pushed down, and held in the body in the form of muscular tensions that eventually become chronic. This can leave the parts of body feeling numb or inaccessible. Haines's somatic interventions include therapeutic conversation, bodywork, and new embodied practices. This type of support allows locked-in contractions to soften and release. It also helps the survivor begin to find new ways to address their needs for safety, belonging, and dignity that match their adult lives.

If you suspect that you could benefit from a more comprehensive type of support that includes the release and healing of trauma, I recommend somatic therapy, somatic bodywork, or a book like Staci's as a next step.

Staci Haines, *Healing Sex: A Mind-Body Approach to Healing Sexual Trauma* (San Francisco: Clies Press, 2007).

Generative Somatics: Somatic Transformation and Social Justice Center, http://www.generativesomatics.org/.

L. D. Salay, N. Ishiko, and A. D. Huberman, "A Midline Thalamic Circuit Determines Reaction to Visual Threats," *Nature* 557 (2018): 183–89.

Bessel Van Der Kolk, *The Body Keeps the Score: Brain, Mind and Body in the Healing of Trauma* (New York: Penguin Books, 2014).

Case Study 1: Erin is an emerging leader and a general badass in the data science industry. When we met, she was struggling to decide whether to stay in her current organization or begin a job hunt. She was ready to step into greater leadership, but her company was relatively small, and the opportunities didn't exist. Over our two years of working together, Erin was able to raise the ceiling by first opening a new office, then recruiting a new team, then receiving a promotion and ultimately training her new boss—all the while continuing to build a solid data science infrastructure for the new biotech product her company was developing. But it wasn't easy at first.

An initial 360-degree feedback process revealed that Erin was great at her job but that her superiors didn't like her attitude. This took some time for us to understand. Eventually, we realized that the attitude they were referring to was part of the cover story for her Core Dilemma—the infamous "whatever." Erin was a powerful creator when she put her mind to it. But when she faced what appeared to be an intractable challenge (particularly of the people-and-relationships type, e.g., "Leadership is not really backing us," or "the other department is just trying to get their way"), she would show up to the meeting having already decided that it wouldn't go well. And when she did, she would disengage, silently judge others and the process, and fail to advocate for her side. "Whatever," she would say to herself (or out loud). "It's not gonna happen even if I try."

This pattern was Erin's *internal* glass ceiling. By challenging her own tendency to give up before the deal was done, Erin was able to start bringing her full creative resources to the biggest, most important challenges. She learned to stick with it *even when she might fail*, and eventually she become a powerful influencer at work.

Case Study 2: Becca and I met via LinkedIn and had an instant affinity toward one another. She was working in HR, aiming to build great culture at a manufacturing company at the time, and her future looked bright. When she became my coaching client a year later, I discovered that her exciting new job had turned out to be a disappointment. Not long after we began, we *also* discovered that Becca had had a hunch about the job's downsides before she even started.

Becca, it turned out, was a highly intuitive person. But she also grew up in a family where she had to hide a lot of what she knew in order to fit in. This led her to doubt herself and defer to others frequently. It also contributed to a long-standing habit of choosing environments that weren't quite the right fit, where she couldn't quite be herself. This was Becca's Core Dilemma. A deeper look revealed that this self-defeating habit played out both at work and in her dating life. It created a loop that went like this: I want this, but I probably shouldn't; it seems to be going well, but I feel insecure; it's not going well, and now I've wasted all this time; I should have known better; I'll never find the right thing.

Through our work together Becca made a powerful decision to attract and choose opportunities (and men!) who were exactly what she needed and wanted. After leaving her job, she went into business on her own, using her culture change and leadership training skills to do consulting for other firms. Through an eyes-wide-open process of trial and error, Becca is learning about what type of clients and partners are a great fit—and falling in love with her unique gifts, talents, and desires in the process.

I hope these examples are helpful. As you can see, the Core Dilemma can take different shapes, depending on who you are, and the unique life you have lived. As you begin the journey of uncovering yours, here are a few additional guidelines:

- The Core Dilemma is a behavior, conscious or unconscious, that tends to trip you up.
- While it may seem like it doesn't make any sense as a "strategy," there is a way it has worked to protect or help you in the past, or is currently working in your favor, or both.
- It may be connected to any behavior you've ever referred to as your Achilles heel.
- It may be a behavior you learned from one of your parents, or a behavior your adopted in order to make yourself different than your parents.
- It probably has an upside *and* a downside.
- It might be something you're ashamed of, embarrassed or even frustrated about.
- It might seem like an inherent part of you that's impossible to change—"this is just my personality."

- It probably has an impact on both your work and your personal life.
- It probably showed up in any 360-degree feedback process you've received at work.
- It may be the thing your spouse or friends lovingly tolerate about you.
- It may be related to the biggest excuse you make when you fail. It may also be the thing you secretly think is helping you to succeed.
- Most likely, it's linked to a deeper fear. Or it has roots in unconscious self-preservation or self-promotion of some kind.

Now that your head has been filled with a lot of information, your next step is to take a deep breath, forget everything I said, and begin your reflection process. Don't try to figure it out. Rather, set an intention that the insights you need will come. Then, open yourself to receiving them.

In order to support your discovery, I have included a lengthier-than-usual set of questions below. These questions will help dig up some raw material that *may* be related to your Core Dilemma. Don't worry too much about how your answers fit together. Some of them may not be end up being useful. Imagine you are trying to enter a round maze from a number of different possible doors. The goal is to find your way to the center.

I suggest that you answer these questions all very quickly right now. Literally run through them in three minutes or less. Answer each one from the top of your head, in just a few words or one sentence each. Don't think about it; just write. First thought, best thought.

Then set your answers aside. Come back to them again later. As part of your practice this week, take a second pass, giving yourself a full thirty minutes (three to four minutes per question) to answer them more thoughtfully and deeply. For now, quick and dirty. Trust that a mini brain-dump can be disarming—and revealing.

Ready? First thought, best thought. Go!

Know Thyself: Reflection Questions

- What do you now believe is your Achilles heel—the behavior that you hate to admit you even do but that you can't seem to change about yourself?
- What do you *most want* in life that you can never seem to have?
- What is the sneaky fear that grabs you when you least expect it, and no matter how rational you try to be, you can't seem to shake it?

- Were there any major life events that impacted you in a strong emotional way, either early in your life or more recently, that feel connected to your typical behavior?
- What is the emotion that flows forth *today* when you lose your cool that you wish would just go away?
- What do you blame others for that you have a hunch might be partly your fault?
- What baggage do you know that you carry from your past and that you have no idea how to heal (an event, an overall emotion, something you had to overcome or cope with)?
- What do you do *today* in order to belong that isn't really that effective?
- When you're about to fail (or afraid you *might* fail), what do you consciously or unconsciously do instead?
- If you met a fortune teller who could answer anything, what is the one question, in any domain of your life other than your leadership, that you would want to know the definitive answer to? Why are you so concerned about this?

The Practice

The practices in chapter 6 are designed to help you to uncover and understand architecture of your Core Dilemma—the one thing that's in the way of you becoming your most conscious, sustainable, and thriving self as a leader. Since there is no "right way" to uncover your Core Dilemma, I suggest you start with what most intrigues you. It's also okay to design your own self-discovery practice. This week, your primary focus is to gather some data.

Consider yourself to be on a Scavenger Hunt. When it comes to uncovering the Core Dilemma, it's often the case that one realization leads to another, leads to another, leads to another. Literally. Even if you make discoveries that are ultimately tangential, you will most likely complete this module knowing more about yourself. Some of these threads may prove to be useful in later chapters, so be sure to take good notes along the way.

Let's dive in.

PRACTICE 1: DEEPER REFLECTION

Revisit the questions from the Know Thyself section. Set aside about thirty minutes to write in your journal. Give yourself a good three or four minutes per question. You might try setting a timer for each one so that you don't rush through. Let your hand fall on the page and write what comes to mind. Don't stop moving your pen. Keep writing. Or sit in silence if your thoughts go blank. Wait. Allow the possibility that some new or unexpected thoughts eventually show up in the silence.

Or you might decide to bring some of the questions into your physical movement practice. This is a great way of opening yourself to new realizations, without trying so hard to "think it through." You can jog the questions. Dance the questions. Drive or take a shower with the questions. Include them as part of your weekly routine and trust the wisdom of your body to provide some answers.

ACTIVE INGREDIENTS slowing down, automatic writing, deep reflection

WHY IT WORKS Typically, underneath the first thoughts that come to our minds, there are multiple layers of subconscious answers. This practice allows them to surface.

PRACTICE 2: CATCHING YOURSELF IN ACTION

Catching Yourself in Action is an embodied self-observation practice that you can do in real-life moments at work and at home. It doesn't take any extra time, but it does require that you bring a greater level of mindful awareness into your day. The goal of this practice is to leverage your bodily sensations to help you notice when your Core Dilemma is playing out in your behavior in real time.

Here's How

- **First,** choose a period of time for your research. Typically, I recommend that my clients do this over the course of one week.
- **Then,** take an intention to "catch yourself" anytime you're doing something that you think might be a form of self-sabotage. You might not know what that will look like (or you might). Your intention engages your self-awareness.
- **Also,** commit to not judging yourself. The goal is to catch yourself *for the sake of learning*—not for the sake of blaming or beating yourself up.
- **Next,** observe. Take note when it happens. In particular, notice the bodily sensations and emotional feelings that are present during that time. If you're comfortable pausing briefly to write down a few notes, they can be incredibly helpful in your self-discovery process. Jot down 1) what happened, 2) what feelings or sensations were happening in your body, 3) what you did (i.e., behavior), and 4) what happened as a result.
- **As the week goes on,** pay closer attention to your bodily experience. When you notice similar physical sensations or emotional feelings arising, check in with yourself: *am I moving into self-sabotage now?*
- **At the end of the week,** go back and look at your notes (or simply take some time to recall the various moments). Write a summary and any themes from your observation. If you adjusted your behavior in some way, you can also celebrate!
- **Finally,** consider these additional questions: Why do you think you do that? What function does it seem to serve?

Remember, your Core Dilemma can present itself as an Achilles heel or an act of self-sabotage in the moment. It's the reason we can't succeed, the reason it's not our fault, and it's the reason we may as well not bother trying. As you do this practice, I encourage you to take yourself lightly. Approach the assignment (and yourself) with compassion.

ACTIVE INGREDIENTS	self-observation, mindfulness, tracking bodily sensations and emotions
WHY IT WORKS	The Core Dilemma typically operates below the radar of your conscious experience. Setting a clear period of time, and taking a strong intention, can help you turn up the volume on your attention and notice things you may have otherwise missed.

A FEW MORE THOUGHTS

As I said in the beginning, chapter 6 takes you to the *bottom of the valley* of your *Guts and Grace* journey. Each of these practices offers a unique opportunity to get clearer about the one thing blocking your path to a more conscious, sustainable, and thriving leadership approach. And you don't have to figure it out in a single week.

If you do catch yourself in the act of self-sabotage, there is no need to change anything immediately. Just get to know *how* you do it. Use the next few weeks to stalk your Core Dilemma. Learn when it plays out. Notice what affect it has on you, your work, and your relationships. You could even ask some colleagues or friends for feedback on what *they* observe. It's okay to take your time with this research. When you do, it makes space for your reflections—and your intentions—to penetrate your subconscious.

In the next few chapters, I will be giving you all the tools you need to make a lasting shift. You will learn practices that ignite a new level of clarity about your vision, your strengths, and the next iteration of your leadership purpose. For some of my clients, the Core Dilemma becomes abundantly clear *only* when they have fully crystalized their next-level goals. It's totally possible to pull these two threads (releasing the old and moving toward the new) in parallel. In fact, it's pretty much the definition of being human.

Trust that while you may not solve the puzzle of what's *most* likely to stifle your success in just one week, you have laid some solid groundwork already. The information, stories, and practices in chapter 6 are designed to shift things in your body–mind system over an extended period time. And, when you do become clear about your Core Dilemma, the real magic of your unique leadership journey will begin to unfold.

Be bold. Trust the process. It's your life, and it's worth every step you take.

REFLECTIONS ON THE CORE DILEMMA PRACTICES

- How did the practice go? What did you uncover?
- What struck you or surprised you about your observations?
- Across all of your reflections and observations on your Core Dilemma, what central themes seem to be emerging?
- Who else could you ask for feedback on your self-sabotage behaviors? Ask them.
- If you haven't done the Catching Yourself in Action self-observation practice, what's still holding you back?

Guts and Grace Playlist Recommendations

"Show Yourself" – Ayla Nereo

"Waiting on the World to Change" – John Mayer

"Get Free" – Major Lazer

"Beautiful Ugly" – Muph & Plutonic

"Ghosts" – Ibeyi

"It All Can Be Done" – Nahko and Medicine for the People

Activate

"As we let our own lights shine, we unconsciously give other people permission to do the same."

—MARIANNE WILLIAMSON

Activation is about honesty of purpose. Simply put, great leaders are driven by something larger than themselves—and larger than the next rung on the organizational ladder. True activation requires knowing what matters most to you, both in your personal life and at work, and taking aligned action. It's also about listening to your inner longing and not selling yourself short by playing small. In this section, I introduce practices that help you cultivate the courage and clarity to take greater risks and claim your real visions for personal, institutional, or community-wide change.

LEADERSHIP MYTH

Real, lasting change is not possible.
People, teams, and organizations
stay the way they are.

LEADERSHIP TRUTH

Real and lasting change is both harder—
and easier—than you think. It's definitely
possible. In fact, it's what you're built for.

Chapter 7

THE NORTH STAR

What happens when your soul
Begins to awaken in this world
To our deep need to love
And serve the Friend?
O the Beloved
Will send you
Wonderful and wild companions!

—HAFIZ

DECLARING A POWERFUL INTENTION

Take a deep, cleansing breath. We're about to turn a *big* corner. From here forward, things are going to get lighter. And I can't *wait* to share this next practice with you.

Have you ever found the traditional process of setting goals to be . . . a bit underwhelming? Maybe, as Hafiz writes later in the poem "What Happens," you make heroic promises that you know you can't keep. Or perhaps you're fantastic at achieving the goals you set, but on the other side of accomplishing them—when every item on the to-do list has finally been crossed off—things aren't that different, really.

As a society, we're not very practiced at creating real and lasting change. In fact, many of us doubt (either consciously or unconsciously) that change is really possible. *I was born this way. It's just my personality. That's just how we've always done things around here.* Yet this is another leadership myth: ***Real, lasting change is not possible. People, teams, and organizations stay the way they are.***

While we learn early in our careers that it's important to set goals and go after them fiercely, we tend to select challenges that keep us inside the proverbial box. When we're *still* not satisfied, we make those goals more specific, more actionable, and more relevant. We define the time frame, and we measure them well. But even the SMART-est of goals are bound to disappoint when they're born of our focusing on the *wrong things*. The truth is, ***real and lasting change is both harder—and easier—than you think. It's definitely possible. In fact, it's what you're built for.***

In chapter 7 you will develop a new relationship with goal setting. You will learn how to choose an intention that has enough power to transform your life, your work, and your relationships. You will learn how to leverage your own longing, express it with confidence, and rally others to support your cause. And, between chapter 7 and chapter 8, you will learn how to *embody* your new intention through simple, relevant *Daily Practices* that literally reshape your leadership, so that you can rise to meet any challenge you deem worthy of your time.

But let me not get ahead of myself.

Over the past few weeks, you identified the one thing that's most likely to sabotage your leadership today. This week, we'll focus our energy on creating a new type of goal—a North Star Intention—that will support you to authentically transform your habits in that same domain. Later, you can apply the North Star practice to *any* area of your work or life, once you get the hang of it.

By focusing this practice on your Core Dilemma, you will begin harnessing the power of your entire body, mind, and spirit to unlock the hidden power and potential *underneath* the self-sabotage. Instead of holding change as equivalent to losing a part of yourself, you will learn to expand your range in a way that naturally supports your healthy and graceful evolution. Through this process, you will keep the good parts of your old habits and develop new ones, so that you can make more effective choices in the moment. You will also proactively challenge any voices inside you that might be whispering things like "No way! Not possible" or "It's just too hard to change."

As William Hutchinson Murray writes in *The Scottish Himalayan Expedition*, "the moment one definitely commits oneself, then providence moves too."[21]

Are you ready to commit?

FINDING NEUTRAL (A.K.A. CENTERING)

If you want to set a powerful new intention that leverages the wisdom of your body to create real and lasting personal or professional change, the best place to start from is neutral. In other words, it's important to ground yourself and take the pulse of your own body–mind–spirit system, before you shoot for the stars. This will help ensure that you set your compass from a true state of *generative creation* rather than a state of *reaction*. It will also help you avoid decision traps like the *IRS* ("I really should"), which I come back to in chapter 10.

On the macro level (e.g., the level of your entire career or your entire life), getting to neutral can be a lengthy process. That's why we spent the last few chapters engaging in emotional and mental clearing practices. In essence, we've been tilling your internal soil and casting out some weeds, so that you'd be ready to plant important new seeds this week.

That said, there are also a variety of simple actions you can take to find neutral on a micro level (e.g., the level of this day or this staff meeting) in a matter of minutes. Often called "centering practices," these actions help you slow your breath, relax any unneeded tension, bring awareness to your bodily sensations, increase your clarity, and prepare you for more effective action.

Here's how they work. Using a powerful metaphor, nationally renowned composer and sound healer Dr. John Beaulieu compares the human body to a musical instrument. With use, the body can become out of tune. His and other scientific studies suggest that the frequency of resonance in the body can be disturbed by outside stressors. Like an instrument, it can also be brought back to resonance at the optimal frequency through the use of sound waves and other interventions.

Dr. Beaulieu calls the state of optimal human tuning "neutral." In other disciplines, like the martial arts, we might call this same state "operating from center." In every session, the first goal he takes with his client is to bring the body back to this neutral state. Likewise, in the martial arts, practitioners aim to bring their bodies into a state of calm relaxation before performing any feat of strength or agility. Experienced athletes "get into the zone" before a match or competition. The practice of yoga is designed to bring the body into the most balanced, relaxed, and aligned state before beginning meditation. In each of these disciplines, the practitioner finds neutral before taking an important next step.

Similarly, when I facilitate a group coaching session, I typically invite participants to begin with a very simple centering practice. This practice is inspired by my training at the Strozzi Institute. It is also mentioned in the Practice section of chapter 4. Here again are some basic instructions:

First, sit straight up in your chair. Place your feet on the ground. Keep your eyes open. Take a few deeper breaths. Sense the length of your spine in space. Imagine a string is pulling you up from the top of your head, and your body dangles effortlessly below. At the same time, feel your feet connected to the ground. Gently root down. Breathe. Sense the sides of your body. Expand your energy from your core, out past your shoulders and hips. Taking up more space. Sensing your width. Breathe. Finally feel the front of your body, and allow your energy to expand into the space in front of you—your metaphorical future, including all the hopes and intentions you have for your future. Then feel your back and allow your energy also to expand behind—into your metaphorical past, including all the people and events that have supported you. Last, feel your insides. Your lungs. Your heart. Your guts. Enjoying a sense of depth and roundedness. Breathe. Relax your shoulders. Relax your jaw. Breathe and feel.

This simple, physical practice can be done several times a day, as a way of relieving stress and coming back to your emotional baseline in the face of challenging life events. It's one example or the topic we cover in chapter 8: *Daily Practices*. For now, as we prepare to set some powerful new intentions, you can use it to help you find neutral.

If you're skeptical like I am, you may be wondering, "Can this simple action truly make a big difference in my life?" I get it. I used to think the same thing. I would do it once or twice, and, when no big fireworks seemed to happen, I'd start to doubt that it was useful. It's such a little thing. How could it possibly improve my leadership?

But I've changed my tune. After committing to do it consecutively for thirty days, I found my own powerful answer to the question, "Why bother?" Let me tell you why I have used this simple practice, almost daily, for the past ten years.

No matter one's age, gender, race, ethnicity, or nationality, there is at least one universal, biological truth that applies to the human body: when scared, surprised, or threatened, the body's fight-or-flight response kicks in. This response serves as a powerful and important protection from danger throughout our lives. However, the effects of sustained exposure to the chemicals produced by this natural response are undeniably damaging to our physical, mental, and emotional well-being.

When we fail to "reset" our systems and come back to neutral, we end up hanging out in an emotionally amped up, adrenaline-filled state for far longer than our bodies can tolerate. We end up depleted and exhausted, at best. At worst, we find ourselves at risk of heart attacks and other serious diseases.

Why would our greatest source of protection also have the power to cause us harm? And why don't other animals suffer the same consequences? Of course, we share this physiological mechanism with most other organisms on the planet. Their muscles get tense, their heart rates rise, and blood flows away from their brains toward their limbs as they prepare to attack or run away. Yet in most other species, the response is mediated by natural habits that bring the body back into a state of relaxation and calm. They run. They shake. (Hence the expression "shake it off.") They release tension through sound. We human beings, however, have fallen out of the habit of coming back to neutral. A basic centering practice—whether done through breath and body posture like the practice I described above, through chanting relaxing sounds, or through mind-calming meditation—is a way to press the reset button.

Over the past decade, I have seen over and over how this simple practice can make a huge difference for me. It's especially useful when I start to lose my cool in the moment. As a trainer who is committed to trying any tool I might use with clients, I have spent hundreds of hours and thousands of dollars learning wonderful techniques to enhance my own body, mind, and spirit. Yet I always come back to centering. Through my exploration, I've learned that centering (simple, accessible, and cheap!) can serve as a basic foundation upon which all my other personal development practices can rest.

In a moment, I'll connect the dots between *starting from a neutral state* and *setting a powerful intention*. But first, here are a few more things I've learned about finding neutral that may be useful. (*Note:* I use "centering" and finding neutral interchangeably below.)

- To get the greatest benefit, it helps to do it every day. Multiple times a day.
- Practicing when *I don't need it* helps me build the muscle, so that I can do it when *I really do need it.*
- The goal isn't to never lose my center. The goal is to admit that I will lose my center—often!—and to come back as quickly as I can.
- When I'm out of tune, if I try to do anything else other than coming back to neutral, I end up at best ineffective. At worst, I make a huge mess.

- Cheating doesn't work. It is not possible to pretend I'm centered and act effectively "just to get through it."
- Typically, finding neutral involves both making physical (body-based) adjustments *and* changing my thoughts or emotions about the situation. The body-based adjustments can be done immediately, and they affect the mind and emotions, so they're a great place to start.
- There's no way to do it wrong. Just *deciding* to center and doing my best to shift *something* in my body and breath is better than not centering at all.

Whether or not the specific centering practice I shared above resonates for you, I encourage you to take on a practice of finding neutral this week. If needed, you can adjust the practice above so that it suits you well. Ideally, I recommend picking a regular time once a day to do it. At that time, spend three to five minutes returning your body, mind, and emotions to a centered, neutral state. Notice what shifts for you each time.

If you work in a hectic environment, or you're prone to feeling a lot of tension during the day, you might also try doing a centering practice "in the moment." For example, slow down or pause a conversation that isn't going well. Take a time-out or a deep breath when you feel frustrated. Feel your body, and relax any strong contractions (e.g., neck, shoulders, jaw, forehead, belly). You might imagine your favorite icon of relaxed, centered presence (e.g., a teacher, leader, or famous figure that emanates this quality). Allow your body to mirror the shape, energy, and attitude of that person. Bring their essence into important or difficult situations. Notice when your breath gets shallow. Deepen it again.

That's all it takes. You've found neutral!

Finding Neutral: Reflection Questions

- Do you currently have a practice for finding neutral? If so, is it working for you? How do you think you could benefit from doing basic centering practice regularly this week?
- Did you try the centering practice just now? If so, what do you notice? If not, why not?
- What, if any, resistance do you have to the idea of taking a pause and coming back to neutral throughout your day?
- Think about your work week. Where, when, or with whom would a centering practice be most useful to you?

UNCOVERING YOUR INTENT

Now that you have a practice that brings you back to your physiological baseline, let's return to the focus of this chapter—*setting a powerful new intention*. The truth is, there are two ways that a daily centering practice can support you here. One, it can help you discover (or *uncover*) your deeper goals, intuitions, and intentions. And two, you can use it to *anchor* those intentions with your entire body, mind, and spirit.

First, let's explore how to use the centering practice to design the most powerful intention possible for your professional growth right now. Let's assume that you want to set an intention about stepping out of your Core Dilemma so that you can become a more conscious and effective leader this year. Let's also assume that you are the clearest, most hopeful, most resourced, and wisest version of yourself when your body-mind system is resting in a neutral state. In that case, centering can help you listen more deeply to your body in order to discover what you *most care about* when you're no longer operating in a reactive state. In other words, the practice can literally help you *uncover your intention*.

Here's How

- First, find neutral. Using the basic centering practice, or another practice that works well for you, bring your body-mind system to baseline.
- From this state, feel and listen more deeply. Ask your body questions: *What's important? What matters? What do I deeply know? How do I want to feel? How do I need to grow? What do I stand for? Who am I becoming? What do I want to create?*
- With each question, wait patiently for the answers. Even if nothing obvious comes, trust that you are planting seeds that will eventually bear fruit.

It's important to keep in mind that there is no wrong way to engage in this enquiry. At this stage, your primary goal is to let your body-mind system know that you are listening. Expressing trust and exercising patience will typically (and counterintuitively) expedite the process. In fact, many of us already know at a very deep level what's needed next when it comes to our professional or personal growth. Uncovering your intention is about creating space for that *knowing* to be revealed.

If you've never tried this before (or you've tried but have come up blank), you might be curious about what you can expect to find. Here's a hint: often, our bodies speak *first* in very simple words, phrases, images, or sensations. I call these shorthand messages *Qualities*.

What do I mean by "Quality"?

In the English language, we often use physical "quality" words to describe the characteristics we observe in people. For example, you might say something like "He's a really *solid* guy, like a rock," or "She gave me a *cold* stare before she walked away." In fact, while we are not always aware of it, these metaphors play a big part in the way we understand the world around us.

For example, call to mind your ideal image of a caretaker. You might think about a nurse, nanny, or hospice worker. Now, imagine that you are deciding whether or not to entrust the care of a loved one to this person you have envisioned. On paper, the person appears to have all the right credentials. Yet when you meet them in person, they clearly lack one Quality: *warmth*. Allow the image in your mind to adjust . . .

Do you suppose you would hire them?

Most people would say *no* without much deliberation. In this way, the Qualities we embody affect both our actual capability *and* our believability in the eyes of others. When you want to grow in your leadership, identifying the new Quality you will need to embody is a useful stepping-stone. What's more, your body will probably give you clues, if you are willing to listen.

Here's another example. One morning, I was practicing a series of martial arts moves (called kata) with a wooden staff (called a jo). I had done the same sequence hundreds of times in the past. Yet, on this particular day, one of moves kept catching my attention. This move involved executing a forward-facing overhead strike while going down on one knee. I kept losing my balance while doing the move. I also noticed that I usually didn't put my knee all the way down on the ground.

After pausing for a moment to consider what my body was trying to tell me, I laughed out loud. For about a week, I'd been reflecting on how to appropriately use power and directness in my leadership. From time to time, I would enter a conversation at work with such fierceness that my colleagues would pull away and ignore my input. My body's resistance to *going down on one knee* felt related. In order to explore this hunch, I brought myself to neutral, then tried the move again a few times, taking an intention to put my knee down fully. The Quality was now totally different. I felt a sense of *humility*, whereas before it had been entirely lacking.

Ah. Yes. Powerful *and* humble. Not my forte. This felt like a new intention that I could really get behind—one that could help me evolve my leadership that year. What's more, because the message came from my body in the context of my practice, I had a clear sense of how the shift might *look* and *feel* day to day.

Do you see what I mean?

In this story, I was engaged in a physically active practice—performing the jo kata. But the basic centering practice you learned in the last segment is an equally good place to start. The physical distinctions in the centering practice may immediately open doors for you. For example, sitting upright may connect you with Qualities like *strength* or *dignity*, while sensing your back may bring forth Qualities like *patience* or even *confidence*.

It may also be the case that your revelation comes at the *end* of the practice, when you pause and ask your body a question like "What matters today?" At this moment, the answer may come to you as *words*. Or you may get a felt sense through the shape and Quality of your presence. The key is to remain open and to trust.

A quick caveat here: uncovering your intention is not about "acting" something out. Rather, it's about letting your body show you where your real growth edge lies. In fact, I hold this practice as a *counterpoint* to some of the more traditional body-language training approaches. Here's why.

Some public speaking trainings focus on giving leaders a list of things to do with their bodies in order to guarantee success: stand this way; use that hand gesture; always make eye contact. I believe this approach is a massive oversimplification of what is needed in order to build a compelling presence. At best, it feels awkward. At worst, it can lead to an army of cookie-cutter speakers that put an uncomfortable mask over their real selves in order to make the grade.

Moreover, applying this one-size-fits-all approach can be akin to "faking it." And while your colleagues *may* believe you're "fine" when you put on a happy face to cover up your anxiety, most people can tell the difference. A genuine, authentic shift is required in order for the people you lead to respond in kind.

The same can be true of old-fashioned goal setting. Let's say you want to lose weight, so you set a SMART goal: you're going to work out five days a week, for thirty minutes per day, at your target heart rate, over the course of the next month. Let's say you chose this goal because we've heard that other people have had success doing it this way, but let's say it feels totally unnatural and misaligned to you. This type of goal, chosen in this way, is more likely to *override*—rather than *work with*—your body's natural instinct to thrive.

In contrast to these types of mind-driven "good idea" approaches, Quality words and phrases that come from the body are modern-day somatic tools that can help you align your body-mind system with your real mission in a more holistic, believable way. Uncovering your intention by listening to your body, then pairing a simple, powerful Quality with a regular daily practice, is a doable bite-sized way to begin evolving your leadership . . . *for real.*

This week I invite you to begin the process of uncovering your intent. Using the approach described above, come up with a first draft. In the sections and chapters that follow, we will continue to refine what you've uncovered, ultimately crafting a simple, clear intention that supports you to become a more conscious, sustainable, and thriving leader, day by day.

You may also find it helpful to review your notes from the last chapter, where you identified one thing you most need to shift right now. With that in mind, ask yourself, "What one or two Qualities would I need to embody more fully in order to leave my Core Dilemma behind?"

Here are a few more examples of embodied Qualities, to spark your discovery process: *warmth, strength, dignity, kindness, passion, flexibility, reliability, rigor, softness, rigidity, generosity, transparency, structure, speed, flow, aliveness* . . . You can also choose trait words like "trust" "confidence" or "dependability," though you'll have to do the extra step of discovering what that trait *feels* like in your body . . .

Uncovering Your Intent: Reflection Questions

- Whether you judge them as good, bad, or neutral, what are some Qualities that you *currently* embody? (Include a wide range, both positive and negative.)
- When you imagine yourself making progress on your Core Dilemma, what behaviors do you need to change or stop? What new actions would you need to take? What new Qualities would you be displaying?
- When you do the basic centering practice (from the last section), what shifts in your presence? What new Qualities, if any, do you notice in yourself when you come back to neutral?

THE SCIENCE: GROWTH MINDSET

Still not sure it's really possible to change? Stanford University psychologist Dr. Carol Dweck's research suggests that it might be worthwhile to adjust your mindset. According to Dweck, *mindset* plays a major role in achievement, impacting how much confidence you have in yourself, how long you persist on difficult tasks, and how likely you are to learn from your mistakes. It also impacts the degree to which you believe that your own characteristics are *malleable* or can be changed over time.

In her early research on coping with failure, Dweck discovered that some children are able to remain in good spirits, even when facing very difficult challenges. When these resilient youngsters had a tough time completing puzzles in her research study, they kept on trying. These children believed that they were *getting smarter* through their efforts. They hoped their performance would eventually improve. And it did. In contrast, Dweck herself had learned at a young age that traits like intelligence weren't going to change. If you weren't smart, you did your best to hide it or compensate in other areas. And you avoided publicly making mistakes.

Dweck calls these two frameworks *growth mindset* and *fixed mindset*. Neither mindset is inherently bad. However, Dweck's research shows that world champion athletes, inspiring business leaders, and other highly successful people tend to operate from a *growth mindset*. This belief allows them to do their best in the moment, improve over time, and learn from setbacks along the way. While these beliefs get set at an early age, Dweck also argues that it's possible to *change your mindset* in adulthood. First, notice the ways you explain away your failure or talk yourself out of trying. Then, reconsider your goal and break down the small steps you could take to improve your results the next time around. Making small increases in progress over time helps you to trust that growth is indeed possible.

Carol S. Dweck, *Mindset: The New Psychology of Success* (New York: Ballantine Books, 2006).

YOUR NORTH STAR

How did it go? If you're getting the hang of finding neutral, and if your body is starting to give you some hints about new Qualities, congratulations! While every*body* has the ability do this type of reflection, it doesn't always come easy at first. If it's starting to work for you, you might be feeling clearer about where your real growth edge lies—perhaps you've uncovered some Qualities that resonate or you had a breakthrough in the centering practice.

On the other hand, if you're feeling a bit scrambled from your work in the last section, don't worry. It's all part of the magic. You're starting down a path that will ultimately reprogram your mind-body system (in a good way, of course!). It can be confusing, or even disorienting, at the start. Keep breathing and trust the process. It's totally okay at this stage if you have a few puzzle pieces but aren't sure how they fit together.

Wherever you're at in the process, please trust me on one thing: this exploration is not a competition. There is no way to lose or fail. Rather, it's purely a *learning* game. You are learning how to receive information from your body and leverage it to support your professional growth. You won't be graded on the accurateness of the intentions you uncover. My aim is to help you find a new way to cocreate your own conscious transformation—a way that takes the body into account and leads to lasting, positive change.

If you feel ready to take the next step, we'll spend the rest of this chapter putting it all together. We will refine and crystalize your new intention, so that it carries the most possible power. If not, you can always pause and devote a few more days to your research. Or you can practice tolerating ambiguity and continue moving forward anyhow.

In 2017 I wrote a blog entitled "Big Enough: Why 'Right Sized' Challenges are Far Too Small." In it, I explained why *waiting for the right moment* to go after your dreams is a strategy that is destined to fail. The goal of this blog was to highlight the importance of setting an intention *big enough* to call you into your own greatness. Rather than worrying she'll never be ready—a fear that comes from the ego and is *designed* to keep you safe but small—I encouraged the reader to think of her challenge like a difficult mountain climb, and to trust that *the climb itself* is what shapes her into the kind of woman who is able to reach the summit. In the blog I also featured Kate, the client I mentioned a few chapters back.

At that time, Kate was working as the executive director of a nonprofit organization that supported women leaders. Day after day, she would encourage her clients to step up and pursue their dreams. Yet Kate herself was wilting inside of a business partnership that failed to make space for her to truly flourish as a leader. The state of affairs had an impact on her mood—and took a definitive shape in her body. Kate would show up to our sessions hunched forward, with her shoulders and back rounded, head forward, and eyes cast down. It was the shape of resignation. Yet the idea of changing her situation felt like a mountain that was impossible to climb. I knew that for Kate to take the next step, it would take a *powerful intention* that she felt 100 percent committed to achieve.

In one of our coaching sessions, I guided Kate through a centering practice. I encouraged her to drop her shoulders back, raise her head, and extend upward along the length of her spine. Her eyes sparkled mischievously. When I asked her how she felt, she said, "Better!" Then, "Like I could be *the leading lady of my own life*." The words bounced off the walls of my office and rang loudly in both of our ears. That's it! We agreed that she had just landed on a profoundly resonant new intention—one that could guide her leadership in the weeks and months to come. I asked her to speak it again, out loud: "*Starting today, I am committed to being the leading lady of my* own life."

Thus, Kate's *North Star Intention* was born.

Like a compass that points us toward our own greatness, the North Star Intention—or embodied declaration—is a simple, compelling sentence that ties you to the future state you most desire. It both paints a picture of the future and sheds light on the path. It also resonates at the cellular level with the natural longings of your own body and soul.

Kate's North Star included some touching words. But it *also* included a particular type of body posture (shoulders back, spine straight, relaxed muscles, eyes looking forward), as well as a unique mood (bright, confident, and a bit mischievous—even sassy). Over time, it became clear that this North Star also required new behaviors—speaking up, trusting her desire, taking a stand for what she believed in, and being willing to say an honest "no." While the declaration is based on a powerful phrase, your North Star Intention is a coherent package that, when embodied, feels believable to yourself and to the world.

So how do you create one?

There is no cookie-cutter way to craft your North Star. Sometimes—as in Kate's story, it suddenly becomes obvious. Sometimes, it takes a while to find the words that feel most meaningful. In all cases, however, it should bring you right to your growth edge. Sometimes saying it out loud even brings a shiver or shock of electricity through the body—a mix of excitement and fear—that lets you know you're on the right track. Here are a few more examples to help you get the creative juices flowing.

Recall my story about relationship drama and self-sabotage from the last chapter. At that time, I realized that the one thing I most needed to change was my addiction to toxic intimate relationship dynamics and victimy commiseration. I was conscious that my tendency to get lost in negative emotions was derailing both my personal life and my work. When I decided to change, I used this declaration as my North Star to stay the course:

I am a commitment to transforming or ending my toxic relationship this fall.

And I did.

In my case, the declaration pointed to a specific outcome that I had no idea how to achieve but I was totally committed to pursuing. And it had an end date—about six months after I made the decision to begin. Both of these elements helped me to identify the path forward and stay true when the going got tough.

Years later, I use a different declaration in my intimate relationship. It is a modified version of my earlier North Star. This version would have been too much of a stretch for me years ago, but it feels true and right-sized today.

I am a commitment to cocreating a loving and supportive relationship where I can be 100 percent myself.

You may have noticed that these North Star Intentions begin with "I am a commitment to" instead of "I am committed to." This phrasing was coined by my teacher Richard Strozzi-Heckler, founder of the Strozzi Institute, as part of his training on embodied leadership. It helps connect us more deeply with our declarations and anchor them in our bodies (rather than outside of, or away from, ourselves). You can learn more about his approach in the book *The Leadership Dojo: Build Your Foundation as an Exemplary Leader.*[22]

For our purposes, there is no wrong way to phrase your North Star—though I recommend "I am a commitment to," if you're willing to try it out. For inspiration, here are a few more examples from my current and former clients:

- I am a commitment to trusting my gut.
- I am a commitment to owning my path and loving what is.

- I am a commitment to putting myself back in the game.
- I am a commitment to loving and living the gray.
- I am a commitment to letting my fears flow through me and embracing my potential.
- I am a commitment to building unshakeable confidence in myself and helping others do the same.
- I am a commitment to speaking up and being seen.
- I am a commitment to letting go of anger and finding my true happiness.
- I am a commitment to pursuing a chief engineer position by the end of this year.
- I am a commitment to visible leadership and pioneering the next generation of leadership strategies that move our organization forward.

While each one of these statements may sound interesting—even inspiring—they are only truly meaningful to the women who chose them. A good North Star is not a bright idea that looks polished on paper or sounds important to somebody else. Rather, each statement has *very* particular meaning to its speaker. The words were born out of weeks of self-reflection, and directly address the Core Dilemma each of these women *most* needed to change in order to grow in their leadership.

- Many of these declarations were *not* obvious to my clients at the start of their journeys. And if I had told them on day one that they would have to tackle these challenges, many of them would have run for the hills. But since they came to their own clarity through embodied practice and deep reflection, they were willing (and able) to go for it.
- Okay, enough examples. It's time to start drafting your own.
- Here's how. Let's say that you have a pretty good idea of your Core Dilemma, and you have clarity about the counterproductive behaviors it leads you to act out. Let's say you've been using the centering practice to come back to baseline, and you've noticed what it takes for you personally to find neutral. And let's say that you've uncovered one or two Qualities that relate to your next level of leadership.

Can you imagine boiling all of this down into one simple phrase—a powerful *declaration* that could serve as your North Star for the rest of the year? If yes (or maybe), ***pause for a moment, grab your journal, and scratch down a draft or two while they are still at the top of your mind.***

If you feel comfortable, I encourage you to use the phrasing "I am a commitment to . . ." in order to remind yourself that you intend to *embody* this new commitment.

(Pause for a moment here.)

Welcome back. If you did scratch something down, good job! I realize that for many of us, "getting it right" can be a barrier to "getting it done." The good news is, whatever you wrote doesn't have to be perfect. It can simply be the starting point for your practice and your reflection. What you've written may not even make a lot of sense. When you bring the pieces together, your North Star may or may not include the quality words you recently brainstormed. Don't worry! You can always come back to them later. It's not important that you include everything. For now, it's okay to just go with what feels the strongest and most charged to you, for now.

That being said, if you look at your first draft and feel it's *missing something* or is *disconnected from* the better part of the reflection you've done so far, I encourage you to keep adding, honing, or refining it over the next few days (weeks, months). It's *typical* that your North Star will evolve over time. When you speak your North Star out loud, and aim to *embody* it during an intentional body–mind practice (the topic of chapter 8), you will *feel* the coherence (or lack of coherence), and you can make adjustments to the phrasing if needed.

This week you will set your North Star as your *new baseline* and (through regular practice) start building your capacity to return to it, like returning home, again and again.

Your North Star: Reflection Questions

- What do you care about *more* than any familiar inertia that keeps you stuck? (E.g., Health? Well-being? Peak performance? The company mission? Your personal mission? Being able to show up for your children in five, ten, or twenty years?)
- If you haven't done so yet, take a few moments and write down a draft or two of your North Star. Begin with "I am a commitment to . . ."
- Put down your pen and speak it a few times out loud. Keep your attention on your body. How does it feel? How does it sound? What do you notice?

The Practice

Let's dive into practice. In chapter 8, you will learn how to create elaborate, custom practices that you can use to fully embody your new intentions. At this stage, however, I encourage you to start with a few basic ones that will help you uncover and refine your North Star. In case it wasn't abundantly clear, your first—and most important—mission for this chapter is to *craft a working first draft of your North Star.*

Your secondary assignment is to do the centering practice, paired with your declaration, at least once a day *when you don't need it.* For example, once a day (in the morning, evening, or at lunch time) go through the centering practice. First, find neutral. Then, at the end, call to mind your North Star. While you hold that declaration in mind, organize your body in a way that resonates. Do this once per day, at a time you select in advance. If helpful, you can also do a shorter version (e.g., fifteen or thirty seconds) as often as you like, as a way of coming back to your intent throughout the day.

That's all you need to know at a high level in order to get started. For those who want more guidance, you will find the juicy details below.

PRACTICE 1: FINDING NEUTRAL IN THE MOMENT

This week, I invite you to practice finding neutral *as often as possible.* When you start from a neutral, relaxed state, your North Star will be easier to create. It may even begin to reveal itself without effort. As I mentioned above, there are a variety of ways to return your body to neutral. Many mindfulness disciplines offer meditations and other techniques that can support you. Earlier in the chapter, I also included guidelines for a *basic centering practice* that can be done daily. (You can find a guided version of this practice on the book website www.gutsandgrace.com/book-resources/).

That said, it's also important to get familiar with how your body *loses center,* so that you can recognize when you might need to come back. You may also find that the particular *way* you lose your center relates to the new Qualities you want to embody. Here's how to practice *Finding Neutral in the Moment.*

Version 1: Practice in Your Regular Movement Routine. When you do your Joy Workouts, or other regular physical exercise routine, track the sensation of neutral in your body. For example, practice putting your attention on your center of gravity as you move. Feel your feet on the ground. Relax your muscles. Even if you're moving fast, slow down on the inside. Imagine you have all the time in the world to complete the next action. Allow yourself to take up more space. Sense your body as tall and upright. Contract and release. Notice what shifts. Can you move faster? Slower? Can you still find neutral?

Version 2: Practice in Life. Track the sensation of neutral back at work or in your personal relationships. It might look like slowing down or pausing when a conversation isn't going well. You might notice when your breath gets shallow and your body contracts, and choose to relax again. You might even remember the last time you did a basic centering practice by yourself and let that memory change your presence. Allow your body to take on the shape, energy, and attitude you felt before.

ACTIVE INGREDIENTS	self-awareness, somatic (body-based) adjustments, conscious intention
WHY IT WORKS	Finding neutral is easier when you're practicing by yourself, at home. By practicing in the moment, you build a strong re-centering muscle that you can use anytime.

PRACTICE 2: REFINE YOUR NORTH STAR

If you've done the activities in the text of this chapter, you should already have a North Star draft that you can use as a starting point. (If not, I recommend you go back and do them first.) Once you have a working draft, there are many things you can do to continue refining the phrasing and enhance its resonance. In addition, it's a good idea to keep track of the other elements that *support* or *connect with* your North Star: body posture, mood, emotions, new thoughts or beliefs, and new actions. I've described a few possible next steps below.

Try This: Write your North Star draft at the top of a page in your journal. Then ask yourself the following questions:

- *If I were living this North Star every day, how would I typically feel?*
- *In order to* EMBODY *this North Star, how do I need to behave?*

- *If I wasn't afraid, and I knew this North Star were possible to achieve, what else would I have to believe (about myself, about other people, or the world)?*
- *If this North Star were already true about me, what actions would I be taking right now?*
- *If my North Star were my natural way of living or leading, what else would be different?*

Try This: Stand in your bedroom, office, or other private space. Speak your North Star out loud. If you have a mirror, you can do this facing your mirror. Notice how it feels. Let your body take on the *natural* shape this declaration inspires (physical posture, mood, emotions). If you were *being* this commitment right now, how would you be? Be careful not to "act it out." Rather, imagine that you are exuding the commitment through your presence in a natural and effortless way.

Try This: Before you leave the house in the morning, remind yourself of your North Star. Decide to "take it with you" for the entire day. When you find yourself in a situation that would typically evoke your Core Dilemma, remind yourself silently of your North Star. Notice what happens. Is it simple enough that you can remember it in that moment? Is it strong enough to support you to stay on track in that moment? If not, what's missing? What needs to change? At the end of the day, make any adjustments you think would be helpful.

These practices can help you uncover, refine, and embody your North Star. Once again, I want to acknowledge that this work is a path—not a destination. The very good news is that you have full permission to continue adjusting your North Star, as needed, for the rest of our journey together. Some of my clients uncover a powerful new intention quickly, then stick with it for as long as several years. Others have trouble at first, trying on several options before finally landing one that resonates. Still others start with one that feels great, and then quickly outgrow it. As their original intention becomes embodied, an even more exciting North Star is ultimately revealed.

In other words, it's *totally* okay if your declaration evolves. You can come back to *any* of the practices in chapter 7, *anytime*. In fact, I HOPE you come back to these practices, year after year. As you become an even more conscious, sustainable, and thriving leader, you can craft a powerful and relevant North Star Intention for every phase of your career.

ACTIVE INGREDIENTS	mindful reflection, self-observation, intention, physiological resonance
WHY IT WORKS	Each of these practices get you into imperfect practice, despite any lack of clarity. This provides opportunities for a spontaneous "aha" insight to arise.

REFLECTIONS ON THE NORTH STAR PRACTICES

- What are you learning from engaging in the North Star practices this week?
- Has your North Star evolved, from your initial draft to now? What's changed? Why?
- What else are you becoming aware of about yourself as a learner or about your own embodied presence?

Guts and Grace Playlist Recommendations

"Man in the Mirror" – Michael Jackson

"Right Now" – Van Halen

"Catch My Breath" – Kelly Clarkson

"That Old Pair of Jeans" – Fatboy Slim

"I Don't Want to Wait" – Paula Cole

"There Is Only Love" – Karen Drucker

LEADERSHIP MYTH

I've read the book; I've attended the training; I've changed my mind . . . so I should be taking different actions, right?

LEADERSHIP TRUTH

The body plays a critical role in real, sustainable transformation.

Chapter 8

MY DAILY PRACTICES

Now to stand still, to be here,
Feel my own weight and density!
. . . all fuses now, falls into place
From wish to action, word to silence,
My work, my love, my time, my face
Gathered into one intense
Gesture of growing like a plant.

—MAY SARTON

THE ROAD TO FULL-BODIED LEADERSHIP

By now it won't surprise you that I believe change happens in the tiny steps we take each day. In fact, I have found that even a dramatic intervention like a major surgery or important relationship breakup can be rendered ineffective when your subsequent daily actions don't line up with the transformation. The same is so for an exciting life change like a wedding or major promotion or a deep energetic clearing by a talented body worker (which I highly recommend!). Too often, we take our own evolution for granted once we've made it through a "big doorway." In doing so, we miss the opportunity to take the simple actions that can really make it stick.

One big difference between embodied leadership coaching and traditional coaching is the strong focus on *supporting practices*. By deciding in advance about the ways your body, mindset, and behavior need to change in order to become the type of leader you want to be, and choosing to take specific new actions every day, you can literally reprogram your own system.

This work is particularly refreshing (and useful!) against the backdrop of a corporate training culture that focuses primarily on knowledge delivery and mindset shifts. Which brings us to our next leadership myth: ***I've read the book; I've attended the training; I've changed my mind . . . so I should be taking different actions, right?*** In fact, many of us believe that changing our minds is a surefire way to change our lives. Yet, even when you're able to shift your mindset through better information, new decisions, or daily affirmations, it's not always the case that your body will conform. Your mind is a powerful tool. But it cannot do the job of behavior change alone.

The truth is: ***the body plays a critical role in real, sustainable transformation.*** Those who work with trauma and physical injuries know from experience that *the body cannot be ignored.* Even when you change your thinking, historical memories can remain stored in the cells of the body. If so, they need to be released or alchemized for lasting change to take place. The body needs to learn, through vulnerable trial and error, that it can indeed get its old needs met in new ways. When we start making new moves—and find that they actually work—our body-mind systems are more willing to let go of old fears and come along for the ride. That's why embodied practice is one of the fastest ways to change deeply ingrained, lifelong habits that have been difficult to shift.

The 1984 movie *The Karate Kid* inspired a generation of young people to trust in their ability to succeed against all odds. Speaking into a context of rampant childhood bullying, the film portrays the journey of a young man who wants to build his confidence through the practice of martial arts. In one memorable scene, the protagonist, Daniel, is asked to spend an afternoon waxing his teacher's car. The sensei, Mr. Miyagi, is a man of few words. He says only: "Wax on, wax off. Wax on, wax off." Giving no further instructions, he promptly leaves. Daniel is furious, but ultimately decides to take on this seemingly menial task, in the hopes that Miyagi will eventually teach him some "real" karate moves. Later, however, he is surprised to find that "wax off" comes in handy, when he instinctively blocks an incoming blow from one of the local bullies in a spontaneous street fight.

This is the power of *embodied practice.*

This story accurately captures the fact that small actions, when taken frequently and regularly, will inevitably add up to new behavior. In fields like athletics and martial arts, experts note that it takes one thousand to three thousand repetitions to feel comfortable with a new move. And it takes about ten thousand reps to master, or embody, it. Similarly, research by K. Anders Ericsson on deliberate practice[23] suggests that it can take ten thousand hours or more of *deliberate practice* to reach expert status in a given domain.

Are you having a hard time imagining yourself doing something ten thousand times? I get it. But think for a just a moment about how many times you've said yes when you wanted to say no. How many times have you stuffed (or lost control of) your emotions? Apologized when someone bumped into you on the street? Held your breath when you were under a lot of stress? As we say in the dojo, "*You're always practicing something. And what you practice . . . persists.*"

In fact, it actually doesn't take that long to perform ten thousand reps of a habit you're doing unconsciously. Choosing to take on a new set of Daily Practices to support the evolution of your leadership will help you consciously replace your unconscious, unhelpful existing habits with some more helpful, effective practices that align with your present-day goals.

By the time you finish the homework for this chapter, you will have designed (and executed) one or two simple, effective, *custom* embodied practices. These practices will bring your North Star to life—and will keep you at your growing edge this year. By pairing a powerful intention with deliberate practice, you are about to harness the power of your body, mind, and spirit to take your leadership to the next level.

Don't worry too much yet if you're not sure *how* to do this. When you start taking action, you will learn everything you need to know. As I say to my clients, *It's in the "doing of it" that things become truly clear.*

CHOOSING YOUR PRACTICE

Now that you've created a draft of your North Star—a commitment to a possible future you—your next step is to pair it with additional Daily Practices that align precisely with your intent. These practices will support you to *embody* your North Star, by making it real in your physical shape, posture, mood, presence, and way of moving through the world. They will also help you teach your body-mind system that it *can* successfully get its old needs met in new ways.

I got my first real taste of the power of Daily Practices in 2008, after getting some pretty tough feedback at work. Around my one-year anniversary at my first consulting job, I was asked to go through an anonymous 360-degree feedback process. Ten colleagues and personal references offered input on my greatest strengths and weakness. Most of their comments didn't surprise me at all. Even at that time, I was pretty self-aware. And when I'm *not* good at something, I'm not shy about owning it.

However, I am also a woman who prides herself on success and has a knack for getting a lot of things done. I had been a straight A student in school, and I was always hungry for my next promotion. When I read through the 360-degree feedback report for the first time, one comment nearly jumped off the page: "LeeAnn can be flaky at times. I don't always trust her to follow through and do what she says she will do."

Yikes.

It took me a while to digest the input. At first, I found my mind racing to figure out who said it, and secretly wondering if they really knew me at all. Then, one by one, I began to write my colleagues off: *Well if it was her, this is why she would have said that, and here's why it isn't true.* There was, however, one person for whom I couldn't find a good way to let myself off the hook: the graduate school professor who had advised me on my master's thesis.

I turned the idea around and around in my head. If *he* said it, then I would want to change. He knew me inside and out. And the more I thought about it, the more I could see *why he might actually have that impression of me.* You see, in my haste to get things done, I often went fast. I was a big-picture gal, and I loved to multitask. And frankly, I had a tendency to miss (or just conveniently ignore) the minor details. If someone was hoping for more precision and micro-level follow-through, there was a good chance my style of leadership would seriously disappoint.

Humbled by the feedback, I decided to take it on. I had just recently learned the jo kata (series of martial arts moves with a long staff) that I mentioned in chapter 7. I decided to put it to the test. Could I improve my attention to detail and follow-through with a physical practice that had nothing to do with work?

As it turned out, the answer was yes.

Using the process you learned in chapter 7, I created a simple declaration: *I am a commitment to mindful completion.* For me, that meant paying attention to details, keeping my word, and seeing things through to the end. Then, I committed to practice the same jo kata five times each day, while embodying my North Star. As I executed each of the thirty-one moves, I paid special attention to the endings and transitions. I focused on the detail and accuracy of each move (*much* more than I ever had before, I discovered). And I made sure to finish one movement *completely* before I started the next.

I did this practice every day for several weeks. In some ways, it was excruciating. Without a doubt, it asked me to pay attention in a very different way. What I also saw, however, was that practicing that level of attentiveness quickly started to impact the quality of my delivery back at work. While none of my colleagues knew what I was doing in my spare time, I started to receive very different feedback.

Anyone who knows me today might actually be surprised by this story. In fact, I was recently invited by one of my teachers to support an event she was hosting precisely *because of* my powerful attention to detail. When that happens today, I laugh to myself.

Another example of the power of practice.

As a result of my commitment to mindful completion, I have been able to build a reliable consulting business, show up for my clients, and even finish writing this book. I will offer a few more examples in the next section. But you may already have enough data to take the first step: *choosing your first practice.*

How do you know what kind of practice to choose? The truth is, it's up to you. In my story, I chose the jo kata practice because 1) I already knew how to do it, 2) it was compact enough that I could complete it in about fifteen minutes, and 3) I could imagine ways in which the kind of presence I wanted to practice could be applied to the moves in the kata.

In the Practice section of this chapter, I introduce a wide variety of different kinds of practices for inspiration. Here are just a few:

- Ten minutes of basic yoga postures
- Fifteen minutes of dancing to music
- Going over my celebrations for the day in my mind
- Doing an activity you typically dislike (e.g., vacuuming) for ten minutes, with a positive intention
- Listening to a specially crafted playlist on your drive home from work
- Releasing anger for five minutes by punching a pillow
- Chanting a favorite yogic mantra or singing a prayer song each night before bed
- Walking from your house (or car) into the office with intention

Of course, the possibilities are endless. That said, it's a good idea to choose an activity that you would be willing and able to do regularly. It's also useful to choose one that is related *in some way* to your declaration.

For example, if your North Star is asking you to become more flexible and cooperative at work, a ten-minute yoga practice might be an interesting fit. Alternatively, if your North Star is about developing more self-respect, you could do ten minutes of yoga while connecting with the bodily sensation of self-respect while you move.

Let's say that in order to embody your North Star, you know you will need to slow down and listen more. In that case, you could choose *any* type

THE SCIENCE: POWER POSING

Your body language not only impacts how others view you . . . it impacts the way that you feel inside, claims Harvard Business School professor Amy Cuddy. Cuddy's 2012 TED Talk entitled "Your Body Language Shapes Who You Are" has received over fifty-two million views to date. In it, she identifies a number of "high-power positions" and "low-power positions" that mirror the expressions of dominance animals make in the wild. Cuddy's research has shown that standing or sitting in a high-power position for as little as two minutes can lead to an increase in testosterone, a decrease in cortisol, and a feeling of increased confidence in research participants. What's more, in a mock job interview protocol, participants who stood in high-power positions were judged by interviewers as more competent and were more likely to "get the job."

According to Cuddy, body language is not just about doing the right thing in order to influence those around you. Her research suggests that your posture actually changes your inner experience—your emotions, physiological sensations, and self-perceptions—leading you to connect with a different version of yourself. Given that power can be a difficult thing to come by, depending on one's gender, race, and social class, Amy's work offers a needed and accessible path toward change that can be practiced by anyone with a desire to learn.

Meanwhile, practitioners in the field of somatics and other body-based mindfulness studies have demonstrated similar results in private practice for more than forty years. Dr. Richard Strozzi-Heckler, founder of the Strozzi Institute and Two Rock Aikido Dojo, drew from these disciplines to develop a series of martial arts-based practices that help leaders become a more grounded, centered, and powerful version of themselves. His book *The Leadership Dojo* offers a basic introduction to the methodology.

Amy J. C. Cuddy, "Your Body Language Shapes Who You Are," filmed June 2012 in Edinburgh, Scotland, TED video, 20:36, https://www.ted.com/talks/amy_cuddy_your_body_language_shapes_who_you_are.

D. R. Carney, J. C. Cuddy, and A. J. Yap, "Power Posing: Brief Nonverbal Displays Affect Neuroendocrine Levels and Risk Tolerance," *Psychological Science* 21, no. 10 (2010): 1363–1367.

R. Strozzi-Heckler, *The Leadership Dojo: Build your foundation as an exemplary leader* (Berkeley:Frogg Ltd., 2007).

of physical movement you regularly do and practice doing it slower and more mindfully. Or let's say you have decided that core strength is one of the main Qualities connected to your declaration. Perhaps working with a favorite Pilates or kickboxing video would make sense.

Are you starting to get the picture?

Let's begin with some reflection on your new practice. Don't worry if you don't nail it down right away—like the North Star, your practice can also be changed or refined later, as needed. At this stage, you also don't need to know exactly *how* to integrate your North Star. We'll come back to that in the next section. Just trust your gut and pick one or two practices that you intuitively feel might relate.

Ideally, I recommend picking practices that you already know you will enjoy doing or at least feel excited to try out—so that you can get in those first one thousand without too much strain!

Choosing Your Practice: Reflection Questions

- Considering your Core Dilemma (the one thing most needed to shift to become a more conscious leader), and the emotions, sensations, and behavior that go hand-in-hand with your North Star, what kinds of practices do you suspect might be a good fit? Why?
- What are one or two Daily Practices you'd like to try out over the next few weeks?
- Describe the skeleton of the practice clearly and precisely: what, where, when, how long, etc. (Again, don't worry about how to pair it with your declaration. Just make some tentative decisions about the basic structure of your practice at this stage.)

PAIRING YOUR PRACTICE AND YOUR NORTH STAR

Now that you have a practice in mind, it's time to pair it with your declaration. I'll give you all the details you need in a moment, but first, let's talk about *why*.

What I've found over the past decade coaching women and leaders is that the *intention* behind your practice matters. As we saw in chapter 1, if you go to the gym with a secret intention to punish yourself for last night's ice cream sundae, you will have a very different experience than the woman who exercises in order to fall in love with her body again. The same is true for our Daily Practices.

Even the simplest practice, like finding neutral, can be incredibly powerful. But it isn't the action alone that makes it so. Think for a moment about the basic centering practice we did in the last chapter. Mechanically, you are shifting your body into a tall, grounded, and open posture. Why? You are doing it *for the sake of* bringing yourself back to a more balanced and accessible state. Shifting to this state makes it easier to take other meaningful actions that you care about. And when you do it regularly, it becomes easier and easier to return to this state.

In contrast, a ballet dancer might shift her body into a tall, lengthy posture for a very different reason—to look beautiful on stage, to control her presence, to transmit a sense of dignity, or to hold a solid frame when her partner lifts her off the ground. She may or may not feel relaxed and accessible. (In my personal experience as a young dancer, I remember feeling quite the opposite!)

As these examples suggest, the power of the Daily Practice lies in the *combination* of your action and intention. Your level of dedication—or regularity—also matters. In summary, a powerful Daily Practice involves doing a simple, repetitive activity on a regular basis, *for the sake of* something you want or care deeply about. When all three elements are in place, the magic truly begins.

When it comes to evolving your leadership by choice, this triad opens up a world of possibility. For any existing Quality you'd like to change about yourself, or any new Quality you'd like to embody in your leadership, you can set a strong intention and create a simple daily practice to support you. Whether you're already a wildly successful leader, or you feel something is missing in your leadership, you can apply this tool to evoke your next level.

When I first met my client Tara, she might have put herself in the latter category. In fact, she had achieved a ton of success as a research scientist at a prestigious university, yet she felt she was in a mid-career slump. Tara had a nagging suspicion that something more was possible, and she wanted to explore it. Her research in the health care field had the potential to support policies for patient advocacy. Yet she lacked the courage to pursue a project that would connect her directly with patient groups.

Tara created a North Star that helped her lean into her next level: *I am a commitment to having a voice.* (This was both meaningful to her personally and also related to the way she hoped to support patients.) In her Daily Practice, Tara discovered an important new Quality: *kind-but-strong.*

She realized that her typical MO was to be "nice." And Tara was tired of being nice. For Tara, embodying *kind-but-strong* involved sitting up straighter, feeling calmer and fuller, with eyes straight forward and a touch of fierceness. She imagined her voice coming up from her belly, and felt her throat open.

Through her Daily Practice, Tara began to develop a comfort with her own self-advocacy, negotiating a 20 percent pay raise, and taking a stand for the official recognition of an underacknowledged committee she'd been chairing with great success. She also decided to pursue a larger and more prestigious grant than she'd had the guts to apply for the year before. *Kind-but-strong* had a powerful impact on her leadership. In fact, it helped her "catch up" on accolades and career opportunities she should have received earlier in her career.

For my client Megan, the path was a lot less obvious. Megan was a high-potential millennial powerhouse, working in a Fortune 500 company in the field of sustainability. She had already racked up a string of successes in her short time in the workforce. She had a great relationship with her boss, and she loved her work. On paper, Megan was all set. Megan decided to hire a coach because she was forward-thinking in spirit, and she wanted to preemptively shift any questionable unconscious habits now, lest they become bigger liabilities later in her career.

Megan had a secret, though: underneath her confidence and visible high performance, she also dealt with anxiety on a daily basis (her Core Dilemma). Megan's North Star was about *releasing the anxiety and changing the world by inspiring others.* At first, it was hard for her to imagine what Quality she could practice that would help her embody her declaration. It seemed like a pretty tall order! But when she did the basic centering practice and asked her body for guidance, her body didn't disappoint. Quickly, she imagined herself as a massive old-growth tree, with roots going deep into the ground. She could sense the solidness and stability in her body. She felt resourced and nourished by the earth.

Megan realized that a tree didn't need to worry at all—it could always trust that it would receive what it needed from the earth itself. She decided to bring the Quality and presence of the tree into her Daily Practice. Given her line of work, it made perfect sense and felt totally inspiring. A few weeks later, when giving a presentation to a large audience, Megan found that her tree Quality practice came in handy, helping her to slow down and connect deeply with her audience while easing the stage fright.

I hope these examples have provided some clarity—and inspiration—regarding how to pair your North Star with an intentional Daily Practice. Let's shift gears and turn the attention back on you.

If you've already chosen your practice, great! If not, pick something—like walking down the street—that can serve as a placeholder for now. Bring the action to mind now, and we'll do a little "walk-through" together to give you a taste of how it works.

Let's say, for example, that you chose a practice that involves doing fifteen minutes of movement each day. Before you begin to move, see yourself in your mind's eye. Begin to take on the Quality you'd like to embody. Start with the feelings and sensations. Imagine how it would impact your body. Without thinking, allow your physical body and your presence to adjust. There is no right or wrong way to do it. Just try not to think too hard.

Now, begin your practice. While moving, keep returning to that sensation and the physical experience it produces in your body. Whether you swim, bike, walk, or dance, allow your primary goal to be *cultivating that Quality in the way you make each move.* Over time, it will become more natural and accessible to you.

Outside of your fifteen-minute practice, you can also make the same adjustments at various points throughout the day. You may be surprised at how quickly it becomes a part of who you are. You may also find that the world begins to respond to your new way of being in positive ways.

Sound inspiring? Let's take a few more minutes to reflect on what's to come.

Pairing Your Practice: Reflection Questions

- Are you willing to commit, for a period of time, to doing a Daily Practice and pairing it with your North Star? If so, why? If not, why not?
- Why is it important to you to embody your North Star right now? What's at stake (at work, at home, in life)?
- What do you imagine you will begin to feel or experience by doing this practice?
- What's your plan to deal with your likely imperfection? What will you do (or not to) to help you stay on the path if you miss a day?

JUST DO IT

You now have just about everything you need to begin practicing. If you feel clear enough to start, I recommend doing your practice for a week *before* you read the Practice section of this chapter. Then, come back to it later for ideas on how to tweak, adjust, or upgrade your initial Daily Practice. If you're not clear yet, and you feel more examples would be helpful, you can check it out first. Just promise not to get overwhelmed. Trust that deep-down, your body *already* knows what to do!

The last thing left to do is *begin*. As you might imagine, it can help to put it on the calendar so you hold it as a real priority—like an appointment

THE SCIENCE: IMPLEMENTING INTENTIONS

To lower the bar on taking a new action without hesitation, New York University psychologists Peter Gollwitzer and Gabriele Oettingen suggest linking your intentions with a critical situational cue: *"If situation X is encountered, then I will perform the goal-directed response Y."* They call these cue-behavior pairs implementation intentions. Their research, based on over a hundred studies, shows that this type of pairing helps to close the gap between setting goals and attaining them, by enabling the brain functions that support automaticity to come online.

Early in the process, when the future cue is selected, the brain creates a mental representation of that situation. This amplifies the brain's tendency to notice the situation when it happens. Deciding in advance *what* you will do in response to a cue forges a mental link between the two. But all if-then pairs are not created equal. According to Gollwitzer and Oettingen, the most effective implementation intentions are those that either dictate an action that *replaces* the original behavior (e.g., If my colleague approaches me with a piece of candy . . . *then I will ask for an apple*) or identify a specific way to ignore the original behavior (e.g., . . . *then I will ignore his offer and continue working*). Implementation intentions that simply negate the original behavior (e.g., . . . *then I won't take the candy*) are significantly less effective.

Peter M. Gollwitzer, "Implementation Intentions: Strong Effects of Simple Plans," *American Psychologist* 54, no. 7 (1999): 493–503.

Peter M. Gollwitzer and Gabriele Oettingen, "Implementation Intentions," in *Encyclopedia of Behavioral Medicine*, vol. 3, eds. M. Gellman and J. R Turner (New York: Springer-Verlag, 2013), 1043–1048.

with yourself. Now, or later when you have your calendar with you, take a moment to add your Daily Practice to your ideal week, and block time in your schedule each day for it. Then, if possible, begin today. Remember that neither your declaration nor practices need to be "right" or "perfect" at the start. Very often, one or the other will evolve as you start doing the practice.

This is usually the point where my savvy clients ask, *And what about those days when I just don't feel like doing it? What if I'm tired or sick or just in a bad mood? Am I really going to be able to show up for my practice every single day?*

Here's my answer: over the years, my Daily Practices have become a place that I come home to. I show up at this place, no matter what my mood, my state of being, my physical health. I don't always do it well or right. And it doesn't matter. It turns out that my practices don't care if I'm perfect, fully present, half checked-out, angry, or half dead. I show up with whatever I've got, and my practices are there to meet me.

The quality of my experience is different every time. When I am tired, my practice slows down. When I have given up on myself, my practice lacks luster. When I am present, I am able to invent new moves that inspire me. When I am anxious about whether or not I am good enough, my practice is wobbly. But the practice is still there, and I still engage.

Is it worth it to do a daily practice—even with such a busy life? For me, the answer is yes, because *it's a daily opportunity to witness myself.* Not to judge, but simply to observe and to know me. In other words, doing a practice isn't about doing it perfectly every time. If anything, it's about *expecting* that it won't be perfect and doing it anyway.

My practice gives me a benchmark of how life is going right at this very moment. I can feel the difference, because I know how it felt yesterday when I was stressed, or last week when I was full of Joy. And because my practice invites me to connect with my body, my practice offers a doorway back into harmony with myself when I've lost my way.

What I have found through practice is that I can access the Qualities I most want to develop while dancing or walking my dog or even doing the dishes. And when those Qualities aren't present, I can choose to tweak something—an attitude, a thought, a movement, a physical location—and immediately sense the difference the change creates in me.

As you begin to experiment with your own Daily Practices, I encourage you to show up for yourself regularly, no matter how you are. That said, it's totally okay to miss a few days here and there. If that happens, it doesn't mean you're not committed. It just means you're *human*. Just recommit and come back again tomorrow. One of the biggest traps I've seen is that we never start (or quit too soon!) because we can't do it perfectly.

Be willing to be imperfect, remember why it matters, and you'll be just fine.

I promise.

Just Do It: Reflection Questions

- What time of day will you do your practice (e.g., morning, lunchtime, after work)?
- How long are you willing to commit to your initial Daily Practice research (e.g., one week, three weeks, a month)?
- For how long will you do your Daily Practice each day?
- How will you know it's working? In other words, what will you be feeling, seeing, thinking, doing, etc., that's different than before? You can think of these as measurable results.

The Practice

Since this chapter is *all about* practice, your instructions are already built into the sections above. Your mission, should you choose to accept it, is to design one custom daily practice and begin practicing regularly, starting immediately.

In case you're still having trouble choosing, I've included a list of different *kinds of practices* below. You will also find more resources on the *Guts and Grace* book webpage (www.gutsandgrace.com/book-resources/). While it can be tempting to approach these resources *buffet style*, I encourage you to instead treat it more like a *fine dining* experience. If you had to pick just one dish that was *just right for you* in this moment, so that you could savor every single bite and feel totally satisfied, what would you choose?

Rather than worrying about making the wrong choice or suffering from FOMO (fear of missing out), I challenge you to trust your gut and make a powerful, definitive choice. They all work. I promise.

PRACTICE 1: IMPLEMENTING YOUR DAILY PRACTICE

For easy reference, here's a shorthand summary of how to design and implement your Daily Practice this week. Deeper instructions are peppered throughout the text of this chapter.

Step 1: Take Note of Your North Star. Write it down or speak it out loud a few times before you choose (and do) your practice, as a reminder of what matters most. Also, remember your key Qualities.

Step 2: Choose One Daily Practice for This Week. Review your notes from this chapter—if you already have an idea about the right Daily Practice for you, you're done! If not, spend some time now to choose.

Step 3: Calendar It! It ain't gonna happen if you don't put it in your calendar. I recommend digging up your work from chapter 2 and looking at the big picture: *How can this practice fit into your ideal week? Are there global adjustments you will need to make?* Make them.

Step 4: Commit and Execute. Decide on your timeline. Will you do this practice for one week? Three weeks? A month? If you're worried you won't stick with it, consider starting with *one week*. Do the practice as many days as possible. Then, if the practice still feels like the right fit, commit to another two weeks. If not, adjust something and try again.

ACTIVE INGREDIENTS	when–then commitment, body-based learning, ten thousand repetitions
WHY IT WORKS	This practice operationalizes your North Star. Through regular practice you are bringing your commitment, and the Qualities you need (and want) to embody, to life.

Kinds of Practices: The List

If you want to begin a Daily Practice but you're not sure where to start, read through the examples below and choose one or two that resonate. Or let it serve as inspiration to create your own. Remember, the goal is to choose something that connects with your North Star.

Embodied (a.k.a. Somatic) Practices: Utilize the shape and movement of your physical body to create shifts in your emotional state and behavior.

- Practicing your new Quality during ten minutes of basic yoga movement
- Happy dancing (or angry dancing) to shift your mood

Meditation/Visualization: Combine physical stillness with a powerful mental intention in order to create a desired state in your body.

- Doing a basic sitting meditation to quiet your mind and emotions
- Visualizing your body's natural healing system defeating diseased cells

Affirmation/Gratitude: Engage the power of your mind to enhance your healing, shift your mood, and create more of what you want to experience in life.

- Speaking an affirmation out loud ten times in front of the mirror
- Writing down your wins, celebrations, or gratitudes before falling asleep

Sound and Voice Healing Practices: Use the transformational power of sound to shift your mood or experience an emotional release.

- Listening to your custom-built playlist on the way home from work
- Speaking or singing your North Star in a tone that embodies your new Quality

"In the Moment" Practices: Choose to replace your typical habits/patterns or reactions "in the moment" *every time the initial trigger comes up.*

- Every time you realize you're giving more than 50 percent, do something for yourself instead.
- Do a basic centering practice when you realize you're stressed.
- Notice each time you say "I need to" and change it to "I want to."

Purpose-Based Practices: Forward your purpose by taking small daily steps toward the work you believe you were meant to do in the world.

- Spend fifteen minutes each evening painting or playing the piano.
- Spend thirty minutes every morning before the kids wake up writing your book.

Note: **You may also uncover some necessary Bold Actions.** As you brainstorm your Daily Practices, another category of actions may come to mind that are more like tasks or one-time to-dos. They may even be big projects, relationship changes, or tough conversations you need to have. We will come back to these a little later in the book. For now, make a list of them in your journal. Call them *Bold Actions.*

A Few More Thoughts

Congrats on designing your first Daily Practice. Enjoy the first week. Rather than strive for perfection, let it be a fun experiment. Remember, you can come back to this chapter to refine your practice at any time—in fact, I hope you will! It may already be clear from my personal stories that this wasn't a tool I used once and then cast aside in favor of the next big thing. Rather, using Daily Practices to support my personal and professional growth has become a way of life for me. My proposal is that these tools could eventually serve you in the same way.

Like I said in the beginning, this book isn't about me giving you a fish.

It's about you learning to fish, so that you can continue crafting your own personal and professional development path over the course of your career. After you've done these activities once, you can then apply them to any domain, any challenge, any big life transition or important career milestone. Your mission this week is to start with what matters *now* and trust that your next steps will become clear in time.

Like many of the tools in this book, Daily Practices will make the most sense when you start to use them. Once you get the hang of it, you will find that you have a powerful reprogramming tool that can be used anytime, anywhere, and with anyone.

REFLECTIONS ON MY DAILY PRACTICES

- What are you learning from engaging with your Daily Practices this week?
- Having done the practice a few times now, what surprises you?
- Compared to your hunches before you began the practice, what do you *now* see about why it's worth it to engage in a Daily Practice? What benefits have you been receiving?

Guts and Grace Playlist Recommendations

"Doin' It Right" – Daft Punk (feat. Panda Bear)

"Make a Change" – Nahko and Medicine for the People (feat. Zella Day)

"You Gotta Be" – Des'ree

"Crystalize" – Lindsey Stirling

"Ceiling Can't Hold Us" – Macklemore

"Energy" – The Apples in Stereo

LEADERSHIP MYTH

Somebody other than me knows best. The information my instincts provide is less reliable than expert advice, data, or "fact."

LEADERSHIP TRUTH

Your own body–mind system is incredibly wise. It constantly provides you with helpful information that can improve your well-being and enhance your leadership—IF you are willing to listen.

Chapter 9

THE BODY'S WISDOM

You are your own answer,
Beyond books and seers,
Psychics or doctors.
Beyond the strength that comes
From what you have accomplished.
Your weakness is as valuable as your strength;
Your helplessness as lovable as your charm.

—JAMES KAVANAUGH

LEARNING TO LISTEN AGAIN

Are you ready to take your relationship with your body and intuition to the next level?

When I first started teaching the year-long women's program that eventually gave rise to this book, I used to begin with a deep-dive lesson on the power and wisdom of the human body. Unfortunately, I found that it ended up being "too much too fast" for most of my clients, who had no prior experience with embodied leadership. Over time, I eventually moved a number of these teachings to the *middle* of the course, so that my clients would *already* have powerful examples and relevant breakthroughs to reference in order to make this section more digestible.

Given that, you may find yourself wishing you'd learned some of these tools *weeks* ago. If so, I encourage you to trust that everything is happing in right timing. My hunch is that you'll actually get much more out of what you're about to learn *now* than you would have when you first picked up this book.

Chapter 9 is about deepening your capacity to trust that *your own body* can provide the information you need on your path to personal and professional transformation. The tools in this chapter run the gamut in application, from highly personal contexts (individual decisions about your health and medical treatment) to concrete, professional contexts (decisions about career changes, business deals, and financial investments). My aim is to give you a deeper layer of education—and a lot of food for thought—about the ways that your body can (and should!) become a reliable and trusted *partner* in your leadership.

Here's why: for many successful women, it can feel critically important to make the "right" next decisions in life. This is especially true when it comes to bigger career moves. Yet this begs the question: *how do you actually know what's "right" for you?* Likewise, many women who struggle to effectively juggle their work and their well-being (a.k.a. the proverbial "work–life balance" problem) are looking for an answer—like a magic bullet—to the question, "How can I have it all?" But again, this begs the question, *What is "it all"? And how will you know when you have it?*

Whether we're aware of it or not, many of us habitually look *outside of ourselves* for answers to questions like these. We secretly believe that *the experts have the answers*—and that all we need to do is figure out *which* expert to ask. This is yet another leadership myth: ***Somebody other than me knows best. The information my instincts provide is less reliable than expert advice, data, or "fact."***

If you're not sure whether you relate to this statement, check in with yourself. Do you watch the news? Buy fashion, or health, or business trade magazines? Do you run Google searches for medical advice? Get second and third opinions? Call your friends for career or financial advice? Consult a mentor about critical business deals?

These actions are not *bad*. Indeed, they can be wise choices, especially when you're operating in a field that is new or unfamiliar to you. But there is also a risk—a big one. Buying into this myth can also preclude taking stock of your intuition or listening to your own deeper wisdom (a.k.a. trusting your gut). And *that* can come with some *huge* costs—including losing access to your own instincts—and even your ability to innovate—altogether.

The truth is: ***your own body–mind system is incredibly wise. It constantly provides you with helpful information that can improve your well-being and enhance your leadership—IF you are willing to listen.*** In fact, your body's wisdom holds the keys to your healing, your most effective, compelling communication, *and* your purpose. While it doesn't always speak in words, it can be even more effective than logic at solving your most challenging problems. As in the excerpt from James Kavanaugh's poem above, *"you are your own answer."*

In this chapter, you will learn to listen to it again. Our practices will focus on accepting your body as a reliable source of information when it comes to important decisions and actions. We will explore how to trust yourself more deeply and take both "expert opinions" and "cultural norms" with a grain of salt. We will also explore the common traps of poor decision-making and how to avoid them. As always, my goal is to help you learn how to fish for yourself, so that you can chart your own unique course as a conscious, thriving, and sustainable leader.

It starts with *trusting your gut* . . .

TRUSTING YOUR GUT

If there's one thing I most want to say to kick off this section, it's that *the "experts" don't always know best.*

How do I know? I used to be one.

Well, sort of. Let me explain. As a PhD student and researcher in the field of personality psychology at the University of Illinois Urbana-Champaign, I was on the path to making a career out of publishing scientific research. To this day, I still place a lot of value on good science. Yet spending a few years in the shoes (and lab meetings) of the "experts" was enough to confirm my suspicion: they are just people—like you and me—with opinions that might be wrong, who make mistakes (and sometimes cover them up to save face), and who (unfortunately) sometimes have agendas fueled by "looking good" and "getting ahead." Just like we all do.

In other words, "the experts" are human beings *just like you.*

During that phase of my life, I also learned that good research—the kind that eventually informs major policies and turns industries on their heads—is often born of a *hunch*. In other words, it's the *gut instinct* of these so-called experts that guide them to analyze the data a different way, ask a new kind of question, and even go down the long road of collecting piles of scientific data in the first place.

Just like you, the experts have ideas that sometimes show up out of the blue. Just like you, they sometimes make mistakes that have consequences. Just like you, they sometimes miss critical evidence that leads them down a circuitous path. And just like you, they sometimes worry that they've got it wrong.

I tell you this because I believe it can be a *big mistake* to give all of your power away to the experts in any field. What do I mean by "give your power away"? For example, have you ever had an intuition about something you needed but went to ask someone else about their opinion before you took action? Has the other person's opinion ever swayed you to change your mind? And have you ever realized in the end that, in fact, your first instinct about the situation may have been the right one?

That's what I mean by "give your power away."

This kind of thing happens all the time. In fact, the very *foundation* of the patriarchy rests on the premise that there are *some* experts (mostly men) who have the only right answers about how things *should* be done. They are right because of science, right because of political power, right because of their family status or social class, right because they were born, and right because God says so (i.e., their religion).

Indeed, this is one of the primary reasons I teach an embodied leadership curriculum *specifically* designed for women. While many of these tools are useful for men in leadership, they are built and curated to serve as keys that unlock what's been locked down for several thousand years of human history. I call this process "dismantling the patriarchy *within*."

In order for a woman to become a fully conscious, sustainable, and thriving leader, she must understand how these forces are working on her—not just from the outside but *on the inside*. In order to do that, she must 1) be able to detect when *what she personally knows* differs from *what the experts say*, and 2) have the confidence to listen to herself in order to challenge the status quo when necessary.

This kind of confidence, when embodied by a visionary woman who cares about people and the planet, can open the door for her to make innovative breakthroughs in social and technological challenges. It can enable her to risk designing new systems and policies and even steward the healing of global conflict. When she trusts her own knowing even more deeply than what the "experts" say, she can muster the courage to follow it, even when nobody else hears the call.

This may sound grandiose, but the practice itself starts at home. It plays out in small and mundane situations. It takes root in your relationship with your own body. It becomes a habit in the daily moments when you choose—or decline—to trust your instincts and take action on behalf of your knowing.

Some of the most powerful mundane examples I've come across fall into the category of health and well-being. Because we all have physical bodies, and most of us do care about our health, this domain can be a unifier. Therefore, I want to dedicate some attention to the practice of *trusting your gut* in the medical context.

While it may seem a far cry from world peace, the truth is that some of these individuals went on to use the advocacy skills they built in the domain of their physical health to transform their organizations and the lives of people around them. If your health is not currently of concern, feel free to take the examples in the next two sections as metaphors you can apply to any domain. However, if you *are* facing any personal health challenges right now, I encourage you to hold them gently in the back of your mind as you continue to read.

Here are a few brief stories of people I know who have trusted their own intuition and questioned the medical industry, to a positive end:

- *A woman is told her melanoma is incurable and that she has only two months to live. Her doctor didn't want to give false hope. But she believes she is meant to live and to serve the world. She completely stopped the melanoma from spreading using visualization and lived over fifteen years, using what she learned to teach leadership and personal transformation.*
- *A man in his eighties is informed that his test results have come back positive, that disease isn't gone and he needs three more months of treatment. His doctor didn't want to risk letting him go too early, but, in fact, it was a false positive, and his disease was gone. By staying hopeful and committing to his life, he was able to marry the woman of his dreams and serve as a critical mentor for youth in his community.*
- *A woman is told there is no problem in her mouth, that the root canal was successful. Her doctor didn't want to admit a mistake, but the problem persisted. Three different doctors and several surgeries later, the infection was finally under control. Because of her fierce commitment to truth, she was able to get through the challenge. She brings this same dedication to her work, where she takes a stand for her staff as a branch leader in the US Naval Air Systems Command.*

Let's be clear. I am not suggesting that anyone should avoid traditional medical approaches, or mistrust doctors point blank. Nor am I making a case that all (or even most) experts will make recommendations that are wrong for you. Of course, both doctors and other experts provide an immensely valuable service to society and can offer a tremendous amount of support when your health is on the line. They have dedicated their lives to the deep study of their field, and they deserve both respect and appreciation.

My goal, however, *is* to use these examples in order to illustrate a particular kind of moment *that often goes unnoticed*—the moment where the expert's recommendation doesn't sync with the patient's intuition. In other words, the moment when your gut instinct is nagging you to *challenge* or *ask questions* rather than *concede*.

Again, I chose the medical industry as an example because it's one of the places we're most strongly programmed to trust the "experts"—especially in Western society where self-healing practices have mostly been replaced by modern medicine. Of course, these kinds of situations happen *all the time* . . . not just in the relation to "scientific" experts.

For example, you're at the grocery store. You pick up a juicy red apple that calls to you, then hesitate and ask the store clerk which kind of apple is better. He points to the yellow ones. You buy the yellow one, take it home, and take a bite. And you find yourself wishing you'd bought the red one instead.

Yes, it can be that mundane. Even invisible. And yes, it happens that fast. Instead of listening to our bodies—our urges, our hunches, our intuitions—we get worried we won't be "right" and look for external validation. It's human nature—especially today, when piles of information are available at the tip of our fingers. But more information doesn't necessarily lead to the best decisions.

In fact, in his book *The Paradox of Choice*,[24] Swarthmore College psychologist Barry Schwartz exposes this dilemma. Drawing on data from dozens of scientific studies, he demonstrates that the more choices we have, and the harder we try to make the best decision, the less likely we are to be satisfied with our choice in the end. According to Schwartz, the *paradox of choice* is that it doesn't actually make us happy.

But he's one of those experts, right? Yes. And, in some ways, so am I. So don't take our words for it. Instead, take few minutes to check in with your own body's wisdom and intuition about the topic *trusting your gut*.

You can use the following questions to reflect.

Trusting Your Gut: Reflection Questions

- Where, when, and with whom do you tend to "give your power away" when it comes to your physical health, your leadership, or your general thriving?
- What does it feel like in your body when you do so? What are the common tell-tale signs your body gives you to let you know you're not listening?

- Do you listen to these signs in the moment? Why or why not?
- What is one intuition you have *right now* about something that you should or shouldn't do in order become a more conscious, sustainable, and thriving leader, but that you haven't acted on yet? Why haven't you?
- What, if any, conflicting advice have you been given lately? What makes it so compelling?
- Can you remember a time when you really trusted your gut and you were glad you did? Briefly describe how that situation unfolded.

THE LANGUAGE OF THE BODY

"So," you may be thinking, "I'm willing to entertain the idea that the body's wisdom has some critical value to offer. But how do I *know* what it's saying? What *is* the language of the body? And how can I listen when it's talking to me?"

There's no doubt about it: your body has an intuition about what it needs in order for you to thrive. In fact, research suggests that the body even knows how to heal itself—physically, mentally, and emotionally—when given the opportunity. It's what the body is designed to do. In service these goals, your body talks to you every day, all the time. You can reap the benefit of this partnership when you learn to speak its language.

How? One of the body's most common languages is the language of *pleasure* and *pain*. Simple, yes. But elegant. When it doesn't feel good, there's something—physical, emotional, mental, or energetic—to pay closer attention to.

The problem is, this type of communication isn't always *convenient*. We're busy. And it doesn't feel good. And it's hard to understand. So instead of getting curious, we numb the pain by taking another Aspirin and plowing forward with our day. Unfortunately, we might just be missing a critical piece of information. And in the long run, ignoring that information could have some pretty big costs.

One of my mentors once shared a story that stuck with me for a long time. The story was about a man whose foot started speaking to him. "Something's out of alignment," it said. "You spend all day standing up. I'm not getting what I need!" But the guy was one of those important fellows who ran a big business and just didn't have time to waste. So, over time, his ankle started speaking up as well. Then his knee got involved and eventually his hip. Finally, when the whole system was ready to shut down, his low back got involved, laying him out for a week in serious pain.

Any chance you can relate?

Time and time again, I'm reminded that when I get too far ahead of myself and take my body for granted, there are consequences. I've forgotten to listen, and I pay the price. I find that deep down I know the difference between a healthy strain and overdoing it. I might pretend I don't. But really? Deep down I usually have a hunch. Ninety percent of the battle is being willing to listen.

Then what? If it feels good, continue. And if there is pain, "tweak" something. Ask for something. Do something else. Get help. Get curious about what's going on. Sometimes even minor adjustments can make a big difference.

It's easy to imagine how this plays out when it comes to our physical health (which is obviously related to our bodies!). So feel free to start there. But the same practice can be applied when it comes to our work and our personal relationships. Have you ever gotten a headache in a difficult meeting? Or suddenly felt sick to your stomach when your significant other, or one of your kids, looked the other way?

In the health-related stories I shared in the last section, the protagonists listened to their own body's wisdom, challenged the experts, and took a stand for their own inner knowing. In each case, they felt something in their bodies that didn't resonate with the advice they were being given. They asked questions, followed their intuition, and requested more information. In some cases, they got a second and third opinion, until the signals finally made sense. Rather than ignore their bodies, or see them as a nuisance, they were able to partner with their bodies in order to successfully achieve their healing goals.

Outside of the health context, the body gives us messages about what's good for us, what we desire, and what we instinctively know. For example, I've literally experienced a pain in my *gut* at critical life junctures when I needed to make a change. Though it seemed overly simplistic, I remember one moment vividly from an early embodied leadership training. It was the day when I uncovered the North Star I shared with you a few chapters back.

I had innocently asked the trainer about a minor ache in my right abdomen, figuring he (the expert) would be able to tell me what it meant. It was yet another moment where I was navigating the emotional dynamics of a challenging interpersonal relationship. Without hesitating, the trainer simply asked, "What is your gut trying to tell you?" To my surprise, the answer came back quickly and crystal clear: "This cycle has to stop."

With the help of the trainer, I'd successfully translated my body's message of pain into something my brain could understand. I listened, trusted the wisdom in that message, and began to adjust my life accordingly. Thus, my first deeply meaningful North Star—*I am a commitment to healing or ending my toxic relationship by this fall*—was born.

The body's messages can be big. They can even be life-changing. But again, they can also be quite mundane. To demonstrate, let's start with a minor and immediate example.

I'm curious: as you've been reading this section, *what messages has your body been trying to give you?* Check in with yourself *right now.* Notice if your legs are crossed uncomfortably. Are your shoulders tense? And (oh yeah!) are you breathing? If needed, *tweak* something. Adjust something. Sense the difference. That's exactly how this practice works. Although the content of the message *can be* minor, or as critical as life and death, the shift happens in the small mundane, moments where we make the choice to listen.

Now, tune in to your body again. Ask yourself: *is there* ANYTHING ELSE *that is nagging—in my body, mind, or emotions—at this moment?*

If so, take note. Then, make some time later today to journal about what its message might be. Below are a few questions that may help you investigate.

The Language of the Body: Reflection Questions

- When and where do you avoid listening to your body? In what relationships, situations, or activities are you most likely to tune out?
- How, specifically, do you tune out or avoid listening? What is your go-to thought or action in that moment?
- What would it mean for you to reconnect with the wisdom of your body more fully?
- What messages has your body been trying to give you lately, and about what important topics?
- Are you ready to listen? Why, or why not?

THE SCIENCE: THE BODY AS A PARTNER

Does the body *really* matter in business? According to a nine-year longitudinal study conducted at the Cornell University Johnson School of Business, it does. In this study, Alexandra Michel followed investment bankers across their careers to better understand what drives their work habits (e.g., putting in a one-hundred-and-twenty-hour work week), and the resulting costs. Her goal was to examine the beliefs behind the high occurrence of burnout in industries like engineering, consulting, investment banking, and law. According to Michel's research, many investment bankers chose their careers for the high compensation, prestige, and marketability. Early in their careers, they saw their relationship with their bodies as adversarial (e.g., "I didn't want to let my back pain interfere . . ." and "You have to fight the biology . . ."). Over the first four years, they did their best to ignore or control their bodies in order to get ahead at work.

Beginning in year four, many bankers experienced severe bodily breakdowns as a result of their work habits. By year six, 60 percent of these bankers still maintained their antagonistic relationship with their bodies. Eventually, this took an even bigger toll on their health and their careers.

On the other hand, 40 percent of the bankers began to treat their body as a subject rather than an object and use its guidance to make choices about their behavior. These bankers built a relationship with their body by attending to and trusting it. They also became more skilled at negotiating between work demands and the demands of their health. Despite the loss of apparent "control" over their bodies, they were more able to realistically choose behaviors that would sustain their energy and ultimately succeed. Surprisingly, these bankers also displayed fewer performance issues and engaged in more productive, creative leadership behaviors at work.

The researcher's conclusion? When people in high-stakes careers learn to listen to their bodies, it can reduce their propensity toward illness and burnout—while improving their ethics, judgment, and creativity at work.

Alexandra Michel, "Transcending Socialization: A Nine-Year Ethnography of the Body's Role in Organizational Control and Knowledge Workers' Transformation," *Administrative Science Quarterly* 56, no. 3 (2011): 325–368.

THREE DECISION TRAPS

Are you starting to believe that this stuff could make a difference?

If so, keep reading. And if not . . . keep reading. We're going to shift gears from the medical domain now and take a look at three major Decision

Traps that have the power to derail your leadership. We'll also explore how to harvest the power of your body's wisdom to avoid these traps and make better, faster, cleaner choices at work.

For my client Jackie, learning about the Three Decision Traps was a total game changer. I met Jackie when she was deciding about whether or not to go back to school for her MBA—again. Ten years into her career, Jackie was feeling stuck. Her leadership potential at her company had capped out when the next possible rung on the ladder was her boss's job. And he wasn't going *anywhere*. On the surface, she was functioning just fine. But deep down, she felt depressed.

It was a big decision for Jackie to hire a coach. She debated and debated. How will I know if it will really be worth it? Will I get the value I'm investing? Are there other coaches that are cheaper? More experienced? A better fit? Should I just go back to school instead? Which strategy would work best? How could she guarantee her success? As is often the case, Jackie's biggest opportunity for growth was the very thing that made it difficult for her to take the leap. The struggles with indecision that had her second-guess our coaching relationship *also* had her second-guessing her need to start looking for a new job with greater upward mobility, despite the boredom and frustration she felt every day.

After learning about the Three Decision Traps, Jackie made a commitment to *trust her gut*. Quickly, we found that she actually had a *very strong* intuition and a knack for innovation that had been lying dormant underneath her dominant logical mind. And that made sense. Jackie had built a successful career in the financial industry. In that role, her skill with numbers, data, and logic had become her claim to fame. What got lost, however, was the deeper thread of her leadership purpose. At heart, Jackie had the spirit of an innovative, instinct-driven entrepreneur. When she allowed herself to trust her gut, she was able to use it as a compass. This enabled her to start moving toward new work that would utilize all of her strengths and genuinely light her up.

As it should be. When something feels deeply off, it usually is. When the going feels easy and hopeful, it usually is. Though the mind is an incredibly powerful tool, it can also tend to overcomplicate things. As in Jackie's case, this can play out in the context of major life decisions. But when you boil it down to its most mundane form, it's really about the simple choices you make day to day. In fact, I'd make the case that it applies at even the tiniest of choice points.

For example, in your yoga class, the instructor demonstrates a difficult stretch. You observe and feel inspired. Then you begin to organize your body into that posture, but it *hurts*! You notice if you bend your knees slightly, the stretch feels great. But you're worried what your classmates will think of you—so you choose not to modify the stretch.

Or you are hungry and decide to go out for lunch. You see a chicken salad on the menu and remember the last time you ate something like that, you felt great for the rest of the day. But you notice it costs twice as much as a hamburger. You think about your dwindling financial resources and order the hamburger.

In both cases, your gut sense of "how it feels" conflicted with another line of thought. These kinds of choice points present themselves all day long. The following are the three most common unconscious responses I see my clients make, both at home and at work. These responses, which I call the *Three Decision Traps*, throw you off the path of least resistance and disrupt your connection with the natural flow of abundance.

Trap 1: Thinking It Through. Human beings think a lot. We gather the data. Look at the pros and cons. Make a list of all the reasons why this choice is better than that one. Don't tell me you've never done it! We learn at a young age that our brains are our biggest assets, and we use them excessively.

In a research study on decision-making, customers who purchased stereos at Best Buy were asked about how they made their choice. Those who tested one stereo, liked it, and purchased it on the spot were *most* likely to enjoy their purchase. Those who compared a lot of stereos, paid close attention to small differences in volume, sound quality, battery life, etc., were more likely to either return them or report dissatisfaction in the end. The moral of the story? The extra information doesn't necessarily improve your quality of life!

Trap 2: I Really Should (a.k.a. The IRS). You know the feeling: *I so don't want to do this, but . . . "I really should."* And you do. And sometimes you do it even if it makes you miserable. When we act out of obligation, we feel *responsible*. Not a bad thing, on the surface. Yet many of us are pre-programmed to take on responsibility *even when it doesn't feel right*. If it was really the right course of action, *wouldn't it feel right at a gut level too?* In other words, there's a difference between a genuine obligation that matters to you (which feels good even in your gut), and a distracting IRS (I really should) that throws you off course.

For example: You feel an obligation to visit your aging mother. You'd rather be golfing, but deep inside you know it's the right thing to do. Although it seems like a drag at first, you enjoy the visit and feel good in the end. Versus: Every time you call your friend, she gets angry with you for not calling sooner. The conversation always goes downhill fast. But you feel an obligation to keep calling because you are a *responsible* friend. Each time you hang up the phone, you feel bad. But you call again a few weeks later and do it again.

What if you went with your gut and based your next decision on *how it feels*? In the first case, your gut may be telling you that seeing your mother matters deeply to you. In the second case, your gut may be telling you it's time to put a little space between you and your friend and let go of the hope that she will change—at least for now.

Trap 3: How It Looks "On Paper." This trap is all about *looking good*. We want to be impressive. If we let ourselves be really honest . . . we may even want to be seen as *the best*. We get the right degrees and certifications. We wear the right clothes, go to the right events, and choose the right business partner (or romantic partner!) who has the right credentials. We polish our marketing materials. We drop names.

Have you ever made a decision based on how well it would fit into the image of who you wanted to be? Or based on how impressive the other person seems at first glance? I hate to admit it, but I certainly have. The problem with this strategy seems obvious: what we get from our choices doesn't necessarily correlate with what we genuinely need. So why do we do it so often? I think the *real* problem with this strategy is that it's nearly *invisible* to us in the moment. It feels true, right, and real. We get pulled in. And the benefits of this approach can be huge. Fame. Fortune. Recognition. Praise. Loud flashy benefits that distract from the little voice in the background whispering, *Something isn't quite right here.*

The other problem with this strategy is: it can take *years* to realize that what looked good "on paper" wasn't really what most mattered in the end.

Do any of these three traps sound familiar? If so, you're not alone.

These three common "mistakes" illustrate the ways we human beings act when we're out of alignment with our deeper knowing. In contrast, there are *other* moments when things are just different. In these moments, we're on the path, in flow, and the stars seem to align.

When I think about the times in my life when things were going very well, I am aware that I was doing something quite different. I was not questioning my instincts. I was not spending long hours thinking about the right course of action. I was not calling the experts. I was not frantically weighing pros and cons. And I was definitely not feeling as though it would take mustering all of my strength to push a giant boulder up a hill in order to finally "get somewhere." Rather, I was listening to my gut. And life was easier.

Not only was it easier . . . but *it felt good*!

Though it may sound like magic, this kind of listening and flow is accessible to every*body*. Think for a moment about the last time you found yourself in a state of flow and ease. Maybe it was just for a few minutes or a few hours. Maybe it was a single day. Take a pause here and try to remember what was *different that time*. Focus on determining which of your actions and sensations (rather than what other people were doing at that time) might have been the cause.

Below are a few questions to help you brainstorm.

Three Decision Traps: Reflection Questions

- Describe a recent time when your gut feeling *was* aligned with your actions. What happened and how did it feel? What were you doing that was special or different than usual?
- Now, describe a recent time when your gut was in conflict with your other thoughts, and you made a poor choice. What happened?
- Which of the three most common Decision Traps do you fall into most often? What typically happens?
- What are your fears about listening to your own intuition and trusting your body's wisdom when it comes to the important decisions in your life?
- What do you feel curious or excited about?

The Practice

I hope the examples in the last few sections have provided some inspiration. In brief, your mission this week is to do an experiment: starting in small, low-risk situations, try listening to your body and basing more of your decisions on your gut instinct. Of course, the long-term goal isn't for you to stop thinking. We're not aiming to replace your powerful, logical mind with intuition. Rather, these practices below will help you cultivate your ability to access your intuition on demand, so that you can *choose* to use it when it makes sense. Like many of the other practices you have been learning, these tools will *expand your range of competencies* as a leader and ultimately give you more options in the heat of the moment.

In case you're not sure how to begin, I've included descriptions for two concrete (simple but not easy) practices below. The first will improve your ability to listen to the sensations in your body. The second is about letting go of one of the Three Decision Traps you just learned. Don't think about it too hard. Just pick one and dive in. Your North Star may also provide some guidance on *which* practice to choose, and why.

Remember, "First thought, best thought." That approach may open doors where you least expect to find them.

PRACTICE 1: TRUSTING YOUR GUT

Option 1: In Your Regular Movement Routine. As you go about your regular daily movement or exercise routine, take an intention to regularly connect with the "brain" in your gut. Physically, practice dropping your weight to just below your navel and shifting your attention there as you walk. Notice when you're pitching forward, in a hurry to get to your next destination. Notice, too, when your energy and your shoulders have risen up around your ears, instigated by the stress of day-to-day life. Drop back down into yourself. Imagine your hips are gliding forward on a smooth track, while your upper body is simply, effortlessly going along for the ride. Imagine that your hips are in charge of your decisions. Or simply feel that you are guided by your gut.

Option 2: In Life. In life, practice bypassing your thinking mind and letting your actions be guided directly by your inner gut voice. If you made that commitment today, what behaviors would you stop? What would you start? What would you continue? How would you remind yourself to check in with your body for its input on a regular basis? Take a few notes on your typical habits. Then, make a decision to try something different for one week and put it into action.

ACTIVE INGREDIENTS	body scanning, self-observation, commitment, in-the-moment practice
WHY IT WORKS	Most of our decisions to bypass our gut-level knowing are made unconsciously. This practice reconnects you with your body's wisdom and builds your self-awareness, opening new choices in the moment.

PRACTICE 2: TRACKING THE THREE DECISION TRAPS

Take a look at your notes from the Three Decision Traps reflection questions. Which one do you fall into most often? Make a commitment to stop doing that, cold turkey, this week. Then, pay attention to your decision-making process closely for seven consecutive days. As in earlier chapters, the goal is *not* to beat yourself up. Nor is the goal to do this perfectly. The goal is simply to stay committed even when you fall off the wagon.

Most women find that the simple act of making the commitment will heighten their awareness, allowing them learn *a lot* about their unconscious habits when it comes to decision-making. This data is invaluable! When you know when, why, and how often you fall into a thinking trap, you're much more able—and likely—to successfully incorporate a new Trust Your Gut practice.

ACTIVE INGREDIENTS	commitment to stop, self-awareness, curiosity
WHY IT WORKS	This practice creates an opportunity for your brain to produce creative new responses (and new neural pathways) by taking its habitual response off the table.

The last thing I want to leave you with is this: *have fun.*

Believe it or not, I spent the better part of my life as a super-logical and -intellectual human being whose brain pretty much always worked overtime. When I started trusting my gut, what I found was that my life got a lot *easier and more enjoyable.* I stopped talking myself out of all the stuff I knew, dreamed of, felt, and wanted, and I stopped spinning for hours while trying to "figure out" what I ought to do next. Instead, I started deciding more quickly—and finding myself in *flow.*

It can feel good. It can be easier.

And it starts today.

REFLECTIONS ON THE BODY'S WISDOM PRACTICES

- Which practice did you choose this week, and why?
- What are you learning from your experimentation?
- What new actions, behaviors, or approaches are becoming accessible as a result of your practice and that you feel curious or excited about?

Guts and Grace Playlist Recommendations

"Human Nature" – 2Cellos

"Free" – Illumine (feat. Shannon Day)

"100 Years" – Five for Fighting

"Listen" – Goddess Alchemy Project

"Breathe" – Anna Nalick

"Rafiki" – Zap Mama

Inspire

"If you have knowledge, let others light their candles in it."

—MARGARET FULLER

Inspiration is where the rubber meets the road. It's the act of taking what's inside and sharing it with others. What good is your vision if nobody knows that you (or it) exist? When we dare speak up in a way that invites others to stand beside us, we become the catalysts for the changes we wish to see in the world. In this section, I introduce practices that help you become truly generous—rather than stingy—with what you think, feel, see, and know, so that you can inspire others to follow.

LEADERSHIP MYTH

It's hard to find, and live, your purpose.

LEADERSHIP TRUTH

Your purpose is a path. Following it may seem like an unwieldy task, but you're up for it. It's what you feel guided to do, it includes all parts of you, and its backed by grace.

Chapter 10

THE GIFT OF PASSION

Now is the time to know
That all that you do is sacred . . .
Now is the time to understand
That all your ideas of right and wrong
Were just a child's training wheels
To be laid aside, when you can finally live
with veracity, and love.

—HAFIZ

LIVING YOUR LONGING

Do you believe you were born with a unique life purpose? Have you ever worried that you might not fulfill your potential?

In theory, passion and purpose should be exciting topics that energize your leadership and ignite your career path. Instead, many of my clients feel *the most* anxiety in the face of this conversation. Why? Because knowing and living your purpose can feel like a lot of pressure at times.

That's one of the reasons I wait until chapter 10 to bring it up. The other reason is this: until you've done all of the necessarily emotional, mental, and physical clearing to ensure that you know the difference between operating from your Core Dilemma and operating *on path*, it can be tough to tell whether the purpose you *think* the Universe (God, The Mystery, Allah, etc.) has in store for you is *actually* what you were born to do. And the uncertainty can be frustrating.

What I've found is that many traditional leadership training programs take people immediately into the question of purpose, long before they're ripe. The unfortunate cost is that these leaders can end up feeling *behind* in some way rather than feeling right on track. This leads to another leadership myth: ***It's hard to find, and live, your purpose.*** Its symptoms include: I'm supposed to know what it is, but I don't; I know what I'm supposed to do, but I can't seem to make it happen; the resources aren't showing up, the connections haven't appeared, and the money isn't coming. Am I too young? Am I too old?

Just what is it I need to do in order for things to finally click?

You need to know who you are. You need to tune into the mundane. And you need to be ready—as Hafiz says—"to know that all of your ideas of right and wrong were just a child's training wheels, to be laid aside" in order to embrace your true genius.

But the truth is: ***your purpose is a path. Following it may seem like an unwieldy task, but you're up for it. It's what you feel guided to do, it includes all parts of you, and its backed by grace.*** Over the course of your awesome lifetime, you have been acquiring *all of the skills and tools you need* in order to pursue your purpose. And whether you're aware of it or not, you're probably already on the path. My aim in the first part of this book was to help you peel away enough layers—and provide the right kinds of tools—such that you're able to move more quickly, starting now.

In chapter 10 we'll take stock of the ways you've already been *on purpose* every day, since the day you were born. We'll also take a look at how you hide, ignore, stifle, and otherwise run from your purpose, even as it stalks you. You will learn that your purpose is *not* a mystical unicorn—but it *does* often require some tenderness, care, feeding, and even coaxing in order to let you ride it on demand.

If you've spent the last five, ten, twenty, or fifty years wondering about your greater purpose—wishing you knew what it was or lamenting that you haven't quite been able to step into it—that's all about to change. Hold onto your hat and get ready for the ride. The practices in this chapter will incite clarity and help to remove the blocks. On the other hand, if you're one of those magical women who already has 100 percent clarity about what you were put on earth to do, congrats! You've got one thing going easily for you—though I realize that *knowing your purpose* doesn't necessarily mean you've had an easy time living it day to day. I can also relate. While my own purpose is nuanced enough that I didn't step into it at twenty, I've also followed what felt like a very strong thread for as long as I can remember.

Sometimes, having great clarity about your purpose can be *even more* challenging than not knowing. People may not "get it." You may have had to explain it over and over again. You may have heard things like "you're crazy." You may have even believed it. Again, the practices in this chapter can help.

We will look to your body, and your past experiences, for clues. Though you may have tolerated tremendous amounts of personal challenge—in the recent months, in your distant past, or both—you may also find that there's a calling that whispers in your ear, when the voices of fear and doubt are quiet. This chapter is about learning how to tune in to that calling and use it as an inspiration that propels you toward your future. You will harness the power of your strengths and gifts in order to take actions that have a bigger impact on the world. You may also find that you're tapping into a more sustainable source of energy as you make upward-spiral choices that require less push and invite more *grace.*

But you have to allow it.

PERMISSION

A while back, I was sitting in the grass, under a shade tree in Central Philadelphia's Rittenhouse Park. To my right, a man sat under a statue, fiercely playing his guitar. Passersby clapped lightly as he paused between songs to tune up. It wasn't perfect. But it was good. And he was giving it away, there in the park for free, without a second thought. It had me wonder, what does it take for us to give ourselves *permission* to be all of who we are—to shine and to offer our much-needed gifts courageously—to the hungry world?

Unfortunately, many of my talented female clients hold back from sharing their real gifts, genius, and even purpose with others. Surprising, yes. But true. And sometimes, I can relate. It feels like this:

There's a way I keep it locked up tight.

It's mine. And you can have some, *maybe.* If I'm feeling generous. If nobody came along and questioned me today. If nothing has thrown me off my center. And if I'm in *just* the right mood. But that doesn't happen very often. Don't get me wrong, I like to share. So it's not that I don't want to give it to *you*. No . . . it's far more personal than that. It's about me. Not giving it *from* me. Because somewhere along the way, I just might have learned that *giving it* wasn't entirely okay.

When it comes to being fully visible in our greatness, many of us women have experienced pains that now cause us to hold something back. We tell half-truths. We downplay our talent. We perform in our zone of excellence, consciously or unconsciously avoiding our true "zone of genius."[25] I wonder, what would the world be like if we weren't playing this way?

To be honest, I believe that most of us human beings were born with a hunch about our purpose. We knew what we showed up here on Earth to say and do. Then, somewhere along the line, we forgot. *Watch out*, people told us. You'd better not be too sure. Too happy. Too excited. Too loud. Too fulfilled. You'd better not show up as too sexy. Too knowing. Too eager. Too smart. And, consciously or unconsciously, we started to believe them.

You'll see, they admonished (sometimes unknowingly), challenging the childlike parts of us that were born with absolute clarity and zero fear. Unpleasant things can happen when you want something too much. When you show you're too talented. When you let *it* too far out of the bag. And what is "it"?

What is YOUR "it"?

As you make your way through this chapter, I invite you to consider: What is the *it* you were born to embody—to be, do, say, or stand for—that *somewhere along the way* may have gotten a bit lost? What is the *it* that you've been keeping quiet for too long, that is dying to be reclaimed? Is it your fierce nature? Your excitement? Your voice? Your sexuality? Your deep inner knowing? Your bold and natural leadership? Your compassion? Your healing gifts? Your spirituality? Your courage? Your competence? Your commitment to your stakeholders? Your love for the planet? Your dignity? Your true strength?

Even if you've been living a very full and successful life, there may still be a next level for you here. Even if you've already come "out of the closet" about your true passion long ago, I encourage you to check in with your body, heart, and soul one more time. Is there something else? Something you haven't quite been ready to see fully until this moment?

If so, *the time is ripe to pull back the veil and smile.*

As part of our exploration together, I will challenge you to consider taking a chance. Which chance? The one you've been wanting to take for some time.

When my client Natalie dove into this lesson, she was 100 percent clear about the chance she needed to take. She also found it to be 100 percent terrifying. I met Natalie when she was still recovering from some challenges in her personal life that left her quite shy to speak up and be visible at work. But Natalie had a very big vision for her organization, and it was obvious to both of us that her tendency to hide was holding her back.

Natalie was afraid that people would disagree with her ideas and stop inviting her to the table if she spoke up too boldly. But finally, she took the chance to speak about her vision for an evolution of the company-wide workforce development strategy out loud. She spoke it to our community of women. Then to her bosses and mentors. Then to anyone who would listen. This led to a promotion that included both the support and the budget to tackle the project head on. She was invited to solve the problem for a much larger division and eventually build a model that could be replicated by other teams across the organization.

Natalie's vision was big enough to propel her out of hiding. With a few nudges and some powerful encouragement from her peers, she finally gave herself permission to make a massive impact. And, as with any powerful declaration, she found that *Providence moved too.*[26]

Like Natalie, I dare you to ask yourself the question, *If I weren't afraid of the repercussions, what would I . . . say? Do? Risk? Buy? Ask for? Pursue? Let myself become?* You may also ask, *What do I long for?* These are questions for your intuition, so you can draw upon tools you've been learning up to this point. Feel your body as you ask. Pay attention to your sensations and emotions. Notice if something lights up. Encourage it. Or you may notice that some part of you contracts or pulls away. Invite it to soften.

When an answer does come, speak it out loud to yourself in the mirror—or speak it to the mundane God who fills the room in which you happen to be sitting at this moment. Speak about your *it.* Don't censor. Let *it* roll off your tongue and listen to the sound of your own voice, which may be tentative at first. Then say it again, louder and more confident. *It* is yours.

When you've had your fill, let the sound of your own voice fade away on the breeze and sit in the silence of the state of potential you just created. Can you tolerate the sensation of electric? Are you willing to leave the door open for just a little while?

Are you willing to give yourself *permission*?

Permission: Reflection Questions

- If you weren't afraid of the repercussions, what would you . . . say? Do? Risk? Insist upon? Ask for? Let yourself become?
- What do you secretly long for?
- What is one chance you've been wanting to take that you've been holding back on?
- What is one thing you have always wanted to do with your life, for as long as you can remember, but you have sometimes been hesitant to admit?
- What would you do if you knew you could not fail and the money would definitely come?

WHAT ARE YOU BUILT FOR?

Now that *it's* out of the bag, let's spend a few minutes talking about *purpose*. It's a big little word that gets tossed around in the leadership world regularly . . .

. . . *but what exactly does it mean?*

In order to live a truly fulfilled life, some of us have an inner sense that we'd like to be taking more action "on purpose." In other words, not just doing things at random. But rather, doing things that give us the feeling: *Yes! This is something I was born to do.* From a positive psychology perspective, this may happen when you're fully engaged, using your core strengths.

From an embodied leadership perspective, the simple and profound sense of *bodily resonance* might just be enough to let you know you're on track. (Recall our reflections in chapter 1: *if it feels right, do it again!*) If you've felt this kind of sensation before, you may have already discovered how to use it as a homing device. If you've never felt this before, or you have but you can't yet access it *at will*, then we still have some work to do.

Perhaps, for example, you're not sure you were built for a specific purpose. I can relate. I spent a lot of time resisting the idea, though in a positive way. As an American, and the daughter of baby boomer parents, I grew up hearing "You can be anything you want; you just have to try." Maybe in some ways, under some circumstances, it's true. In theory, I *could* be. From this perspective, "What's your purpose?" can be a pretty big question. Yet I am increasingly aware that I have a package of talents and strengths (as well as weaknesses) that allow me to perform some actions with less effort than others. This is true mentally, but it's also true physically and energetically. This approach offers a simpler, more concrete way to reflect on your purpose.

As a starting point for data collection, let's take a look at your body itself. Not through the eyes of the fashion industry standards of beauty or the fitness industry standards of strength, but rather with a curiosity for *form* and *function*. Form: what particularities do you notice about your body? What's unique? What's interesting? And function: given those characteristics, what's possible? What's easy?

In other words, *what are you built for?*

In order to explore purpose from a unique angle, you can use your physical body as a metaphor for the rest of your life. It's easiest to notice in motion. When you're moving, you can more easily feel and see the type of activity that suits your body's physical form. Think about your natural relationship with movement. While dancing, or doing other movement practices, what do you love? What comes naturally in movement for you? How would you characterize the typical quality of your movement? Are you strong? Flexible? Slow? Agile? Solid?

If you're an athlete, you probably already have some answers. For example, "I'm a sprinter" says a lot about the sort of race you're built to run, bike, or swim. It also may speak volumes about the kind of business you naturally do best—or even the way you typically behave in intimate relationships.

Here's my own example. My physiology is very good at intentionally increasing energy. When I dance, I go into a zone as the music peaks and we ride the wave toward greater intensity. When I cycle, I'm the first one to the top of the hill. At work, I love facilitating group dialogue, where I can ask powerful questions such that the first person's breakthrough leads to another, and then another. In my writing, I enjoy producing short story-bursts that bring about a new idea quickly and leave an open-ended conclusion (hence my love for blogging, which led to the content of this book you now are reading). It took me *honoring* that strength before I could imagine publishing my first full-length book.

This line of reflection may or may not bear obvious fruit at first. Nonetheless, I encourage you to try it out. Sometimes mission-critical puzzle pieces are hidden behind the most unlikely doors. Take a few minutes to explore—through physical movement and metaphor—the question, "*What am I built for?*"

You can use the questions below as a guide.

What Are You Built For? Reflection Questions

- When you ask yourself the question, "What am I built for?" what is the first answer that comes to mind?
- If you think about the way your body loves to move, what metaphors, if any, come to mind that can help you understand your leadership strengths?
- Compared to other people, describe yourself in motion. Try starting with "I tend to be . . ." (*Note:* Judgments like "clumsy" will be less helpful here. See if you can translate them to more neutral observations, like "I move in a lot of directions at once.")
- What is one hidden talent that you really love but are not currently using?
- What do people constantly invite you to do or express gratitude to you for?

THE SCIENCE: SIGNATURE STRENGTHS

Strengths-based leadership assessments have become a popular trend in workforce leadership development. These approaches are simple and appealing: If you're good at something, focus on doing more of that rather than trying to fix weaknesses or change your style all together. While the overall premise of this approach is fantastic (do what you're good at, and what you love!), the approach *can* lead to overly simplistic training interventions that may prevent long-term professional growth.

In their 2011 *Journal of Positive Psychology* paper, Robert Biswas-Diener and his colleagues propose a more dynamic approach to the use of strengths. Citing over twenty years of research, they argue that strengths are not fixed traits that are consistent across all settings and times. Rather, they are *potentials for excellence* that can be cultivated through awareness and effort. They argue that strengths should be used in varying capacities and degrees, depending upon what is called for by the situation. And they explain how personal interests and values interact with strengths, moving a person toward some situations and away from others.

In other words, the pursuit of passion is not as simple as "I have a hammer, so let me go find some nails." Instead of aiming to use your strength "even more" or "becoming even better" at one particular strength, it's important to consider the interaction between your strengths, your passions and interests, and your environment. Discovering *what you're built for* is only the first step.

R. Biswas-Diener, T. B. Kashdan, and G. Mihnas, "A Dynamic Approach to Psychological Strength Development and Intervention," *The Journal of Positive Psychology* 6, no. 2 (2001): 106–118.

IN LOVE OR FEAR

I hope the last two sections have sparked some new insights. Before we go any further, I want to set a standard: this chapter is *not* about discerning everything about your purpose immediately. Rather, it's designed to help you collect raw data that may (in a moment of synthesis or a stroke of insight) lead to a breakthrough in clarity. This is more likely to happen if you don't put too much pressure on yourself. Depending upon your current relationship with purpose, this chapter may also add color, or nuance, to the clarity you already have.

One of the toughest things about coaching women on their purpose is that there's no right (or wrong!) answer about how to find it. That's why I typically teach about *the path*: how to track it, what it looks and feels like, and, of course, what can get in the way.

When I first met my client Hanna, it was obvious that she'd been living just a few degrees off her purpose for over ten years. Right away, she told me about an earlier career in social services. I could hear the sparkle in her voice when she spoke about that work as compared to her current job. It gave me the baseline. I thought to myself, "When Hanna is *on purpose*, she's likely to light up in this way."

As we got to know each other, it also became clear that she had a secret desire and one pretty big roadblock in the way. The roadblock was money—but not how you might think. Hanna was actually pretty good with money and had reason to believe she could wield as much of it as she needed to tackle the low-income housing crisis in her community. But Hanna *also* had a lot of negative beliefs about money, and about people with money, that prevented her from seeing herself as the boss/lady/benefactor she was built to be.

Because she was so afraid of embracing that part of herself, she had literally hidden the road to her purpose just out of her own sight. She felt frustrated about her work and anxious about her next step. Through our brief work together, Hanna got more comfortable with the path and started taking action to get herself back on track. She started to see *universal accessibility in the housing industry* as part of her purpose. As soon as she told me about the new project she was planning to pursue, I could feel the sparkle come back into her voice.

What I've found is that purpose begets flow. On the other hand, resisting purpose is hard work. When we are *on purpose*, we begin to experience a greater sense of ease in our lives. Rather than bumping into walls and feeling stuck, things begin to fall into place more easily. Rather than focusing on what isn't working, we see a path that is before us, and we take each day in stride. With a little bit of intuition and a lot of faith, we are able to walk out onto the invisible bridge that is ours to create, step-by-step.

Of course, declaring that purpose begets ease doesn't necessarily mean that it always comes always come *easily*. In the process of putting the final touches on this book, for example, I bumped square into some *incredibly compelling* limiting beliefs and self-sabotaging behaviors. As I got closer and closer to the doorway of completion, their pull got stronger and stronger. In my case, approaching my purpose can lead me into doubt, fear, and worry about my competence or can even cause me to mistrust others who are trying to help. But fear and resistance can play out in many ways.

Like me, you might actively derail yourself with thoughts and actions that don't make sense. Or, like Hanna, you may feel distracted, off track in your work. You may even feel a sense of anxiety, despite the fact that things are going well. For example, you walk into your first appointment of the day. In the back of your mind, you are rehearsing your performance. In parallel, you begin scanning for friends and foes. Who will judge this idea? Who won't take well to the way I come across? Who might challenge me? At what moment am I likely to feel most embarrassed, and how can I make sure to avoid it?

With all of the internal dialogue, entire segments of the landscape may get missed. A friendly hello. An offering of connection and camaraderie. A caring mentor who wants to support you to grow. Suddenly, you're wrapped up in your thoughts, fears, and protective stances when ultimately what you most crave is an authentic sense of purpose and belonging. In fact, this might just be an indication that you're close to an important doorway.

Here's another example. A few years back I coached a client who habitually talked too much. In fact, it became his overarching reputation. Unfortunately, he was often on the receiving end of eye-rolling and not really listening as a result. In one coaching session, we finally uncovered what was driving him in those moments. His greatest need was *to feel seen and valued for his unique contribution.* In other words, he was longing to feel *on purpose.* When we named it together, we felt both surprised and relieved. Finally, his incessant overcommunication made sense. When he was afraid that this need wouldn't be met, he'd keep talking to ward off the fear, trying and trying again to contribute. The irony, of course, was that his strong desire to contribute left him feeling (and being!) ineffective. It even pushed people away.

I could relate to his struggle. Sometimes the very behaviors that are driven by my longing to contribute are the same ones that sabotage my effectiveness in the moment. When I'm off purpose (or just worried about not fulfilling my potential), I may unconsciously take actions to feel safe or to soothe myself. I may over-effort and end up creating the opposite effect. I may even create a compelling smokescreen that prevents me from seeing an important next step (which also serves as an *excellent* excuse in the case that I should fail).

This is why I approach the topic of purpose with equal parts fierceness and empathy. Real personal growth and professional growth requires us to face into the very opportunities that terrify us and fall in love with the vulnerable stretch. These exciting and challenging situations tend to increase (not decrease!) in frequency and strength the closer we get to our purpose. Progress, then, is not about "fixing ourselves" once and for all. Rather, it's a path that we keep walking moment by moment.

The beauty of life *on purpose* is that it connects us, makes us more effective, and brings out a resonance (or spark) that people gravitate toward. We exude a kind of love—pure passion for what we care about—that helps us know we're on track. And hopefully, it makes the journey feel worthwhile.

Take a moment and reflect on your own dance with love and fear when it comes to sharing your gifts, strengths, and passions at work. Consider *what's been getting in the way* of you finding, or fully living, your purpose.

In Love or Fear: Reflection Questions

- What are your biggest fears about living in alignment with your life purpose (even if you're already doing it)?
- What behaviors do you fall into that end up distancing you from your sense of purpose?
- What behaviors do you engage in that are "look-alikes" to living on purpose but actually throw you off course? What do you do, unintentionally, that gets in the way of you making a genuine contribution in the world?
- What if you weren't afraid? What would it mean to live "on purpose" minute to minute, day to day?
- If you knew you could not fail, and you could be sure that the money would follow, what would you do with the next ten years of your life?

PURPOSE LEAVES BREADCRUMBS

One of the most concise and compelling pieces of writing on purpose and passion that I've ever come across is a short poem called "The Way It Is,"[27] by William Stafford. It begins: *"There's a thread you follow. It goes among / things that change. But it doesn't change. / People wonder about what you are pursuing. / You have to explain about the thread."*

I love this poem mostly because I can relate. For much of my life, "people wonder about what you are pursuing" has felt like both a burden and a blessing from God. As a very young person, I was fiercely committed to both healing and truth—deeply devoted to the body and logic—and the relationship they have with one another. These two essentials have led me down a winding path. The journey has been both terrible and wonderful at the same time.

Having grown up in a small town in Western Pennsylvania where available jobs included teacher, shopkeeper, factory worker, pastor, doctor, lawyer, and a few others I couldn't really understand, I didn't have a lot of adults around who could reflect my essence back to me. Following the thread of purpose wasn't easy. Rather, it felt like the scene in the Indiana Jones movie when the protagonist steps off the edge of a cliff and *trusts* that the bridge will appear. If you're worried that *your* purpose is too complex, too unusual, too subtle, or too hard to find, just know that I get it. I really do.

Today, it's getting easier. While I didn't know how to put all of the pieces in the same sentence at first, I am now clear that I'm built to help unlock the human spirit in people—especially women—of every age, culture, and creed who hold the keys to a more conscious way of living, leading, and doing business. I understand that my role is to serve as a guide—to help people let go of old programming, more deeply trust themselves, and step into the work they were born to do. I see that my purpose is to help humans—including rational humans who excel in business—to remember that the body itself is encoded with the information we need to heal ourselves, embrace each other, and live on the planet in a good way. I know that embodiment, dance, and music are lost languages, not meant for the minority but for the masses. And I get that my work is to help reintroduce those languages to the mainstream.

Yet, before I was able to speak my truths in this way, I was still walking the path. It would have been impossible not to. Each and every step you take leads somewhere. Whether you have 100 percent clarity or not, you are making progress. As long as you don't beat yourself up, or think you're supposed to be clearer, you will be just fine. And if you start paying attention to the sensation of *resonance*—that body-mind *zing!* that happens when you're doing something you're truly built for—you will start to see how the pieces connect.

As it turns out . . . *purpose leaves breadcrumbs.*

One of my favorite stories about purpose comes from the book *The Big Leap.*[28] Author Gay Hendricks describes a counseling practice he set up in

THE SCIENCE: JOB CRAFTING

What happens if your purpose is a far cry from your current work? According to Yale psychologist Amy Wrzesniewski, the *kind* of work you do is less important than the *relationship* you have to your work. Dr. Wrzesniewski studied people whose jobs involved difficult or unsavory manual labor (e.g., building maintenance). She found that some people saw their contribution to be much bigger, and more meaningful, than their job descriptions would suggest. For example, a hospital cleaner saw herself as responsible for helping to heal the patients whose rooms she regularly maintained. She interacted with the patients in meaningful ways and took extra steps to make them happy (e.g., rotating the paintings in front of their beds).

Wrzesniewski calls this approach to work a *Calling Orientation*—a mindset that helps you see every part of your work as a potential contribution to your greater calling. People with a Calling Orientation seek out work that fulfills their need for meaning. But, like the hospital cleaner referenced above, they also consciously practice making their current work as relevant to their calling as possible. This practice, called *Job Crafting*, involves making cognitive changes to the way you perceive your work (e.g., I am a healer vs. I am a cleaner), as well as physical changes to the tasks or structure of your work (e.g., moving paintings as part of tidying the room), in order to experience a greater sense of meaning and purpose—without necessarily changing jobs. People who engage in Job Crafting experience more joy and passion at work.

In other words, if you don't love your current job, but you're not ready to leave yet, there is hope. By making tiny tweaks in your approach, guided by your passion and deeper purpose, you can begin offering your gifts to the world *immediately*.

Amy Wrzesniewski, "Finding Positive Meaning in Work," in *Positive Organizational Scholarship: Foundations of a New Discipline*, eds. K. S. Cameron, J. E. Dutton, and R. E. Quinn (San Francisco: Berrett-Koehler Publishers, 2003), 296–308.

his living room when he was six years old. He invited his family to come for help solving their problems. Though the road to his true calling as a powerful executive coach was winding, that early moment foreshadowed his later calling with surprising accuracy.

In my own story of gifts and passion, I carry a vivid joyful memory of myself at five years old, dancing at a cousin's wedding. I remember thinking, "Don't stop. Just don't stop." I was *sure* that my dancing was making somebody smile and adding to the jubilation, so I kept on doing it for several hours. It wasn't good or bad dancing. It just was me dancing. My goal was to share the Joy. And I was giving it away as a gift to everyone who happened to pass by.

Can you find a single memory from that early time in your life, before self-consciousness had set in? It doesn't have to be a big, important story. Sometimes the most silly or mundane memories work the best. Do you remember what it was like to act, speak, or move without censorship, as though you knew others would delight in your contribution no matter what?

How old were you before you forgot that life is about *giving it away . . . as a gift?* And what might that younger version of yourself have to offer you today?

Purpose Leaves Breadcrumbs: Reflection Questions

- What one or two joyful moments do you remember, like snapshots from your childhood, that stick with you still today?
- In what way might they represent present or future premonitions of your life purpose?
- Think about any difficult experiences you may have endured in your childhood. How might they have set you up with a capacity, skill, or competence that you now give back to others as an adult?
- What gift, desire, talent, idea, or secret hope from your youth would *radically impact your life* if you were to own up to it today?

The Practice

Are you ready for another layer? Below you will find two practices that are designed to help you uncover, or clarify, the Gift of your Passion. *Wherever you are* on the path—from fully activated in your purpose and talents to still trying to convince yourself there *is* some rhyme and reason to your life—these tools can offer a starting point for the next phase of your professional evolution.

In fact, according to my client Jane, these tools were some of the most impactful ones in our year-long engagement. Jane was a fifty-five-year-old self-proclaimed "seeker" who had worked in several industries, volunteered heavily in her community, and fully embraced her love of music as a hobby. She wasn't purpose-starved by any means. Jane actually had a pretty good handle on what she was built for. Yet she found it incredibly helpful to take some time to synthesize what she already knew. And she uncovered some new themes along the way that helped her to plan for her next career move—retirement.

Trust yourself. Enjoy the process. And *make the time*. It's worth it.

PRACTICE 1: RESONANCE

At the start and end of this chapter, I reference a body-based sensation that I call *resonance*. This sensation can be experienced in many ways by different women. Yet it usually has a positive tone and feels good in the body. My first memory of this sensation was the wedding party dance event that I described above. In my body, resonance feels something like a cross between being tickled and running a vibrant, bright white electrical current through my nervous system. I associate the feeling with Joy. But it can happen in tender or serious moments as well. Today I often experience it with my clients, in particular when doing an embodied practice and we're on the verge of a breakthrough.

The Resonance Practice is simple: spend one week tracking your own emotions and bodily sensations for moments when you feel yourself "light up" or feel a "zing!" that might be your version of resonance.

Step 1. Send an intention to track and learn about your version of purpose resonance. Get curious about what sensations might be clues that you're on track.

Step 2. For one week, pay attention to the bodily sensations you experience. In particular, track the moments where you feel something like sparky, a full-bodied yes, a zing, a strangely positive fear, a strong sense of joy, aliveness, or electricity. Write them down. (*Note:* Your sensations may differ, these are examples to get you started.)

Step 3. At the end of the week, review your notes. Are there any common themes? Are there similarities in the situations where you felt that zing? If so, take note.

Step 4. The following week, make an effort to place yourself in a few more of those kinds of situations. Do you feel more *on purpose*?

ACTIVE INGREDIENTS	mindfulness, body scanning, daily note-taking, synthesis
WHY IT WORKS	When you're plugged into purpose, and fully expressing your gifts, your body tends to let you know. Learning to speak its language will help you make more purpose-aligned choices each day.

PRACTICE 2: STALKING YOUR ESSENCE

The *essence word* is another useful way to think about purpose and passion that helps to make it a daily practice. Rather than hold your purpose as something you need or want to fulfill *someday*, what if you held it as the thing you can't help but do *all the time*? In service of their leadership goals, many clients have come up with a *single essence word*, or word combination, that captures their purpose thread. They then use it—and the feelings, thoughts, actions, and sensations that connect with it—to check in every day about how *on purpose* or *off purpose* they feel.

Here are a few examples:

- *Unlock/Open*
- *Awakener*
- *Advocate*
- *Empower*
- *Entrepre-innovator*
- *Truth-teller*

There are three ways to approach your word:

Option 1: Harvest It. If you were able to identify a memorable early-life moment that reminds you of your adult purpose thread, you can look for your essence word in that story. Who were you being, or what were you doing with or for others, at a simple and basic (essential) level? (*Note:* You can find more detailed on-purpose story-writing on the *Guts and Grace* book website, www.gutsandgrace.com/book-resources/.)

Option 2: Stalk It. If you've already done (or are committed to doing) the resonance practice described above, you can use your learnings in step 4 to help crystalize an essence word. What were you doing in the moments when you felt *resonance*? Again, look for the most fundamental way to describe it.

Option 3: Ask for Feedback. This approach works particularly well if you're the type of person who struggles to see the good stuff about yourself. Choose three to five people who know you relatively well. First, ask them about your top three strengths. Then, ask them, *What's the essence of what I bring to any situation, problem, connection, or opportunity?* (You might also choose to ask a few people at work who barely know you. It's surprising how much an almost-stranger can see!)

When you feel that you've gathered enough data, generate a few possibilities. Then, speak each one out loud and observe how they feel in your body. Does it feel exciting? Does it sound like you? Does it even feel a bit outrageous, like "Wow! Could that really be *my* word?" If so, you're probably on the right track.

As a caveat, many of us women have essence words that we've FULLY embodied when doing for *others* but that are also the very things we struggle to do for *ourselves* (e.g., my client who chose the word *empower* is an excellent mentor, coach, and consultant, but she isn't yet skilled at elevating herself in way she elevates others). This doesn't mean it's not your word. In fact, it probably is! This also offers a good indication of the inner work you will need to do in order to more fully step into your purpose.

ACTIVE INGREDIENTS synthesis, self-reflection, personal storytelling, body listening

WHY IT WORKS When you stop thinking about purpose as a place you could get to "someday" and start seeing it as a moment-to-moment experience, it becomes easier to align your actions with your gifts day to day.

I encourage you to have fun with these practices. When you don't put too much pressure on yourself, stalking purpose has the potential to be a Joyful and uplifting experience. Use the time you spend on these activities to truly honor yourself. You are a beautiful, brave, and inspiring woman, and you deserve it!

REFLECTIONS ON THE GIFT OF PASSION PRACTICES

- What are you learning from engaging with the practices this week?
- If you're relatively new to exploring your purpose, what initial insights did you gain this week? What are you *most* curious or excited about going forward?
- If you've been aware of your purpose for some time, what new insights or questions are opening in your mind and heart this week?
- What's one thing you've discovered that you want to spend more time thinking about, or practicing, longer term?

Guts and Grace Playlist Recommendations

"Unwritten" – Natasha Bedingfield
"Standing Outside the Fire" – Garth Brooks
"Money on My Mind" – Sam Smith
"Wonder Woman" – Lion Babe
"Love Letters to God" – Nahko and Medicine for the People (feat. Zella Day)
"Grateful" – Nimo

LEADERSHIP MYTH

Telling the truth will get me in trouble. If I want to succeed, it's better not to speak or ask about new, controversial, or potentially difficult topics.

LEADERSHIP TRUTH

Speaking up—however radically unpopular the topic may be—is the doorway to activate your real potential for impact as a woman and a conscious leader.

Chapter 11

FREEING CONVERSATIONS

What is hope?
It is the pre-sentiment that imagination
is more real and reality is less real than it looks.
It is the hunch that the overwhelming brutality
of facts that oppress and repress us
is not the last word . . .
That the frontiers of the possible are not
determined by the limits of the actual . . .

—RUBEM ALVES

FREEING CONVERSATIONS AND RADICAL TRUTH-TELLING

When your passion finally gets ignited, it can be hard to keep it quiet. On the other hand, it can also be scary as hell to finally tell the truth about what you want, what you dream, and what you love. There is nothing more powerful than a leader who knows what she wants and goes for it. Nonetheless, that first step can still be a doozy—*especially* if it requires you to speak up on an issue where you've held your tongue in the past.

What's left standing between you and embodying the kind of leadership you most desire?

Basically . . . just doing it.

But because we're human beings, and it's hard to do *anything* completely alone, the very first step often involves talking to other people. And, for a wide variety of reasons, *that* may not be easy. Radically telling the truth about what you see, what you want, what you know, or what you believe must be done takes a massive act of courage. This is true in all contexts, but it can be extra confronting in industries where there are very few women in leadership roles.

Depending on your history (both childhood and early career), you may have learned some version of the next leadership myth: ***Telling the truth will get me in trouble. If I want to succeed, it's better not to speak or ask about new, controversial, or potentially difficult topics.*** You may even have some strong, solid evidence to back up your concern. If that's the case, you may still be holding back on a specific action, conversation, or courageous declaration that could ignite your next level of leadership.

Think for a moment about your insights from chapter 11. Think, too, about your North Star. When you imagine yourself diving fully into that vision, do you have any hesitation? For many of us, the voices of our pasts come up at the point just before we begin to take action. They whisper all the reasons it's best to keep on keeping our big mouths shut. And, unfortunately, the more we obey them, the more anxious, resentful, and depleted we become.

That's because if we can *see* it, it's actually our work to do. And the longer we hold back, the farther and farther we move from the thread of our leadership purpose. The truth is: ***speaking up—however radically unpopular the topic may be—is the doorway to activate your real potential for impact as a woman and a conscious leader.*** It's also the doorway to deeper relationships, more authentic collaboration, and a freer, more creative expression of your unique passion and gifts.

Chapter 11 is about having the conversations that will set you free.

Not sure that you're the kind of woman who holds back? It's possible you're right. Perhaps you've already started to take action, and you are already having all of the important conversations required in order to set your big vision in motion. If that's the case, you might consider the other domains of your life: at home, with your family, your spouse, your doctors and health care providers, your children's nannies or teachers, your accountant, your lawyer, your financial advisor, etc. Are you having 100 percent successful conversations in all of these arenas, or is there room for an upgrade?

If there's room, this chapter can probably help. It's true: there are a *lot* of other methods for success when it comes to difficult conversations—many of which you may have already studied. This chapter is not designed to teach you the *basics*. I'm assuming you've got that covered. Rather, it's designed to offer a few critical (and nuanced!) tools that will help you become more effective in communication of all kinds.

And if you *haven't* yet taken some of the critical steps associated with your purpose or North Star, the reason you're not already doing it probably relates to an important soon-to-be-identified conversation. If that's the case, we will uncover it together this week.

For example, there may be a giant *no* you need to say to someone (or something) in your life, in order to make room for your passion and purpose to grow. Or perhaps there is someone to whom you need to declare your intention, so that you can take next step on the path. Maybe there is even a request you need to make—for money, for love, for support, or for forgiveness—so that you can move forward with integrity and grace.

My hunch is that even without reading the chapter, you already have an inkling about what truths are waiting to be told. My aim in chapter 11 is to offer you some useful insight regarding when, and how, to speak those important truths out loud.

In this chapter, we'll take your lofty ideas and bring them right down to the ground. And when we do, life can start moving fast. Grab your hat, and let's get moving!

COCREATING THE DANCE

Have you ever had a conversation that felt perfectly in flow? The kind where something clicks, and words volley off one another. Perfectly served. Artfully returned. The kind where the leader becomes the follower and the follower becomes the leader in turn—where no one speaks for too long, and everyone remembers to listen all the time?

If so, you know what it feels like to Cocreate the Dance.

A few years ago, I began studying blues and fusion dance. It was completely different from my other movement practices, and something about it blew me away. Around the same time—likely not a coincidence—I noticed that both my work and intimate relationships began to change. Different than salsa or the waltz, blues dance is a *conversation* created between two equal partners. Both make choices that inform the next move. There are no predefined steps. There are no required patterns. There are no strict guidelines about who should lead and who should follow. Improvisation is the name of the game, and deep listening is the only rule. To Cocreate the Dance, you must listen to the music, your partner, and, most importantly, yourself.

As in any healthy intimate relationship, there are sometimes disagreements to negotiate. There are moments of hesitation and uncertainty. There are times when you stumble or even fall. As in any healthy intimate relationship, it's important to take responsibility for your gifts and your mistakes, not giving too much credit to your partner for a good idea, nor laying too much blame for a failure. And, as in any healthy intimate relationship, neither one nor the other partner is more responsible than the other for the ultimate expression of life that gets created.

Many of us women crave deeper intimacy. We desire an even exchange in our connections. Yet often we may still struggle to find this kind of flow.

As a woman—in life, in love, movement, and conversation—it can be tempting to just go along for the ride. (Apologies if this sounds old-fashioned. But check it out for yourself.) We've been told what to do in the past, and, out of habit, we let others dictate the direction we go in. Be it with our parents, our friends, our bosses, or our lovers, we may unwittingly give up our fair share of control. We may even think we're being strong by doing so. We do it out of love. We do it out of service.

And, I believe, we do it unconsciously, out of fear of taking responsibility to lead.

The flipside is equally seductive. As a man—or a woman who favors her masculine side—it can feel critical to appear "in charge." Because you feel it's your job, you make sure that nothing gets dropped along the way. You invest your energy and your self-worth in the achievement of a successful outcome. And, in so doing, you may find yourself steamrolling the very people who could help take somc of the burden off your shoulders. You do it out of duty. You do it at service.

And, I believe, you do it unconsciously, out of fear of taking responsibility to insist on healthy cocreation.

Of course, those are generalizations. Many of us women play both sides at different times, or in different contexts. I certainly do. What I've found, however, is that we typically get *more attached* to one. And when we do, it prevents us from achieving full mastery in the conversational space. Rather than make the right move at the right moment, we make the move that seemed to get us ahead in the past. We make it by default again and again and again—to our ultimate detriment over time.

Regardless of your default habit, this week I invite you to explore what it takes to consciously Cocreate the Dance. Imagine you were committed to crafting a collaborative partner dance . . . in your relationships, in the studio, in the conference room, it the dinner table, in bed.

Could you do it? What would you need to change?

The truth is, this kind of partnering is available *everywhere.* The secret is letting go of your attachment to leadership or followership, and letting the roles be dictated by *what's needed in the moment.* In a Cocreated Dance, the leader and follower changes regularly. In order to partner in this way, you will first need to be honest about whether your typical move is to stay in control—to lead—or to give up control—to follow. Then, to break your habit, try doing the opposite for a few days or weeks. Finally, when you start to get the hang of it, try doing some of both. Notice how it feels. You can do this collaborative practice with both people and forces—your partner, your boss, your fitness instructor, the coach, the terrain, the music, your physical body, your intuition, even God.

Two of my clients, Lindsey and Tara, used this tool to negotiate fairer pay. In both cases, they became aware that they were seriously underpaid as compared to the market for their roles. They weren't happy about it and they wanted to negotiate a raise.

For Lindsey, Cocreating the Dance involved doing her homework and coming to the table with a clear proposal *before* her scheduled performance review meeting, rather than waiting until her boss confirmed her suspicion that he was planning to give her the standard 5 percent annual raise. Lindsey saw that her boss (who was super supportive of her evolving leadership) was willing to give her the reins when he realized she had clear evidence that a change was needed.

For Tara, Cocreating the Dance involved making a spontaneous, strong leadership move *several times* during the negotiation process. Tara broke her typical habit by making the first volley. Yet she found that she received pushback on her request. Having been offered a small raise in a "drive by" interaction that was *better than nothing* but still not *fair*, she was surprised to hear herself say "no" and propose an alternative number. The eventual cocreative conversation lead to a 20 percent pay increase for Tara and a lot of well-earned self-respect.

Tara's commitment to cocreate the negotiation from beginning to end enabled her to insist, in a moment where she would have previously let go. She couldn't have planned that moment in advance, but when it happened, her body–mind system knew what was needed and made the move spontaneously. The rest felt like flow.

When you make the conscious choice to Cocreate the Dance, you get to observe what unfolds and learn from the ride. Just curious: what doors do you imagine would open on your path to purpose and passion if you made that commitment today?

Your mission this week is to break one old habit that has you go "unconscious" in your relationships or communication. In other words, a habit that leads you to stop assessing what's really needed in the situation and simply execute a default move. If you typically take the lead by default, try giving a little more leeway to the other person, while still remaining connected to your important goals. If they won't take that leeway at first, stick with your intention. Find gentle ways to insist.

If you typically follow by default, try taking charge this week. Use your commitment. Use your intelligence and drive. Use your sense of humor. Use your skillful and seductive nature (when appropriate!). Use whatever it takes to coax the other person into handing over the reins for a while. Who knows? It could be what they've been longing for all along.

If you're not sure of your typical habit—or even if you think you're sure—I encourage you start with some self-observation. Take a look at yourself in conversation with an extra truthful eye this week. Many of us (myself included!) are good at tricking ourselves to avoid the prospect of change.

Cocreating the Dance: Reflection Questions

- Where in your life are you letting yourself follow *by default* instead of *Stepping In* to "Cocreate the Dance"? In which conversations do you hand over the reins too quickly or easily? (Even if you think you tend to be controlling, challenge yourself to find at least one answer to the question.)
  - How is that affecting your ability to fully lead with passion and purpose?
  - What is the cost of not taking responsibility right now (for you, for them, for the collective, etc.)?
  - What possibilities might await you if you were willing to take the risk? What excites you about that?
- Where in your life do you insist on holding the reins, when you could or should be letting someone else lead? In which conversations do you hold on too tightly or for too long? (Even if you think you tend to let go easily, challenge yourself to find at least one answer to the question.)
  - How is *that* affecting your ability to fully lead with passion and purpose?
  - What is the cost of taking too much responsibility right now (for you, for them, for the collective, etc.)?
  - What possibilities might await you if you were willing to take the risk? What excites you about that?

BE MORE GENEROUS

When we begin practicing cocreative conversations, things can start to change fast. Sometimes, however, we end up bumping smack into one of our long-standing internal barriers. For example, there's the fear of being a burden or being "too much."

Have you ever held back a comment for fear of taking up too much airtime in a conversation? Or held back a request for help for fear that others would feel pressure to accommodate your needs? There is a pervasive phenomenon among women: we just don't want to become a burden. And we don't want to be burdened. We want to be impactful, but we don't want to make a negative or unnecessary impact. For many of us, these fears run under the surface our interactions, and they stifle our capacity to experience the abundance we so desperately long for.

As a society, we have the habit of being stingy with time, with money, with feelings and emotions, with trust, and with love. We have been hurt before and don't want to be hurt again. And we don't want to hurt others. We are afraid there won't be enough to go around, so we keep it to ourselves. We think there isn't really space for us, or that others can't handle us, so we don't give all of ourselves in any given moment. We don't offer our gift to the world because we're not perfect—yet—and we might not do it right. We save up because one day, when disaster strikes, we might really need it.

The problem with holding back—at least, one of *many potential problems*—is that we make it very hard for our communication partners to *win with us*. Think about it: *if you don't make a clear request, how will anyone know what to do, be, or say that will finally meet your needs?*

I am fortunate to have an unusual friend who is incredibly *generous* with his communication. He says what he feels, and he speaks loudly. He offers care and compassion without hesitation. He talks with his hands, gesturing frequently and fiercely. His emotion shows on his face. When he disagrees—or agrees—he doesn't hold back. When he sings, his rich, deep voice resonates throughout the room in a way that catches your attention immediately and holds it for the duration.

Spending time with him is refreshing and sometimes jarring at the same time. I am simply not used to seeing another human being interact with the world around him so freely. In his company, my boundaries (the ones I am so sure I need to maintain in order to keep myself safe) begin to melt. My own history tells me that I should worry about shining too brightly, because it's not safe. My own body does a very good job of containing Joy. After years of overgiving and getting hurt, I learned the importance of saying *no*. And yet, in all of that, I realize that something subtle goes missing when I live my life this way.

And frankly, he makes me want it back.

When I think about this man, I sometimes find myself feeling resentful. He's a man—and that comes with a certain set of privileges that (may) make it easier for him to own his voice and express himself with ease. I also know his life story. I know that he's suffered abuse and discrimination, and that he chooses to share of himself anyhow. This gives me hope that each of us—regardless of our gender—can make choices in our communication that help the world see us, feel us, understand us, meet us, and ultimately "win" with us.

As you move through the next few days, I invite you to explore what it might mean to "be more generous" in your giving. Perhaps you could expend a little more energy than usual, trusting that your inner supply is abundant enough to last as long as you need it. You might breathe more fully, show more joy, or take up more space. Regardless of how you choose to express it, notice how generosity feels in your body. Is it easy or difficult for you? What emotions or sensations does it bring up?

I realize that just a few chapters back, you may have worked hard to set some boundaries. And I realize that this suggestion may seem to directly contradict that practice. Trust me that it doesn't. In fact, it's a complement. The more you're able to say what's true, show yourself, take up your own space, and make real requests, the more sovereignty you will have over your own time, space, and life.

Though it may sound counterintuitive—especially if you're an *overgiver* when it comes to doing things for others—use this week to take stock of your "stingy" side. In what relationships and situations do you hold really strong communication boundaries? Who are they keeping out? And how are they holding *you* back? Is there room to be more generous there?

When my client Meria heard a deeper calling to evolve her leadership, she faced some really tough choices. These choices asked her to speak her truth to an entire community of people who respected and valued her leadership. Having served as a community organizer and the founder of a local nonprofit that helped promote minority-owned small businesses, Meria had stood *against* big business for years. She and her colleagues particularly frowned upon the exorbitant amounts of money being spent in the corporate sector and felt frustrated about the economic divide.

Then one day, as Meria followed the thread of her own purpose, she began to see that she could create the change she wanted to see in the world *even more directly* by working to help executives in corporations see the bigger picture, value diversity, and understand the blind spots created by their privilege. In fact, she could see how the lessons she'd learned *in the community* had helped her develop exactly the types tools these corporate leaders most needed. In her gut, Meria knew that something had to change, and she was *well*-equipped to drive it. She also knew that many of her closest relationships had been built on us vs. them (community vs. big business), and she was concerned that sharing her new vision would rock the boat.

Meria's bold leadership move involved "coming out" to her community about her desire to do critical work on the other side of the divide. While some people initially received her decision as a betrayal, the work Meria is doing now ultimately has an even bigger impact on the problems she was built to solve. Had Meria held back due to fear, she wouldn't have given her community the chance to benefit from her new vision. By being generous in her communication, she inspired an evolution of the dialogue in her community about how the different parts of society can learn from one another. And many early naysayers are now backing her cause.

Take a moment to think about your own leadership next-level. Think about the important conversations you find yourself in day to day. Do you see something on the horizon that you know others would benefit from hearing about?

First, take stock of whether you are willing to say the tough things to the people who need to hear them. Are you an *activist* for your own cause? Do you take a stand and insist? Do you speak the difficult truth that needs to be said?

And . . . here's the tough one . . . if you *are* already an *activist*, are you ready and willing to also become an *advocate*? While an activist will stand up and point out (often with passion and flare) what's not right in the world, an *advocate* dares to make a request. An *advocate* is defined as *a person who publicly supports or recommends a particular cause or policy.* More than simply calling the world out, an advocate is also willing to vision a new future and will go to great lengths to ask for change.

You may see some connections to your larger work in these distinctions. Nonetheless, I encourage you to *first* start your practice close to home. In your day-to-day interactions, how could you be more generous with your voice? How could you give your colleagues, family, and friends the best chance possible to show up and play the role you want and need them to play?

While it may sound like a subtle distinction, I promise you this practice can have a dramatic impact on the quality of your life.

Be More Generous: Reflection Questions

- If you're really honest with yourself, do you *let people win with you*? How or how not?
- In what ways are you stingy in your communication?
- What fears prevent you from being more generous? In other words, what fears prevent you from speaking your mind and making requests more boldly?
- What would being more generous in your communication entail? Be specific. Consider one small example and one large-scale example in your life, work, or relationships.
- Are you a better *activist* or *advocate*? What could be possible if you learned to do both well?

IN CONSCIOUS COMMUNICATION

Big words, yes? What is Conscious Communication, really?

I realize it may sound a bit lofty. But if you're going to be a "conscious leader," it's important that we take a closer look at Conscious Communication. These days, when we hear the word "conscious," it's easy to imagine an enlightened being in a long robe, sitting for hours in meditation. In other words, it's easy to imagine we're talking about something other than a simple, practical approach we might take in our own daily lives.

Instead I'd like to propose that consciousness is, at its essence, a *practice in paying attention*. We are *conscious* when we intentionally bring our awareness to a topic, person, or situation. And, in so doing, we have access to the simple, important truths that—when told—breed realness in relationships and build energy that fuels our lives.

In my work with leaders of all kinds, I've found that Conscious *Communication* involves deeply listening (to both myself and the other party) for what seems to be true in the moment. And then, taking the risk to name it.

Once again, it's a tool that's simple but not easy! And totally worth it.

When these two elements are present in our communication, a whole host of other things begin to fall into place. Genuine, authentic conversations unfold. Needs get met, sometimes intuitively and often synchronistically. People feel seen and heard. Relationships get easier.

Without deep listening and the risk of naming the truth, in contrast, we find ourselves executing on future plans that don't actually make sense in the present tense, and working toward unconscious goals that fail to align with what we most care about. The worst part is we often don't even realize it's happening until it's too late.

THE SCIENCE: HIGH-QUALITY CONNECTIONS

When you are ready to open up more, how do you ensure that doing so will enhance your relationships at work? Is *generous* always *generative*? University of Michigan Ross School of Business scholar Jane Dutton coined the phrase "high-quality connections" (or HQCs) to refer to those interactions—no matter how brief—that leave you and the other person feeling energized and uplifted. High-quality connections facilitate greater physical and psychological health, encourage engagement, and promote learning. When practiced in the workplace, they also enhance cooperation across business units, encourage dialogue among coworkers, and strengthen employees' attachment to the organization.

In her book *Energize Your Workplace: How to Create and Sustain High-Quality Connections at Work,* Dutton offers three pathways to high-quality connection: 1) respectful engagement—engaging others in ways that send messages of value and worth; 2) task enabling—facilitating another person's successful performance; and 3) building trust—acting in ways that convey to others that you believe they will act with integrity, dependability, and benevolence. By holding yourself as the starting point of these three pathways, you can ensure that your interactions will spark (rather than drain) the energy in the room.

While there's no guarantee that your conversation partner will return the favor, it's important to remember that when you are a leader, people are looking to you as a model of how to communicate. By practicing high-quality connections, you become the starting point for a culture of generative communication in your workplace.

J. E. Dutton, *Energize Your Workplace: How to Create and Sustain High-Quality Connections at Work* (San Francisco: Jossey-Bass, 2003).

Here's an example. One evening, I sat down to dinner with a friend. We'd been looking forward to seeing each other for a while, and I couldn't wait to enjoy the delicious meal we had just ordered. Yet something had also been nagging at me in the weeks prior. There had been a few miscommunications between us that had left me feeling hurt. I didn't really believe our friendship was on shaky ground, but I didn't feel truly centered either.

I sat down with an uncomfortable yet ambiguous feeling that issue was important. So important, in fact, that it was the first thing I brought up when my friend asked, "How've you been?" Rather than spend a joyful evening together recultivating our connection *in the moment*, we defensively rehashed the past few weeks and parted ways on slightly tense terms. So much for the executive coach who ought to know how to have "good communication."

In retrospect, it reminds me of a friendship I ended a decade ago with a woman I still hold fondly in my heart. In this story, I sat on the other side. My friend and I lived many miles apart. Because of our busy lives, we would only speak by phone about every six months. One of us would call the other, and we couldn't wait to reconnect. But she would be so upset about the fact that we hadn't spoken sooner that we'd spend the first thirty minutes of every call talking about her frustration. I knew that "feeling abandoned" was a sensitivity she carried from her childhood. *And* I knew that I was not abandoning her.

As you might imagine, I eventually stopped calling. All I wanted was to be with my friend in the moment. I wanted to start from the present and be recognized for the effort I was making to reach out. At least, I wanted to enjoy the conversation and feel closer as we spoke.

Of course, I cared about her needs and her feelings. It wasn't an either–or situation. Conscious Communication isn't about transcending everything. It's not about avoiding feedback and difficult emotions. In some cases, Conscious Communication *calls* us to say the tougher thing—like an activist—and make a request—like an advocate (for example, "I'm hurting right now in response to what you just said . . . what I need is . . . would you be willing to . . . ?"). And those words are important to speak.

That said, Conscious Communication also *asks* us to be *consistent* with our authentic in-the-moment experience and pay attention to whether our pain truly comes from our conversation partner or from some part of our past experience that has nothing to do with them.

When I think about all of the women I've coached, Karen was one of my favorite "turnarounds." Despite our shared commitment to her professional growth, it wasn't a given that she would be able to make a change. Twenty years into her career, Karen was carrying a big chip on her shoulder—and rightfully so. As a young woman she'd been promoted to a mission-critical role, then completely disempowered. Eventually, the entire operation was shut down. Then, many years later, the same project was reinstituted at a higher level, and, instead of promoting her to run it, the company put a much younger and inexperienced gentleman in the role, at much higher pay grade—and asked her to mentor him.

Yep. I get it. It happens. The *problem* that Karen faced was a real external glass ceiling. But it was made *even worse* by the ceiling she'd created *inside*. When I met Karen, her resentment was palpable. She talked loudly and talked a lot. And often, within the first few sentences, she was either getting down on herself, somebody else, or both. Having spent years carrying around her frustration and resentment, she felt heavy, dismal, and pissed off.

Karen was a super-talented, forward-thinking woman. And nobody wanted to work with her. Our coaching primarily focused on bringing her conversations and emotions into the present tense. Karen committed to stop dragging up stuff from the past. She practiced gratitude, celebration, focusing on the upside, and genuinely letting her current conversation partners win with her. The truth was, the company wanted to promote her but had been walking on eggshells around her emotions for years.

By the end of our six-month engagement, Karen's communication was simpler, kinder, and more generous. Two years later I met Karen's new boss, who joined my program precisely *because of* the miraculous transformation he'd seen in her. Karen had been promoted—twice—and was now doing fantastic, fulfilling work as a leader in her mid-fifties, with a good long run ahead of her.

Inspired? I was.

It can take some work to truly evolve our communication habits. But when we do it, the results can literally be life-changing.

This week as you lean into radical truth-telling and envision the conversations you most need and want to have, I invite you to cultivate your capacity for Conscious Communication along the way. How will you know if you're on track? For the sake of your practice, let's look at an example that illustrates how to sense it *in your body*.

So often we make moves to accomplish a results-oriented goal, meanwhile losing consciousness in the process. The next time you're in a meeting, notice if you are driving the conversation *at the expense of* your relationship with your communication partner. See if you can sense, *in your body*, the moment when it happens. You may feel your own body suddenly react to them differently. You may even be able to feel them either disappear or begin pushing back. If so, good noticing. Without giving yourself up or caving in, bring more awareness to the impact of your words, and try tweaking something in the moment. Then, notice if your body feels different.

Positive, proactive change always begins with awareness. As you learned in chapter 9, bringing attention to the sensations in your body can bring a flood of new information that you can use to guide your choices in the moment. References to the *past* and *future* can also be red flags. In Karen's story, resentment about the past demotion and frustration about a slow-in-coming future role sabotaged her connection with people in the present.

As you practice Conscious Communication this week, take careful note when you are thinking, feeling, and expressing yourself from the past or future instead of the present moment. Check in with yourself: is there an unspoken goal you are holding "between the lines" of the conversation? For example, are you diving into a brainstorming session with the "right" solution already in mind? Are you triggered and feeling emotion that has more to do with what your mother said when you were three years old than what your partner actually said just now? If so, can you re-center in the present?

I realize all of this can feel like a tall order, especially if there is historical baggage between you and your conversation partner. Your North Star can also be of service here. What intentions do you have that are more important than your fears and judgments and that could drive you to navigate these deep waters with courage and with heart?

The following questions will help you to reflect.

In Conscious Communication: Reflection Questions

- What conversations do you need and want to have in the next few weeks in order to forward your movement along the path of purpose and passion?
- What would it mean to have them more consciously?
- What communication traps do you typically fall into that you'd like to intentionally side-step this time?
- What goals or intentions do you care about *more than your fears*? How can these serve as motivation to speak your truth and make requests out loud?

The Practice

Over the past ten chapters, you have taken a number of critical steps toward developing more conscious, sustainable, and thriving leadership habits. With just a few more tools to go, you are now in the home stretch. But I don't want you to stop here. Your mission for this week is to take action on one more thing: *a conversation that will create momentum in the place you've been holding back.*

The practice guide for chapter 11 includes just one core tool. Below, you will find instructions about how to prepare for a challenging but important conversation. First, you will make a list of the people with whom you have a hunch (recent or long-standing) that you need to communicate with in order to live the life you envision. Next, you will answer a few questions to help you gather your thoughts. And finally, homework this week is to stumble forward. Send an email, schedule a meeting, or call that person up.

As always, this is a practice. There's no need to get it right the first time. More likely than not, "getting it right" doesn't even exist. Rather, it's about getting on the path. Success this week is simply taking the first step.

PRACTICE 1: PREPARING YOUR FREEING CONVERSATION

Start by identifying one or two difficult but meaningful conversations that could help you to anchor your passion and purpose, further embody your North Star, or build the more conscious, sustainable, and thriving leadership approach you've been envisioning.

Consider the people whom you believe could support you on the path. Also, consider the people who you tend to blame (consciously or unconsciously) for holding you back. Regardless of the ultimate outcome, having a conversation is likely to help set you free. If you haven't completed the questions in each section of this chapter, I recommend doing that first. They will help you to clarify what's important and how you may need to think about those conversations differently this week in order to succeed. Consider how you typically approach tough conversations and what you might want to do *differently* this time. Then choose one or two conversations for which you would like to *take the first step this week*. Follow the instructions below in order to prepare.

Step 1: Identify and Schedule It.

- With whom do you need/want to have a conversation?
- What is the general topic?
- When will you do it, and how will you (did you) make the request?

Step 2: Get Clear on Your Drivers.

- What is your goal in the conversation? Write down the first thought that comes to mind.
- Is that goal good for *you* and good for *others*? If not, are there other (larger or smaller) goals that are also driving you and that could help you find deeper *alignment* with your conversation partner?
- What are your fears about the conversation? Write down the first thought that comes to mind.
- Is that fear about *you* or about *them*? If it's about them, are there personal fears that are also driving you? And could you address them in a way that would keep the conversation feeling *human* and help the other person feel less *defensive*?

Step 3: Activist or Advocate?

- Is this conversation a *tell/declare* conversation, a *request* conversation, or both? Why?
- What part of the conversation is scariest to address? What important part of the conversation are you most likely to leave out?
- Why would it be important to include it, even if it's hard to talk about?

Step 4: Paying Attention to the How.

- What *past* or *future* concerns do you tend to put attention on that could derail the productivity of this conversation?
- Do these past/future concerns really need to be addressed? Or can you have an equally productive conversation that addresses all critical issues, while leaving them aside?
- If they *do* need to be addressed, how can you make sure they play their right role and don't take over for your most important goals?
- What *else*, if anything, matters to you that you'd like to be conscious about?

Step 5: Have an *Initial* Conversation.

- You are ready. At this moment it may feel like a big deal, but, really, it's like stepping off a two-inch cliff. It doesn't have to be perfect. The time is now.

Go do it. I dare you.

ACTIVE INGREDIENTS	thoughtful planning, self-awareness, imperfect action
WHY IT WORKS	There's never a perfect movement to have a difficult-for-you conversation. When you commit and take action, you free up the energy that was previously invested in worry, planning, and procrastination tactics—and prove to yourself that you can do it.

REFLECTIONS ON THE FREEING CONVERSATIONS PRACTICE

- What did you learn from engaging with the practices this week?
- Did you choose a conversation? Did you have it? Why or why not?
- If you had it, how did it go? And what, if anything, is left to do or say now?
- If you didn't, what's holding you back? And what would it take for you to dive in?

Guts and Grace Playlist Recommendations

"Say" – John Mayer

"Stronger Woman" – Jewel

"Back to Before" – *Ragtime: The Musical*

"Clocks" – Coldplay

"Bone Dance" – Deya Dova

"Yo Canto" – Laura Pausini

LEADERSHIP MYTH

It's nearly impossible to make change that sticks. In a few days, weeks, or months, people always go back to the way they've been.

LEADERSHIP TRUTH

When change happens through the body, addresses the real root cause, and is practiced consistently, it's both possible and probable that it will stick.

Chapter 12

THE ANCHOR

Weave real connections, create real nodes, build real houses.
Live a life you can endure: Make love that is loving . . .
Live as if you liked yourself, and it may happen:
reach out, keep reaching out, keep bringing in.
. . . for every gardener knows that after the digging, after the planting,
after the long season of tending and growth, the harvest comes.

—MARGE PIERCY

MAKING IT STICK

Congratulations. At this stage, you've probably taken on some challenging goals and are seeing the light at the end of the tunnel. And what a journey it's been!

You've learned to build energy and resilience while deepening your relationship with your body through Joyful movement. You have taken stock of your time and put in place some important new structures. And you have adjusted your willingness to say no and yes in ways that serve you well.

You have grappled with both your mind and your emotions, and while it may have been a challenge, you've developed some new mastery in each domain. You even faced your Core Dilemma—the one thing that needs to change in order for you to really step into your next level of leadership. You set a new North Star. And you took action, developing practices and having conversations that point you in the direction of your deeper desires.

At this moment you may be thinking, "Oh no! How am I going to maintain this momentum without the support of regular touch points and guided embodied practices?" Or you may be thinking, "Whew! I can't wait for this ride to be over!" In either case, the goal of chapter 12 is to help you to summarize what you've learned that will be most important for you to maintain, and to put some things in place to make sure that happens.

Chapter 12 is designed to tackle one remaining leadership myth that has the power to derail *all* of your progress so far: ***It's nearly impossible to***

make change that sticks. In a few days, weeks, or months, people always go back to the way they've been. One of the reasons we believe this myth is that we don't always go deep enough to address our counterproductive habits at their root cause. And we don't typically build a strong enough foundation of regular practice to fully counter their unconscious influence on our lives. (Remember, it takes ten thousand repetitions!) Lastly, we may be choosing new habits that are "good ideas" or "shoulds" instead of resonant new habits that naturally evolve from our deeper, embodied longing.

Over the past decade, I've had the privilege to witness both individual leaders and leadership teams blow this myth out of the water. The truth is: ***when change happens through the body, addresses the real root cause, and is practiced consistently, it's both possible and probable that it will stick.*** New actions practiced in this way typically become the new normal in about six to eighteen months.

This book was written and organized specifically to address these pitfalls and to help you create *change that sticks*. Because you've dared to do the deeper clearing work in chapters 1 through 6, the new behaviors, attitudes, and physical shape you're growing into now will actually be *a better fit* for you than the ones you are leaving behind. If you trust this, you can leverage your clarity to keep you on the path of daily practice. And, as my mentors often say, "what we practice, persists."

In fact, it's not uncommon for my clients to be surprised when we get to this part of the journey. They look back on their earlier notes and say, "Wow! I used to be like that? I almost forgot." It's like learning to drive a car. When you practice the desired new habits more often than the old ones, eventually you forget what life was like before you knew how to drive. It's one of the reasons I've encouraged you to keep a journal along the way. This week, next month, or next year, you will look back and smile.

Here's the good news: the stories about your own transformation that you will soon be ready to tell have the power to inspire others. You can reference your own progress as you lead, mentor, coach, and guide others. You may find that you end up speaking about these stories on stage or simply sharing them with your kids when they are old enough to understand. They are your victories, hard won, and they make you who you are.

The other good news is that this book is connected to a wider community of practice, which includes virtual resources, live events, and opportunities for deeper support via mastermind groups and executive coaching. You have access to all of these resources—now or later—to support your ongoing development as a leader. I invite you to use them. (You can find more details in the conclusion section of the book and on the *Guts and Grace* website.) I also invite any reader of this book to reach out to me and my team if you're hungry for more hands-on support.

In this final chapter, however, I invite you to simply focus on *Anchoring* your own progress. Chapter 12 is about celebrating. And putting your stake in the ground. I'm proud of you for the work you've done to get here. Enjoy this last leg of the journey.

WHY ANCHOR?

First, let's define what we're up to here. What do I mean by *Anchor*? And why should you bother doing it?

Early in my work coaching women, I started to notice a pretty consistent trend. In summary, it went like this: A client would set a big goal. Then, she'd achieve that goal or at least have a pretty important breakthrough. I would know this because someone else would tell me, or I'd hear it through the grapevine. However, when I'd ask her how her progress was going, she'd say something like, "Well . . . it's been challenging." Or "You know, I still have a long way to go . . ."

I'd then respond by pointing out her success: "Didn't you XYZ last week?!" She'd look a big sheepish, and say, "Well, yeah, I guess that happened." Or laugh: "Oh yeah! I totally forgot about *that*. It's just been such a busy week." And she'd be onto the next thing on her list.

Can you relate? Or maybe it reminds you of someone you know and love?

It's funny. But not really. The *problem* with this trend is that it *perpetuates* our stories about not being good enough. It reinforces our self-doubt. It locks in place the belief that it's hard for women to get ahead in this world. It gives those who look up to us the impression that successes are tough to come by and that progress can't really be made. And it Anchors the myth that *it's impossible for people to change*.

Today, you have another choice. The tools in this chapter are about *taking credit* for the progress you have made, so that it becomes real—both in your eyes and in the eyes of others. Just a few hours ago, one of my clients spoke up on a group coaching call to celebrate a win. "You'll never believe what's happening!" She told us she'd recently decided to apply for a huge research grant. And, while she was nervous at first that people would try to talk her out of it, she got really clear she'd made enough progress in her career and that she was ready. The result? So far, every person she's mentioned it to has reflected her clarity right back to her. "That's a great fit!" they're saying. "You're really ready for it." And that's how it happens—your world *catches up* with the progress you *acknowledge*.

The Anchor is a tool that helps you own your progress and maintain access to the victories you have already won. While the self-sabotaging parts of your ego (including your Core Dilemma) would like to talk you out of it, the Anchor is your conscious choice to remember.

For me, an Anchor works like a stake in the ground that declares, "I have been here before, and so I know it's possible to come back here again." Envision, for example, the American flag being placed on the moon. When I'm working live with clients, and they have an important breakthrough, I'll often ask them questions like "How did you do that?" and "What about it worked?" Recapping out loud helps you to own your progress. It also lets your mind know that you didn't fall into this new state by accident. Rather, you consciously created it through your own empowered action and thus *you can create it again*.

I encourage you to practice Anchoring precisely because it's *so* easy to avoid. (In fact, Your Core Dilemma is designed to make certain you do!) "Sure, I had this awesome breakthrough, but it was just because of XYZ (fill in the blank) . . ." *This* is how we talk ourselves out of creating lasting and desirable change.

For the sake of your life, your work, your leadership, and your most important relationships, I challenge you to *stop forgetting and negating your own progress* this week. Instead, let's build an Anchor.

In the practice of NLP (neurolinguistic programming), a tool used by many of the great coaches, including Tony Robbins, "Anchoring" is a technique used to make certain mind states (like feeling calm) available whenever you want them. It works by pairing an internal response with an external or internal trigger so that you can get there again. For example, through a series of sessions we train your mind to get calm each time you touch your nose. Then later, when you touch your nose, you instantly feel calm. While NLP makes this process *automatic* for the user, I believe there is also value in in the conscious process of returning to a state via your own choiceful actions or intentional body-based shifts. In the latter case, you also build confidence in your own agency.

What I love about the embodied practices you've been learning in this book is that they can short-circuit the voice of helplessness and help you take new actions. Your North Star declaration, and the practices that support it, can *also* serve as Anchors. If you recall your North Star, and you do one of your Daily Practices, your body will remember. No matter how far off course you may have strayed, you have a road home. It simply takes choosing.

Remember my client Susan, who practiced slowing down her pace in order to deepen her connection with others? The choice to slow down reconnected her with her desire to listen more deeply and be more fully present in conversations. For Susan, *a slower pace* served as an Anchor to create more of the results she wanted in her work relationships.

In this way, your embodied practices are now like a home base. Having put in the time and effort to take conscious actions linked with powerful intentions, your body now carries the muscle memory that it recorded during your time of learning. Months after reading this book—even if you stop paying attention and *think* you've forgotten everything you learned—your practices will still be there waiting to remind you.

As we explored in chapter 8, your practices also provide the opportunity to witness yourself and measure your progress. Not to judge, but to learn something else about yourself. Your practices give you a benchmark of how it's going in your life right at this very moment. When you're on track, you will know because you can feel the difference. Your body will remember how the practice felt strained yesterday—or easier and sparkier last week. And finally, because they have a way of inviting you back into conscious relationship with your body, your practices can ignite your own natural resilience.

In other words, the progress you acknowledge, and the body-based practices that Anchor it, can act as a portal. Through this portal, you can choose to access an empowering experience you've created even just once before.

So, without further ado, let's start taking stock of the important breakthroughs you've had as a result of reading this book and using these tools. In service of your own empowerment, decide that you are now Anchoring them in your body-mind-spirit system. Decide that they are a genuine part of you.

Decide that you have created *change that sticks.*

Why Anchor? Reflection Questions

- How do you downplay, or talk yourself out of, your own success? How do you ignore or disown your progress?
- Did you have a breakthrough of some kind while reading this book? Did you find a new doorway, or access a state that you haven't felt before (or haven't felt recently)? If so, take a moment to describe it in detail.
- If so, how did you get there? What physical, mental, or emotional shifts did you make or what actions did you take that helped make it possible? How did you do it?
- Do you have any fears about losing your way back to this location? If so, name them.
- What do you know about yourself, your strengths, and your own resourcefulness that could help you to quell those fears?

BEGINNINGS, MIDDLES, AND ENDS

What is the most embodied way to track progress over time? While people in Western industrialized nations tend to envision life unfolding in a straight line, people who live closer to the earth tend to see life in arcs and cycles. In order to better understand your recent progress, I'd like to propose we use a cyclical map that includes beginnings, middles, and ends.

When I teach movement classes, I take my students intentionally through a carefully designed sequence. This sequence includes several developmental stages, from *Stepping In* to peaking to cooling down and finally to closing in the same way we began. By design, it creates a complete circle from beginning to end. I am inspired by the innate wisdom of these stages, and I see how they contribute to the powerful feeling of wholeness my students often report at the end of class. I've also noticed that the completeness of this sequence can make my classes challenging or confronting for some new students.

As it turns out, most people are less comfortable (and less practiced) in some of the stages than others. Knowing your defaults, and taking care not to skip important steps, can help ensure that you Anchor your transformation and finish strong. Think about you own habits for a moment. *In general, do you tend to prefer the beginning, the middle, or the end of an experience? How do you know? What do you see about yourself in these three stages?*

Now, look back over the past few weeks, months, or years. Can you locate the beginning of a recent and important cycle? If so, pan forward to the present—where would you say you are in that cycle today?

As I mentioned a moment ago, most of us are less comfortable in some parts of the cycle than others. We fail to set our intention, we rush through beginnings, we get bored in the middle, or we leave before it's time to leave. Tracking your beginnings, middles, and ends can bring a greater consciousness to your leadership—and pay dividends on the home front as well. I recommend developing rituals that demarcate your transitions as a concrete great way to start.

Currently, what rituals do you hold for yourself that mark your beginnings, middles, and ends? Do you—actually or metaphorically—stand at the edge of the pool, secure your goggles, and take a few deep breaths before diving in? At the end of a long ride, do you carefully wipe the dirt off your bike before packing your equipment away for next time? Do you end an intense dance practice with familiar stretches or a favorite snack that replenishes your energy?

If so, what role do these ritualized transitions play in your life? Or perhaps you notice that you tend to lack clear beginnings, middles, or ends. Clearly *stepping out*, for example, may not be your strong suit. In that case, explore putting a new ritual in place as another way of helping you Anchor your recent progress.

Beginnings, Middles, and Ends: Reflection Questions

- What is your typical relationship with cycles and transitions? For example, do you rush through or skip certain stages? Do you linger or cling to others?
- Do you have favorite transition-marking rituals? (Even if you weren't aware of them before, capture them here.)
- Have you experienced a cycle, or a number of cycles, while making your way through the chapters in this book? If so, how have you engaged with (or failed to engage with) those cycles?
- Are you ready to *step out* of this *Guts and Grace* learning cycle for now? If yes, how do you know? If no, what do you still need in order to be ready?
- What ritual could you perform to mark the end of this cycle and help you feel complete? How might you use it to celebrate and Anchor your progress?

THE HARVEST

In my experience, the closing stages of an important cycle are a bit like the autumn in a year. For people who work on the land, autumn is the time to harvest the literal fruit of their labors. For those of us choosing office jobs,

THE SCIENCE: RITUAL IN ORGANIZATIONS

Can rituals be used to support larger professional goals? And if so, how does it work? Positive ceremony and ritual is a relatively new scientific field. Yet it offers some exciting ways to enrich our workday, drawing on approaches that have been used by human beings for thousands of years. In the past, rituals helped tribal people to mark important moments, celebrate rites of passage, and create strong bonds that united their group. Similarly, masters of applied positive psychology graduate Katie Wallace demonstrated a link between ritual and whole-system flourishing inside of her organization. Wallace currently serves as the director of social and environmental responsibility at New Belgium Brewery, an innovative employee-owned company in Fort Collins, CO.

Each year employees come together to look at the business strategically and set intentions for the future. This session culminates in a very special ritual—an ownership induction for employees who have reached their one-year anniversary. The ritual, involving shared storytelling, weaves each individual's story with the story of New Belgium. Tears are shed, laughs explode, and vulnerability is shared. By implementing this company-wide rite of passage for new employees, New Belgium has engendered a deep sense of loyalty among community members that helps to fuel engagement, motivation, and ongoing commitment.

In an extensive literature review, Wallace delves into the science behind this phenomenon. She illustrates how rituals that move people from deep inside—including shared experiences of love, connection, music, dance, and play—can galvanize the energy of coworkers in the direction of a shared purpose. According to her review, rituals serve to unite groups of people and build vibrant culture. By supporting belonging, evoking a sense of meaning, and eliciting shared positive emotions, positive organizational rituals serve as an Anchor that promotes whole-system flourishing.

Katie Wallace, "Positive Organizational Ritual: Awakening the Positive Potential of Organizations through Symbols and Ceremony," MA thesis, UPenn College of Liberal & Professional Studies, 2015, *Scholarly Commons*, https://repository.upenn.edu/mapp_capstoneabstracts/86/.

the autumn brings us back from summer holidays—back to work, back to school, back to projects and relationships that we put on hold during the summer months.

When I teach this curriculum live, chapter 12 always falls in late autumn. Thus, our growth process gently mirrors the natural rhythm of the seasons. Regardless of the time of year you are reading these words, however, it can still be useful to hold the end of *this* journey as a time of harvest. In this context, to harvest is to gather what you've learned for the sake of future sustainability.

When I think about the harvest, I get a warm feeling that suggests a sense of abundance. I have planted my seeds, watched them grow, and now I begin to enjoy the fruit. Despite this warm feeling, I am also keenly aware that the harvest can be a challenging, restless time as well. In the rhythm of life, the harvest calls upon us to sustain our energy and fulfill promises made in the spring and summer months.

Personally, my default is to skip the fall. By nature, I'm easily drawn to move quickly from one task to another—to begin with a fresh new idea rather than going more deeply into a more mature project I started months ago. But I also know that coming back to things I started, and creating a sustained relationship with them, allows me to go deeper. And, like the autumn harvest, it enables me to finally reap the benefit of the hard work I put in up front.

When I don't take the time to harvest, I find that I'm much likelier to get depleted in the long run. How about you? Do you take the time to harvest? Do you reap the full benefit of your labors?

The Practice section of this chapter offers some guidance on how to make *harvesting* a regular practice—starting with a harvest of your *Guts and Grace* journey. In the next few days or weeks, as you take these final actions, I invite you once again to notice how your default habits come into play. With eyes wide open, consciously make choices that will serve your deepest goals.

Consider what you've learned, practiced, and broken through over the past twelve chapters. Own your wins. Take note of where you've landed. Notice how you're feeling about your next steps. You may recall that some of the topics we covered felt particularly challenging or rich, such that you would like to come back to them again. You may have notes about projects that you would like to start or even complete in the next quarter, related to what you've learned here. There may even be a New Year's (or new quarter's) resolution you'd like to declare before we complete.

Whether you've practiced all of the tools in every chapter diligently along the way, avoided the tough ones, or simply struggled to make time in your already busy life, *I commend you* for going on this journey. Take a moment to pat yourself on the back for holding a strong enough intention to make it all the way here—to the harvest. Seriously, *no* beating yourself up. Only celebration at this graduation party!

Put aside any critical voices now. Forget about what you didn't do. Instead, take stock of what you *did* gain . . . and what you *are* harvesting at this time.

The Harvest: Reflection Questions

- How do you feel about *completion*? In the past, what's been your relationship with the harvest, metaphorically (I skip by it, I jump to the next thing, I love to savor it, etc.)?
- What's one topic or tool from this book that felt either rich or challenging or both that you'd like to go deeper with in the future?
- Has your learning from this book inspired you to start any new projects or initiatives? If so, what are the one or two most important next steps you need to take in order to move them forward?
- And finally, what is one change you made (permanently or temporarily) while reading this book and doing the practices that you'd like to Anchor in your life or work?
- Describe what you did to create it, why you decided to try it out in the first place, and why/how it made a difference for you.

UNCONDITIONAL

There's just one more thing I want to remind you of before we complete. It's *the power of your own self-acceptance.*

Do you remember the old Billy Joel song "*I could not love you any better . . . I love you just the way you are*"? Wouldn't it be heavenly to hear those words sung sweetly to you by a lover or friend? Hearing this song again got me thinking about the way we tend to love ourselves. *I'll love myself if . . . I'll accept myself when . . . I'll approve of myself, but only under these circumstances or when these criteria are met.*

Many of us women (myself included) do this automatically. Without thinking, we put boundaries and conditions on our own lovability. But cultivating a truly conscious, sustainable, and thriving leadership approach requires us to find another way. This lesson may be tough to learn at work. In fact, we may learn it from the most unexpected of teachers.

In 2007 I adopted a Shiba Inu. While I was realistic about the fact that becoming a dog owner would change my life in many ways, I couldn't have guessed just how dramatic the changes would be. I had done my homework on the breed. All of the research seemed to concur: Shiba Inus are difficult dogs to raise. Yet, although I couldn't put my finger on why, I couldn't see myself adopting any other kind of dog. I share this to highlight the fact that everything could have gone wrong. There were fifty reasons why I could have said, "This isn't a 'good' dog for me" or *anyone else*, for that matter. Instead, I dove in and made a powerful decision to accept her for *exactly* who she was, quirks, flaws, and all. There was no other way, and I never looked back.

Today I can say with 100 percent conviction that I chose *exactly* the right dog for me. People literally stop me in the street to converse with us. "What a wonderful dog!" they say. Our chemistry is dynamic. She is without a doubt my favorite dog on the planet, and I love her *unconditionally*. My Shiba (named Sheba) trained me to enjoy her strengths and work around her weaknesses. She doesn't respond to punishment, so I learned to ignore her mistakes and reward her progress.

Over the years, Sheba taught me to be unconditional with my love—not as a mental concept but as an embodied practice. Her response (or lack of response) to my approach provides instant feedback when I've lost my center. When I am centered, and I am accepting, she responds. When I am angry, off base, or driven my ego . . . well, you don't want to be around to watch. Because she *isn't* a human being, it hasn't made sense to make excuses like "Well, when she finally stops biting me, then I'll love her," or "That's it, she's got to lose five pounds and then we'll see about that new bone she's been wanting."

You laugh? Yet that's exactly how many of us treat *ourselves*!

I will be acceptable when I can finally get the steps right, when I finally stop losing my temper over stupid stuff, when I finally get my finances in order, when I finally reach a size six and stay there . . . No wonder we are forever on edge, falling back into our "bad" behaviors again and again! Isn't it anxiety-provoking to believe that you must change if you're ever going to deserve your own love? And aren't you that much more likely to make "mistakes" when you are anxious and on edge? I certainly am.

As you wrap up your *Guts and Grace* journey, and finish taking stock of your progress, I leave you with one more question as food for thought:

What would it look like to practice the Quality "unconditional" in your relationship with yourself over the weeks and months to come?

At the end of this section, I invite you make a list—an unconditional gratitude list to all of your quirks and imperfections. I encourage you to do this because it's hard. And because *no matter where you're headed*, starting where you are (exactly where you are!) is still the *only* place you can truly begin. Your list may go something like this . . .

Thank you, body, for feeling tired; I know that you need rest.

Thank you, emotions, for shutting down; I know that you are afraid.

Thank you, mind, for your disarray; I know that you are healing.

Thank you, spirit, for feeling so alive this morning; I know I have got enough rest.

Thank you, body, for these extra few pounds; I know that you are keeping me safe.

Thank you, mind, for forgetting the steps; I know that you are learning something new.

Thank you, emotions, for my grumpy mood; I know that you need patience.

Thank you, body, for the gray hairs; I know that you have enjoyed many wonderful years on this planet.

Thank you, body, for being exactly as you are; I know that I am me . . . and there's no one I'd rather be today.

In other words, I accept you *unconditionally*, even if you hurt, you are uncoordinated, you make mistakes, or you feel unfit. And because I accept you so, I will only ask you to do things that are right for you at this time. I will challenge you, but I won't push beyond your limits. And I certainly won't beat you up for things that are beyond your reach. And I promise to *delight* in the things you can and do accomplish!

As you practice the Quality "unconditional" with yourself starting today, notice what *also* shifts in your relationships with others around you and their relationships with others around *them*. You might just find that it's contagious (and wouldn't that be great?).

That's it. Enough. It's time to move on. You are a beautiful, bold, and empowered woman. I am *so honored* to have shared this journey with you. And I look forward to seeing you flourish in the months and years to come.

Good luck. Have fun this week, and please, please . . . make that list!

Unconditional: Reflection Questions

- What would it look like to practice the Quality "unconditional" in your relationship with *yourself* in the weeks and months to come?
- What would you say or do differently? Why would that matter?
- What would you stop doing? What would you start doing? Why would that matter?

The Practice

The truth is, there's not much more for you to do now. If you've made it this far, and you've done your practices along the way, your body–mind system has already been encoded with a new way of thinking, doing, and being that will have a lasting impact on the way that you see the world. The tools you now have in your toolbox can be called upon at any time to support you as you continue cultivating your conscious, sustainable, and thriving leadership approach. And answering the questions in each section of this chapter will help make your learning stick. That said, I suggested a few practices throughout this chapter, and I want to highlight them here.

PRACTICE 1: CELEBRATE (AND FEEL) YOUR WINS

This week take some time each day to celebrate your wins. You might do this out loud with a friend or partner (or even your kids!). Or simply say them to yourself. Stay present with your emotions and bodily sensations as you do it.

I'm proud of myself for . . .

I feel good that I accomplished . . .

I'm celebrating my progress in . . .

I brag that . . .

Be sure to include wins related to your recent *Guts and Grace* intentions, as well as wins that have recently become possible *as a result of* the new tools you've been practicing. This will help to Anchor your recent progress. Your main job in this practice is to let yourself *feel the sensation of your success in your body.* This practice will stretch your capacity to tolerate the bliss of your own achievement. By tying positive, physical sensations to the results you are currently getting, it will also help your mind relax and trust that your efforts really do make a difference.

ACTIVE INGREDIENTS	bragging, tracking body sensations, recapping, allowing emotions
WHY IT WORKS	When you're uncomfortable with our own success, your body contains energy. This practice helps unlock that energy, freeing it up to support your leadership.

PRACTICE 2: YOUR JOURNEY—A YEAR IN REVIEW

Take an hour (or an afternoon) to review the notes you've taken in your journal while reading this book. Harvest important revelations, moments of breakthrough, and practices you want to come back to down the road.

Step 1: Start from the beginning of your journal and leaf through slowly, with a favorite colored pen or highlighter in hand. You don't need to read every word—just turn the pages and notice what catches your eye. Mark things that feel important. If you notice themes, write something about the theme in the margins. Flag pages that feel particularly important.

Step 2: On a new page, make a list of key themes. Which chapters were particularly important on your journey? What behavior kept showing up in different forms? Was there a thought pattern that shifted from beginning to end? A myth you finally stopped believing? Count each of those as concrete progress. Write them down in bullets, where you can find them again easily, in case you forget!

Step 3: If there were particular moments that could make good stories (e.g., that time I took a stand in front of my boss and peers; that night I asked my husband if we could eat what I really wanted, etc.), write them down in a few sentences as well.

Step 4: If there are tools (or entire chapters!) that you feel you didn't quite "get" (i.e., understand, break through, or find useful)—or chapters you totally got, but were especially challenging for you—and you have a hunch you could benefit from coming back to them later, take a few notes about that as well. Write what they are and also write down why you believe it might be worthwhile to revisit them. Ideally, decide when you will do that now. Put it on your calendar.

When you're done, close your journal and place it somewhere that you will see it regularly for the next week. If other themes, breakthroughs, stories, or relevant memories come to mind, open it again and capture them.

ACTIVE INGREDIENTS	synthesis, personal reflection, gut intuition
WHY IT WORKS	**While it may not be possible to review every note from every lesson, scanning at a high level enables your gut instinct** to guide your eyes to some important and memorable breakthroughs so that you can Anchor them.

BONUS PRACTICE: EMBODY UNCONDITIONAL SELF-ACCEPTANCE

In the last section, I encouraged you to write a list thanking your body for all of its quirks. If you haven't done that yet, do it! In addition, here is an embodied practice you can do that will help you Anchor the feeling of unconditional self-acceptance throughout your entire being.

Part 1: In Your Joy Workouts or Regular Movement Routine. When you move or exercise, allow your body to be *exactly* as it is in each moment. Accept it unconditionally, even if it hurts, is uncoordinated, makes mistakes, or feels unfit. Ask your body to only do things that are *right* for it in the moment. Challenge yourself, but don't go beyond your real limits. Don't beat yourself up. Celebrate your body and appreciate what is accessible to you today. Honor your body's way.

Part 2: In Your Life and as a Metaphor. Choose one big thing about yourself to *stop apologizing for* right this minute. Maybe it's your weight, your temper, your mood swings, your insecurity. For the rest of the week, practice loving yourself unconditionally—*even if* you are too fat, too angry, too moody, or too insecure. If you catch yourself thinking or saying *I'm sorry,* follow it up with *No I'm not; that is just who I am today.* Notice what shifts in the relationships around you. See if you can make your new attitude contagious!

ACTIVE INGREDIENTS	body awareness, intentional commitment, mindful self-observation
WHY IT WORKS	This practice enables you to retrain your body-mind system by interrupting old patterns and building new ones in the moment.

A FEW MORE THOUGHTS

While there are many, many more tools I could offer here (and many more I do offer on the *Guts and Grace* website), my sense is that these are enough for now. Feel free to also practice tracking beginnings, middles, and ends and building regular harvest (completion) rituals for yourself over the next few weeks. And, of course, if you've let go of the Daily Practice you designed in chapter 8, picking it back up is a very good way to ensure that your evolution will stick.

All of that said, if something still feels missing to you, I dare you to create your own practice or ritual to help you Anchor your own *Guts and Grace* process. You now have the equivalent of a master's degree in conscious, embodied, feminine leadership.

The next phase of the journey is *yours* to create!

REFLECTIONS ON THE ANCHOR PRACTICES

- What are you learning from engaging with the Anchor practices this week?
- Where else could you use Anchoring that would support leadership or effectiveness?
- Anything else you want to note this week?

Guts and Grace Playlist Recommendations

"Just the Way You Are" – Billy Joel

"The Riddle" – Five for Fighting

"Your Song" – Ellie Goulding

"Beautiful" – India Arie

"Beautiful" – Nimo (feat. Jason Joseph)

"Earth from Outer Space" – Michael Franti (feat. K'naan)

CONCLUSION

GREAT RESPONSIBILITY AND THE LEADERSHIP MIRROR

I walk down the same street.
There is a deep hole in the sidewalk.
I see it is there.
I still fall in. It's a habit.
My eyes are open. I know where I am.
It is my fault. I get out immediately . . .

I walk down another street.

—PORTIA NELSON

PARTING THOUGHTS

If, by chance, you are feeling like your journey has just begun, you're right. The journey you've been through while reading this book is likely nothing in comparison to the journey of your evolving leadership and your beautiful life. The more conscious and mindful you become, the more you will understand the layered nature of personal and professional transformation. Like the words of Portia Nelson, in one of my favorite poems (above), you learn to get out of one hole, and eventually walk down a different street—emboldened, empowered, and confident—only to find that a whole new set of challenges awaits.

This isn't a bad thing. It's simply the cyclical nature of growth. As we take actions to evolve emotionally, mentally, and spiritually, we continue to refine ourselves. As we free our souls from the shackles of our embodied protections and wounds—what I have come to call *the patriarchy within*—we can surpass even our own wildest expectations in time.

My hope is that the practices in this book have opened up a whole new horizon of possibilities for you. For many of my clients, the end of our time together goes hand in hand with another transition: moving to a new city, stepping into a new role or career, getting married (or divorced!), or even having a child. For some of them, it literally makes sense to *return to page one* and start the whole guided journey of self-discovery over again. And so it is that endings become new beginnings, in turn.

My intention was to create a book that can become a true reference for you—not for one year or one season, but for the rest of your life. At least, for the rest of your career in leadership. When I teach the *Guts and Grace* curriculum as part of a live program, I literally do the practices again myself every . . . single . . . time.

It's worth it. And I can't help it. In order to guide others along the journey, the journey itself asks the guide to continually upgrade and refine her own practice. In fact, **the journey is a mirror**. When I am the leader, the outward progress of my constituents will *directly reflect* the level of mastery I have achieved on the inside.

I guarantee the same is true for you as a leader. It can't help but not be.

THE ETERNAL MIRROR

Before I send you on your way for real, I'd like to share two more of my best-kept secrets with you. The first I've just alluded to: the Eternal Mirror.

This tool isn't really a tool at all. Rather, it's an acknowledgement of *the way things are*. When you learn to capitalize on its lessons, you will have the power to find your way out of *any* hole and cocreate *any* new reality that you can envision. But it's not for the faint of heart. So I offer it *only* to those who are ready.

In essence, it dictates the following: *"as on the inside, so on the outside."* In other words, what I'm personally vibing will be *directly reflected* in the results I create. When I'm feeling physically depleted, my employees (or even the finances of my business) will reflect the same. When I feel like I'm fighting against the world, the world will fight against me. When I'm struggling to sustain my own energy, the sustainability initiative I'm leading at my organization will struggle to get off the ground. When I'm giving from a place of ego or greed, the constituents on the other side will receive (or take) my gifts from that very same kind of scarcity and hunger.

It's not our fault. And we can change it.

I believe this is one of the most important and *challenging* lessons for every conscious leader to master. It takes an unshakeable spirit to walk the *very fine line* between self-blame and total personal responsibility for impact. When you begin to track the Eternal Mirror in your leadership, you may find that it shows you the roadmap for business growth via your own evolution.

It may thus be tempting to think that your goal should be to refine yourself as much as possible, so that you can easily accomplish your business goals. You will eventually find, however, that the hologram works in all directions. Could it be, in fact, that the business *exists* simply to serve as an opportunity for you to refine yourself?

Yes, it's a trip (in all senses of the word). When I work privately with clients long term, this tool serves as a guiding light for our deepest and most profound work together. Since you and I are working long distance right now, across space and time, I'll leave you with this one thought as a starting point for reflection: when we're not aware of the Eternal Mirror, we're prone to cocreating messes that reflect our own inner maze. And the bigger the scale of our leadership, the bigger the potential mess.

By holding a healthy reverence for the Eternal Mirror, we can learn to powerfully, smoothly, and cleanly bring our big visions into form.

SELF-MENTORING

The second tool that forms the foundation of this book is called "self-mentoring," coined by Dr. Marsha Carr. In her book *Self-Mentoring: The Invisible Leader Manual*,[29] Dr. Carr urges leaders to learn how to be great mentors *to themselves* and consciously steward their own professional development.

My own "discovery" of the self-mentoring practice happened organically, which illustrates the tool perfectly. Early on in my career I found that the dominant profit-over-stakeholders paradigm of business, and the leaders who were operating within it, simply did not match what I needed in order to reach my full potential. Therefore, I learned to listen—to my own body and intuition to data outliers, and to the energetic field itself—as a way of guiding my personal and professional journey. This process felt like "self-mentoring" to me!

As luck would have it, the industry has now begun to catch up with my originally quite *different* way of leading. But the truth is, it has nothing to do with luck. Any good futurist will tell you that upcoming trends are detectable long before the majority of people get on the bandwagon. When you are able to learn *directly* from those emerging trends, you can mentor yourself into the leader you were born to be.

Here's why it matters: if you see yourself as an innovative or disruptive leader, you'll likely be blazing new trails frequently as part of your work. While the advice given in women's leadership training today is to *seek a great mentor*, it may be the case that there's simply no one around who has done what you want to do or has accomplished what you dream of accomplishing. Or it may be the case that you *already have* great mentors, but they only see *part* of the horizon you are tracking. This may happen because they were born in a different time, under different rules and different pressures, and their method of success *was appropriate* for those exact times.

As I complete the writing of this book in the summer of 2019, things seem to be moving incredibly fast. Industries are dying and being born, organizations are changing the way they do business, technological innovation is happening at what feels like lightning speed . . . and consciousness itself is rapidly evolving.

In order to avoid limiting what's possible for *your* leadership in *your lifetime*, I encourage you to use the tool of self-mentoring—and any of the embodied leadership tools you've learned that you see fit—to evolve *beyond* what any of your leaders, mentors, teachers, and guides could see possible.

Even me.

ONE LAST THING . . . PAY IT FORWARD

I have one very small request in parting. I'll keep it short. Every great conscious leader knows that her tiny actions have the power to create massive ripple effects. I'd like to see you create some ripples.

If you feel inspired by the message I've shared here, or you received value from the tools in this book that you know could benefit other women in your life, I want to challenge you to pay it forward. Specifically, I recommend gifting this book to two women in your life who need it: one woman who you love, and one woman who you *admire* but sometimes don't *like* or who you worry about. On the *Guts and Grace* website, you can also access more embodied leadership tools and join a global community of women who are blazing a new trail together (www.gutsandgrace.com and www.gutsandgrace.com/book-resources/).

While it may sound selfless, sharing is a great way to build allies that can ultimately support your continued learning. It also helps to build a world where oppressive old-paradigm myths get busted and conscious, empowered female leaders can truly have one another's backs.

Thank you for going on this journey of a lifetime with me.

ACKNOWLEDGMENTS

This book would not have been possible without the love and support of my partner Jorge Evalyn Cortez, my father Walt Mallorie, and the women in my family who taught me how to live, lead, laugh, and love—Karen Gerber, Sylvia Seybert, Della Traister, Lorin Mallorie, Marsha Saylor, Ann Weast, Barbara MacIsaac, and Patricia Walker.

I owe my joy—and my sanity—to my friends and collaborators Jodi Adams, Lise Melvin, Jennifer Petrini, Megan Buchman, Jodie Preiss, Lisa Merlot-Booth, Suzanne Reeves, Kanna Scoville, Alejandra Silberman, Maggie Williams, Andrew Brady, Nadine Keller, Hye-Jin Yu, Terry Eccles, Ron Jennings, Michael Kalikow, A. J. Pape, Amber Johnston, Malia Lazu, Mansi Goel, Dan Tam, Kate Keough, Kim Quick, Angela Harris, Erica Wexler, and many others—as well as my coaching clients and all of the women who have graduated from my earlier programs, Permission to Thrive and Be the Change.

I must also acknowledge my teachers and the lineages of body, mind, emotion, and spirit training I've been blessed to learn from over the past two decades, including Richard Strozzi-Heckler, Staci Haines, and the lineages of Morihei Ueshiba, Morihiro Saito, George Leonard, Randolph Stone, Ida Rolf, Moshe Feldenkrais, Fernando Flores, Wilhelm Reich, and many others. My business mentors and coaches Angelique Rewers and Phil Dyer, Jayne Warrilow, Barry Schwartz, David Bayer, David Neagle, and the lineages of Tony Robbins, Napoleon Hill, Raymond Charles Barker, and many others. My spiritual mentors Maria Owl, Nilima Bhat, and the spirits of Hathor, Isis, Sekhmet, and Saint Germaine. Samantha Sweetwater and the lineages of Rudolf Laban, Irmgard Bartenieff, George Bertelstein, and the grandfather spirits. Anna Halprin and Gabrielle Roth. Carioca, Chonon Yaca, and the grandmother spirits. The lineage of yoga and the lineage of vipassana meditation, as brought by various teachers to the United States. Regina Thomashauer, Nicole Daedone, and the lineages of Lafayette Morehouse. Debbie and Carlos Rosas and the lineages of the nine movement forms, Stanley Keleman, and many others. Clare Nuer, Lara, and Noah Nuer; Shayne Hughes, Marc-Andre Olivier, and the lineages of O. Carl Simonton, Maxie Maultsby, Aaron T. Beck, Werner Erhard, and many more. Silvia Nakkach, John Beaulieu, David Darling, Ysaÿe Barnwell, Pauline Oliveros, David Worm, Gary Muszynski, and the lineages of music therapy and sound healing. Martin Seligman, the legacy of Chris Peterson, the global positive psychology tribe, Jonathan Fields, Charlie Gilkey, Jadah Sellner, and the 108 tribe. Charles Behling and the University of Michigan Program on Intergroup Relations. Eileen Fisher and the Lifework Institute. Michelle Stransky and the Wisdom Women movement. Mary Oleksy and the Stanford WIM program. And authors Oriah Mountain Dreamer, Julia Cameron, Dawna Markova, Paulo Coelho, David Whyte, Rumi, Hafiz, Mary Oliver, Barry Schwartz, Tom Rath, Arianna Huffington, Eckhart Tolle, Brené Brown, Anne Wilson Schaef, Gay and Katie Hendricks, Robin DiAngelo, and many more.

Immense and deep gratitude for the guidance you have provided along this incredible journey.

Thank you.

NOTES

1 Julia Dawson, Richard Kersley, and Stefano Natella, *The CS Gender 3000: The Reward for Change* (Credit Suisse Research Institute, September 2016), https://evolveetfs.com/wp-content/uploads/2017/08/Credit-Suisse-Reward-for-Change_1495660293279_2.pdf.

2 Henry David Thoreau, *Walden*, chapter 18, p. 430 (1966). Originally published in 1854.

3 A physical training facility where martial arts are practiced; literally "the place of the way."

4 G. Mindlin, D. Durousseau, and J. Cardillo, *Your Playlist Can Change Your Life: Ten Proven Ways Your Favorite Music Can Revolutionize Your Health, Memory, Organization, Alertness, and More* (Naperville, IL: Sourcebooks, Inc., 2012).

5 Anna Halprin, *Returning to Health with Dance, Movement and Intimacy* (Mendocino, CA: LifeRhythm, 2002).

6 M. E. P. Seligman, *Flourish: A Visionary New Understanding of Happiness and Well-Being* (New York: Free Press, 2011).

7 D. Rosas and C. Rosas, *The Nia Technique: The High-Powered Energizing Workout That Gives You a New Body and a New Life* (New York: Harmony Books, 2005).

8 Ibid.

9 Brené Brown, *Daring Greatly: How the Courage to Be Vulnerable Transforms the Way We Live, Love, Parent and Lead* (New York: Gotham Books, 2012).

10 Tom Rath, *Are You Fully Charged: The Three Keys to Energizing Your Work and Life* (Arlington, VA: Missionday, 2015).

11 Julia Cameron, *The Artist's Way: A Spiritual Path to Higher Creativity* (Los Angeles, CA: TarcherPerigree, 1992).

12 O. C. Simonton, J. Creighton, and S. M. Simonton, *Getting Well Again* (New York: Bantam, 1992).

13 Karen Reivich and A. Shatté, *The Resilience Factor: 7 Keys to Finding Your Inner Strength and Overcoming Life's Hurdles* (New York: Three Rivers Press, 2002).

14 Regena Thomashauer, *Mama Gena's School of Womanly Arts: Using the Power of Pleasure to Have Your Way with the World* (New York: Simon & Schuster, 2002).

15 Byron Katie, *Loving What Is: Four Questions That Can Change Your Life*, in collaboration with Stephen Mitchell (New York: Three Rivers Press, 2003).

16 O. C. Simonton, J. Creighton, and S. M. Simonton, *Getting Well Again*.

17 Barbara Fredrickson, *Positivity: Top-Notch Research Reveals the 3-to-1 Ratio That Will Change Your Life* (New York: Harmony Books, 2009).

18 Brené Brown, "The Power of Vulnerability," filmed June 2010 in Houston, Texas, TED video, 19:51, https://www.ted.com/talks/brene_brown_on_vulnerability.

19 David Whyte, "The Poetry of Self-Compassion," recorded lecture, April 1, 1992.

20 Marshall Goldsmith, *What Got You Here Won't Get You There: How Successful People Become Even More Successful*, in collaboration with Mark Reiter (New York: Hachette, 2007).

21 W. H. Murray, *The Scottish Himalayan Expedition* (London: Dent, 1951).

22 Richard Strozzi-Heckler, *The Leadership Dojo: Build Your Foundation as an Exemplary Leader* (Berkeley, CA, Frog, Ltd., 2007).

23 Karl Ericsson, Ralf Krampe, and Clemens Tesch-Roemer, "The Role of Deliberate Practice in the Acquisition of Expert Performance," *Psychological Review* 100 (1993): 363–406.

24 Barry Schwartz, *The Paradox of Choice: Why More Is Less* (New York: HarperCollins, 2004).

25 Gay Hendricks, *The Big Leap: Conquer Your Hidden Fear and Take Life to the Next Level* (New York: HarperCollins Publishers, 2010).

26 Murray, *The Scottish Himalayan Expedition.*

27 William Stafford, "The Way It Is," in *The Way It Is: New and Selected Poems* (Minneapolis, MN: Graywolf Press, 1999).

28 Hendricks, *The Big Leap.*

29 Marsha L. Carr, *Self-Mentoring: The Invisible Leader Manual* (Scotts Valley, CA: CreateSpace, 2016).

POETRY

Introduction

Markova, Dawna. "I Will Not Die an Unlived Life." In *I Will Not Die an Unlived Life: Reclaiming Purpose and Passion*. Boston: Conari Press, 2000.

Chapter 1

Hafiz. "Cast All Your Votes for Dancing." In *I Heard God Laughing: Renderings of Hafiz*, translated by Daniel Ladinsky. Walnut Creek, CA: Sufism Reoriented, 1996.

Chapter 2

Whyte, David. "What to Remember When Waking." In *The House of Belonging*. Langley, WA: Many Rivers Press, 1997.

Chapter 3

Oliver, Mary. "Wild Geese." In *Dream Work*. New York: Atlantic Monthly Press, 1986.

Chapter 4

Norris, Gunilla. "Sharing Silence." In *Sharing Silence: Meditation Practice and Mindful Living*. New York: Harmony, 1993.

Chapter 5

Rilke, Rainer Maria. "XXIX: Let This Darkness Be a Bell Tower." In *Sonnet to Orpheus II*. Munich: Insel-Verlag, 1923.

Chapter 6

Nelson, Portia. "Autobiography in Five Chapters." In *There's a Hole in My Sidewalk: The Romance of Self Discovery*. Los Angeles: Popular Library, 1977.

Chapter 7

Hafiz. "What Happens?" In *I Heard God Laughing: Renderings of Hafiz*, translated by Daniel Ladinsky. Walnut Creek, CA: Sufism Reoriented, 1996.

Chapter 8

Sarton, May. "Now I Become Myself." In *Collected Poems: 1930–1993*. New York: W. W. Norton, 1993.

Chapter 9

Kavanaugh, James. "You Are Your Own Answer." In *Quiet Water: The Inspirational Poems of James Kavanaugh*. Kalamazoo, MI: Steven J. Nash Publishers, 1993.

Chapter 10

Hafiz. "Now is the Time." In *The Gift: Poems by Hafiz, the Great Sufi Master*, translated by David Ladinsky. New York: Penguin Compass, 1999.

Stafford, William. "The Way It Is." In *The Way It Is: New and Selected Poems*. Minneapolis: Graywolf Press, 1999.

Chapter 11

Alves, Rubem. "Tomorrow's Child." In *Tomorrow's Child: Imagination, Creativity, and the Rebirth of Culture*. Eugene, OR: Wipf & Stock, 2011.

Conclusion

Nelson, Portia. "Autobiography in Five Chapters." In *There's a Hole in My Sidewalk: The Romance of Self Discovery*. Los Angeles: Popular Library, 1977.

LeeAnn Mallorie, MAPP, began her career as an executive coach in 2006, working with leaders and teams from around the globe. Yet she soon found something was missing—the body. This led her on a personal journey of physical, mental, and spiritual healing that took her into the depths of her soul and the heights of her consciousness. Committed to the belief that transforming business is the keystone to solving many of our world's stickiest problems, she brought each of these lessons back to her clients in the corporate sector. As the founder and CEO of Leading in Motion, LeeAnn has now spent over a decade helping leaders face bottom-line challenges while combating both meaning-depletion and burnout. She does this by using practical embodiment tools to bridge the gap between the hard-driving logical mind and the deeper wisdom of the soul. Her leadership curriculum offers a concrete, actionable doorway to greater power, resilience, influence, ethics, and impact at work.

ELEVATE HUMANITY THROUGH BUSINESS.

Conscious Capitalism, Inc., supports a global community of business leaders dedicated to elevating humanity through business via their demonstration of purpose beyond profit, the cultivation of conscious leadership and culture throughout their entire ecosystem, and their focus on long-termism by prioritizing stakeholder orientation instead of shareholder primacy. We provide mid-market executives with innovative learning exchanges, transformational storytelling training, and inspiring conference experiences all designed to level-up their business operations and collectively demonstrate capitalism as a powerful force for good when practiced consciously.

We invite you, either as an individual or as a business, to join us and contribute your voice. Learn more about the global movement at www.consciouscapitalism.org.

CPSIA information can be obtained
at www.ICGtesting.com
Printed in the USA
LVHW082029140120
643591LV00012B/239